Angels and Demons

A Radical Anthology of
Political Lives

D0281211

Also by Tony McKenna

The Dying Light (a novel)
ISBN-10: 1910705888

The Dictator, the Revolution, the Machine: A Political Account of
Joseph Stalin
ISBN-10: 1845198263

Art, Literature and Culture from a Marxist Perspective
ISBN-10: 1137526602

Angels and Demons

A Radical Anthology of
Political Lives

Tony McKenna

Winchester, UK
Washington, USA

First published by Zero Books, 2019
Zero Books is an imprint of John Hunt Publishing Ltd., No. 3 East St., Alresford,
Hampshire SO24 9EE, UK
office1@jhpbooks.net
www.johnhuntpublishing.com
www.zero-books.net

For distributor details and how to order please visit the 'Ordering' section on our website.

Text copyright: Tony McKenna 2018

ISBN: 978 1 78904 020 3
978 1 78904 021 0 (ebook)
Library of Congress Control Number: 2018933760

A CIP catalogue record for this book is available from the British Library.

Design: Stuart Davies

Printed and bound by CPI Group (UK) Ltd, Croydon, CR0 4YY, UK
US: Printed and bound by Edwards Brothers Malloy 15200 NBN Way #B, Blue Ridge Summit,
PA 17214, USA

We operate a distinctive and ethical publishing philosophy in
all areas of our business, from our global network of authors to
production and worldwide distribution.

Contents

Acknowledgements

I am grateful to the publishers of the following works for permission to reuse copyrighted material from them as the basis for the chapters indicated:

"Hugo Chavez and the PSUV in Light of the Historical Process in Venezuela". *Critique: Journal of Socialist Theory*, February 2009 (Taylor & Francis, Oxford).

"Christopher Hitchens: Pathology of an Imperialist Ideologue". *Socialism and Democracy*, March 2014 (Taylor & Francis, Pennsylvania).

For María del Carmen

Introduction

When I was 19 I read *The History of the Russian Revolution* by Leon Trotsky for the first time. It is a remarkable book for many reasons. It depicts a monumental event in all its sweep and grandeur, it describes with great literary verve and pathos the historical conditions which boiled over into the revolutionary eruption, it outlines the revolutionary process in clinical and precise terms yet also perfectly captures the atmosphere of flesh-and-blood struggle and heady freedom such an event entails. And it all flows from the pen of one of October's central political actors. But there was one chapter which was particularly resonant to me and would have a marked effect on my own development as a journalist and historian. Chapter four of the first volume of Trotsky's *magnum opus* offers a vivid and intimate portrayal of the Tsar and the Tsarina and the atmosphere of the royal court which had now entered into its end of days as the revolution drew close. I would go as far as to say this chapter offers up one of the greatest literary and psychological accounts of the human personality which has ever been penned; it illuminates fully the souls of the Tsar and the Tsarina by way of a writing which is beautiful, profound and scathing in terms of its bitter irony.

It was, however, very different from the conventional psychological approach of the time, the psychoanalysis of Freud. Freudian psychoanalysis offered up a hermetically sealed individuality whose internal laws and patterns operate in an immanent and pristine space, retaining a high level of abstraction and independence from the external world and any historical context. According to Freud, every child goes through several stages of personality development – oral, anal, phallic etc. – and it is the ability to navigate these stages successfully which can determine whether the personality of the fully formed adult is aberrant, neurotic, healthy and so on. Freud would argue, for

1

example, that those individuals who demonstrated a particularly strong attachment to the anal phase in early childhood would, as adults, often take a compulsive interest in the accumulation of money: "The original erotic interest in defaecation...makes its appearance as a new interest...the interest in money."[1]

Expanding on Freud, Eric Fromm of the Frankfurt School argued that the rational bureaucrat – the sociological "type" of capitalist which Max Weber had described with all its orderliness, efficiency and routine – was something which had much in common with Freud's anally retentive personality, only Fromm would re-classify such a personality in terms of a "hoarding orientation". So we are privy to a precise methodological operation; a fully formed and generic individuality is called into being, and this becomes the central impetus, the prime mover, of the historical process. Moving from psychology to historiography, a similar approach was popularised in the nineteenth century by Thomas Carlyle, both a philosopher and a historian, who argued that the "history of the world is but the biography of great men".[2] In this theory, world history is little more than a blank canvass which the great individual personality then stamps with its colour and quality. But the problem with such an approach was, just as with Freudianism, it first presupposed the independent existence of a generic individual abstracted from any socio-historical process; as Herbert Spencer would write so tellingly of Carlyle's "great man" – "[b]efore he can remake his society, his society must make him."[3]

Trotsky's account of the Romanovs provides a tonic to this, the abstract individualism which has become the default template for biography writing in the modern epoch. Trotsky certainly does not deny the importance of the individual, of the "great" man or woman, but he begins from the notion that the key to describing a true and authentic individuality is found in the historical conditions in which it achieves fruition. In the case of the Tsar and the Tsarina, Trotsky describes the twilight of a whole historical epoch. A decaying empire spanning a vast territory was overseen by a decadent state; a feudal absolutism whose power was enshrined by an aura of medieval religiosity and appeared more and more as some gargantuan and monstrous relic in the context of modernity. In the context of the mass migrations which were taking place from the country to the town, the rapidly developing urban populations, the rise of the new industries, and the demand for radical new political forms and expressions. The contradiction between the modern and the archaic was increasingly volatile, increasingly tested; from the Decembrist revolt in the mid-1820s, reformist and revolutionary movements had been gaining steam, and the rise of the new super industries and the vast concentrations of workers in great industrial hubs meant that Russian forms of Marxism and anarcho-syndicalism were fused by steam and fire into a particularly potent product.

But, argued Trotsky, to "that historic flood which was rolling its billows each one closer to the gates of his palace, the last Romanov opposed only a dumb indifference. It seemed as though between his consciousness and his epoch there stood some transparent but absolutely impenetrable medium."[4] The principle of monarchy itself had become historically degraded. The absolutist institution was as some grotesque museum piece, cordoned off from the living social forces and developments which were everywhere springing up, and so it inevitably ossified, becoming ever more cumbersome, ever more demented, ever more rabid – maddened by the fact that the modernity it had suddenly and rudely been thrust into seemed to it incomprehensible, alien and senseless. In Trotsky's account the personal and political achieve a harmonious but terrible synthesis for in the person of the last Tsar is embodied all the decadence, fatality, pettiness, self-deception, brass ignorance, denial and hopelessness of a historical tendency which has entered into an inevitable, mortal freefall. Trotsky quotes from the Tsar's diary after the country had entered its revolutionary paroxysms during 1905 and the writ had been issued to open the state Duma: "April 14. Took a walk in a thin shirt and took up paddling again. Had tea in a balcony. Stana dined and took a ride with us."[5] The great revolutionary observes that such apathy, such utter spiritual inertia, lies at the core of a historically doomed personality:

> [He] would interest himself generally in the little rubbish of the day's doings, while thunders roared over him and lightnings flashed...his ability to control himself in the most extraordinary circumstances, cannot be explained by a mere external training; its essence was an inner indifference, a poverty of spiritual forces, a weakness of the impulses of the will. That mask of indifference which was called breeding in certain circles, was a natural part of Nicholas at birth.[6]

As the revolutionary forces rumbled ever closer to the gate, the royal court seemed to go into lockdown; the hangers on, the bribed officials, the stodges and the lackeys proliferated – a rotten, mouldering network of corruption hung around the state machine like a noose: "Special official purveyors arose...forming a powerful Upper Chamber attached to the monarch. There was no lack of bigoted old women with the title of countess, nor of functionaries weary of doing nothing, nor of financiers who had entire ministries in their hire."[7] In the same moment a thick miasma of medieval superstition descended on the royal court in a poisonous fug: "soothsayers and hysterics were imported for the court...[an] unchartered competition of mesmerists and sorcerers...The more isolated the dynasty became, and the more unsheltered the autocrat felt, the more he needed some help from the other world."[8] The Tsar himself was at home in such an environment which housed both flatterers and ignoramuses, fakirs and frauds, men and women of meagre creativity and dull intellect, possessed only by low cunning and brute greed: "Nicholas recoiled in hostility before everything gifted and significant. He felt at ease only among completely mediocre and brainless people, saintly fakers, holy men, to whom he did not have to look up. He had his *amour propre*, indeed it was rather keen. But it was not active, not possessed of a grain of initiative, enviously defensive."[9] Indeed, observes Trotsky, even the Tsar's sadism was characterised by a certain malignant introversion:

> This dim, equable and 'well-bred' man was cruel – not with the active cruelty of Ivan the Terrible or of Peter, in the pursuit of historic aims – What had Nicholas the Second in common with them? – but with the cowardly cruelty of the late born, frightened at his own doom. At the very dawn of his reign Nicholas praised the Phanagoritsy regiment as 'fine fellows' for shooting down workers. He always 'read with satisfaction' how they flogged with whips the bob-haired girl-students, or cracked the heads of defenceless people during Jewish pogroms. This crowned black sheep gravitated with all his soul to the very dregs of society, the Black Hundred hooligans. He not only paid them generously from the state treasury, but loved to chat with them about their exploits, and would pardon them when they accidentally got mixed up in the murder of an opposition deputy.[10]

Trotsky's account is as eloquent as it is damming, but most significantly, it is able to reveal the historical necessity which lies behind the distinctive and unique traits of an individual character, it is able to demonstrate, in poetic free-flow and with scathing irony, just how the narrow, dissipated characteristics of the Tsar were "individual scratches made by a higher law of development".[11] In the ten chapters which follow I want to utilise Trotsky's methodological approach – and vicariously that of Marxism – to provide a series of examinations of historical figures, both contemporary and classical; I want to demonstrate that the philosophy which these figures espouse, or the art and literature which they create, or the political activity in which they engage – are the products of personalities which are shaped in and through constant dialogue with the historical conditions from which they emerge. To be sure, they are not reducible to mere abstract cyphers, the personal representatives of mechanical, anonymous historical forces, but rather their art and activity, their interests and individuality, only resonates its full uniqueness and meaning in the context of the historical epoch, and the underlying social and political contradictions which set the basis for it.

Having provided a cursory outline of my methodological approach, I would like to say a word or two about why I have chosen to look at the individuals who appear in this particular gallery. The men and women who adorn these pages can loosely be divided into "angels" and "demons" – or more precisely "radicals" and "reactionaries". Obviously these categories are not hard and fast; different people will exhibit more radical or more reactionary forms of politics at different points in the course of their lives. Nevertheless, I think it is fair to make an "overall" categorisation: and so the radicals in the collection are comprised of Victor Hugo, Hugo Chavez, Rembrandt Harmenszoon van Rijn, Andrea Dworkin, William Blake and Jeremy Corbyn – while the reactionaries are made up of Christopher Hitchens, Arthur Schopenhauer, Donald Trump and Hillary Clinton. In addition, the reader will note that there is a division between the explicitly political figures and actors such as Hugo Chavez or Hillary Clinton – and those who are first and foremost artists or writers, such as Rembrandt or Hugo. Again, the line is not hard and fast, both Rembrandt and Hugo, for instance, were clearly political animals of the first order but primarily within the remit of their art.

In any event, the clear political actors in this collection are

Hugo Chavez, Jeremy Corbyn, Hillary Clinton and Donald Trump. I chose these figures partly because this book provides a series of attempts to mediate the broader historical development with the thought and activity of the individual in question, and in all four of the above cases I would argue that it is the modern form of neoliberalism in particular which provides that historical development and comes to impact decisively on the shape of their political lives. In the case of both Chavez and Corbyn, we see very clearly that their politics have been marked by a strong opposition to this tendency. In the case of Hillary Clinton and Donald Trump the situation is more complex. I wrote their profiles for this book around the time of the Trump inauguration, when not only those in the US, but also many around the globe were in a state of shock, unable to fathom how someone so gaudy and demagogic – such a clownish, cruel caricature – could have possibly won the highest office in the land. The liberal-left offered up a deeply pessimistic and sardonic explanation for such an electoral travesty: we had entered into a kind of political dark age; reason and rationality, embodied by sleek professional politicians, the eloquent directors of a more humane, liberalised and inclusive capitalism – *a Democratic Party type of capitalism* – were being usurped in favour of the rabid irrationality and apocalyptic bluster of the far right. Trump had been chosen over Clinton. A monster had been birthed, and at the behest of a population whose frustration and ignorance – especially that of the poorer elements – had bubbled over yielding a toxic age of unreason, or so the pro-Clintonite line went.

But something else was at work here. In actual fact it was not that Trump had achieved a barn storming election success, indeed Clinton herself had a 2.8 million lead in the number of popular votes.[12] What had happened was that voter turnout overall had decreased across the board, and the Democrats in particular had paid the price for this. In 2008, when Barack Obama swept into the White House on the heady promise of "change" 61.6 per cent of those eligible to vote in the population did so.[13] In 2016, when Hillary Clinton was the Democratic candidate that number had fallen drastically to 58.1 per cent[14] – millions of those who turned out before, now chose to stay at home. Why? Because Obama's 8 years in office had failed to deliver on the alternative and transformative politics voters had been encouraged to expect. Obama promised to close the prison camp and torture hotbed of Guantanamo. He didn't. He foreswore to rescind all US troops from the bloody quagmire of Iraq, but US forces were still being sent there during the final year of his presidency. He helped create a more militarised police force and under his watch the slaying of unarmed blacks, including children, became epidemic. While Trump's toxic anti-immigration policies are sufficiently well known, what is not common knowledge is how under Obama's tenure significantly more than 2.5 million people[15] were deported, a figure which exceeds that of any previous president. Obama broke his pledge on introducing "card checks" – a system which would have made access to union membership for workers easier. At the same time he fortified the rapacious and corrupt cabal of bankers and financiers who had helped facilitate the global economic crisis by barring the justice department from prosecuting those at the top of the largest banks. And, of course, he would continue to bail those same banks out.

From the liberal purview, however, the movement from Obama to Trump – and the defeat of Clinton – is not conceived of in terms of the shattered promises made by those at the top of the Democratic Party as they endeavour to better grease the neoliberal machine in and through the promotion of a glittering financial elite and the prosaic, murderous routines of empire – rather it is recast in a melancholy lament for a more rational age, whereby a more humane set of political actors are eventually and tragically consumed by a political barbarism which has been foisted upon the nation courtesy of those at the bottom. I wanted to write about Trump because he is truly a fascinating and horrifying individual, because he represents in visible form a heady, grotesque brand of vulgar eighties casino capitalism married to the glitzy sensationalism and unbridled cruelty of the worst forms of twenty-first century reality TV. But I wanted to write about Clinton in order to expose her own awfulness, duplicity and absolute ambition, to show how she has been the sleek, purring representative of neoliberalism as that same historical tendency enters into acute crisis, and to puncture the idea that there is any real kind of moral, humane or progressive politics behind the PR facade which she exudes. Most of all I wanted to show how she and Trump are the monstrous aberrations of different wings in a ruling class which has all the pity and humanity of the court of Caligula. I wanted to attack once and for all the idea that Trump represents a radical break with something fundamentally more humane which came before; indeed it was the Clintonite/Obama epoch which helped make Trump possible.

I chose to write about Chavez and Corbyn for the fact they represent the antithesis of all of this, and for this reason, in my view, they offer up great hope. Hugo Chavez emerged on the crest of a mass movement in Venezuela which was forged out of the deprivations visited upon that country by one complicit president after the next. Small ruling cliques in the pocket of the International Monetary Fund (IMF) that were able to enjoy lives of untrammelled luxury in inverse proportion to the privations and material extortions the masses were made to endure through the implementation of neoliberal policy, policy which received much of its impetus from the leaders' political paymasters back in Washington. In a country where contempt for the poor was such that maps often didn't bother to print the images and names of the streets of the shanty towns and the poverty-stricken districts of the hills, the explosion of Chavez onto the political scene suddenly made the dark-skinned, impoverished majority who had languished in almost apartheid-like conditions, visible again. In the case of Jeremy Corbyn, he too was brought to prominence on the cusp of a mass movement. For years, both the mainstream parties, Labour and Conservatives, had promoted the same stale consensus; the same neoliberal economic policy which protected and nurtured a clique of the super wealthy, rendering the banks sacred and eviscerating the poor. Corbyn's election to Labour Party leader, and the influx of people, mainly young people – the swelling tide of the mass movement which carried him forward – this also spoke to a question of visibility, as for the first time a credible alternative to the neoliberal politics of "austerity" was floated. For the first time, a mainstream politician would help change the ideological tide, by refusing to condemn poor immigrants and benefit seekers for the economic crisis, and instead lay the blame squarely where it belonged – on the rich cabal of bankers and high financiers and the privileged clique of complicit politicians who had facilitated them.

Beyond their individual personalities, both Chavez and Corbyn represented a shift in the historical pendulum, the moment when the interests of millions of people now received a heightened political expression, a movement whose radicalism and transformative energy was refracted through the person of the leader, and all at once the sense of politics as being an unchangeable crucible manned by a powerful and distant elite began to deteriorate, and more and more ordinary people entered the political field as protagonists. These movements were emancipatory, heady, vibrant and profoundly democratic, and helped shape and fortify the politics of the men stood at their head. They also incurred a visceral reaction from the status quo which in the case of Corbyn took the form of a sustained campaign of hatred and calumny on the part of the press along with an internal plot to displace him; with Chavez, the counteraction was graduated into a *brutal coup d'etat* which physically removed and incarcerated the democratically elected president, and was thwarted only when the masses flooded the streets and the squares in their millions. Here we can see how polarised historical forces reach their greatest conflict and crescendo in and through the individual destinies of two key political actors, figures who represent a moment of rupture with the status quo.

If both Clinton and Trump express different aspects of establishment power, Chavez and Corbyn represent in some way the antithesis of that same power. In the case of Andrea Dworkin and Christopher Hitchens we are confronted by a similar kind of political antipode. Both writers were political journalists of exceptional abilities and literary stylists of the highest order. And yet, when Dworkin died in 2005, her death was little noticed in the mainstream media, with a couple of the bigger liberal papers publishing curt, polite obituaries either in the back pages or on a blog. When Hitchens died in 2011, the reception could not have been more different; papers all over the world featured his face, sometimes on the front page, with countless discussions involving innumerable contributors on the nature and importance of his literary and political legacy, while broadcasters such as the BBC featured interviews with his colleagues and friends speaking of the loss incurred by the broader culture now he was gone. Throughout the twenty-first century, Hitchens' articles had graced the pages of some of the world's biggest media outlets such as *The New York Times* or *Vanity Fair*, while Dworkin often struggled to get her blazing and poetic prose published.

And yet both Dworkin and Hitchens had begun their political lives as outsiders. Dworkin championed the rights of women, and was determined to render their political and cultural discrimination – so ubiquitous and yet so unremarked upon – visible in and through the most eloquent and tragic exposition of their suffering. For his part, Hitchens took up the cause of the oppressed in Third World countries across the world, and his became a strident, witty and ironical voice raised against US imperialism and its shady or sleazy orchestrators, the Henry Kissingers and the Bill Clintons. In 2001, however, following the awful attacks on the Twin Towers, Hitchens' political make-up was radically reconfigured; he became the most articulate and bellicose champion of American capitalism and saw its expansion through invasion and war into Third World territories – particularly those of the Middle East – as essential to transporting civilisation and democracy to those places and peoples who lacked the cultural wherewithal to attain it under their own steam.

In other words, he produced an updated ideological version of "the white man's burden" notable for a particularly virulent strain of the type of Islamophobia which was conducive to Western domination in the Middle East and had become common currency following George Bush Jr's invasion of Afghanistan and then Iraq. Dworkin, on the other hand, never lost a profound and empathetic identification with the oppressed, her radicalism remained pure and uncompromising. For this she was pilloried in the press, demonised as the archetypal irrational man-hating feminist, slandered, harassed, abused and raped. She died an early death, very likely the result of her brutalisation at the hands of the same power she so vividly decried. I wanted to write about Dworkin and Hitchens in this collection because their individual fates say a lot about struggle and reconciliation, literature and tragedy, rebellion and compromise, and their individual lives also say a great deal about the social forces, historical agencies and political contradictions which inspired them.

Like Hitchens, Arthur Schopenhauer was an ideologue and thinker whose philosophy was visibly and indelibly marked by the historical currents of its time. But whereas Hitchens began as a radical, only to have his political philosophy inexorably warped into a militant, enthusiastic, nationalistic and rather thinly veiled *apologia* for ruling class and imperial power –

Schopenhauer's philosophy, like his life, was from the start set in a type of gloomy melancholy. And while it certainly does eternalise ruling class power and class oppression as elements which reflect the broader, underlying and eternal nature of the universe itself – nevertheless the lugubrious philosopher never goes as far as to celebrate these things. His philosophy is reactionary to the core; it represents in particular a concentrated attack on the Hegelian dialectics and historicity which would eventually come to underpin revolutionary Marxism. And yet, at the same time, it is infused with the loneliness, isolation and anomie of the modern epoch, of social life being broken down before the relentless and inhuman force of a generalised market economy – the sense of peering into the abyss – and thus it contains within itself the melancholy of a whole epoch. I would go as far as to say it becomes a form of historical poetry, for its most powerful and moving element lies in its artistic aspect, the fact that it conveys a historical mood aesthetically, rather than in the strength of its conscious, philosophical conclusions which are often retrograde and rather weak.

And it is history embodied in the aesthetic which brings us to the final three figures who appear in this collection. William Blake and Victor Hugo in some sense form a natural couplet; they were roughly contemporaneous, both were poets, artists and writers, and through the work of both there runs the same aesthetic tendency – that of romanticism, which is something of particular interest to our investigation. For the romanticism of Blake and Hugo flows from the same historical source; it comes out of the anxiety which permeates the industrial revolution, its increasingly mechanised forms of labour and their dehumanising effects on the individual who is subject to them. Romanticism provides a critique of capitalist alienation but from the purview of a more whimsical past, the vision of an organic individual – a throwback to a more innocent time – rendered whole again, often through some spiritual uplift or religious rapture. For Blake, of course, the religious impulse is particularly important, and religious themes pervade his art and poetry; indeed the romantic rebellion of the individual against the industrial order is recast in his epic poetry as a cosmological battle between opposing deities. And yet, this romantic, religious vision on Blake's part is also tempered by an incredibly potent identification with the struggles of the oppressed masses, and these confluences in his aesthetic corpus are once again profoundly shaped by the volatile contradictions which were being played out across the historical panorama at the time.

Last, but by no means least, we come to Rembrandt Harmenszoon van Rijn. Rembrandt is the earliest of the figures in this collection, and his life belongs to the period of time when capitalism itself was in its infancy. He was born in 1606, the point at which Dutch capitalism was on the verge of freeing itself from the yoke of the Spanish Empire and spreading across the world, creating a vibrant global market which energised the rapidly expanding cities back home, cities which throbbed with diversity and colour, drawing into themselves a never-ending stream of exotic commodities from the furthest reaches, creating a new commercial bourgeoisie whose glittering wealth flowed into a rapidly expanding art sector such that paintings and artefacts flooded the market. Often, even those of humble and plebeian origins could find the means to secure a painting or two for the hearth. Rembrandt was the artist who expressed this democratic expansion of art as it permeated every pore of his society, and he also expressed the vibrant power of a youthful capitalism which flourished in a global empire. Rembrandt himself was driven and aspirant, and his precocity and brilliance assured him a rapid, dramatic success and early entry into the very highest level of the social elite. His painting had all the technical confidence and ingenuity of the new economic model on which it was premised.

But at the same time there was a dark side. Dutch capitalism had embarked upon a massive project of social engineering, a brutal, callous and systematic regulation of the beggars and the dispossessed in order to create new working-class formations and to discipline and subordinate labour. At the same time, the big Dutch capitalists, the shareholders in the newly created joint stock companies, were investing in projects which routinely employed slavery in the colonies and some decades later began to supply slaves *en masse* for sale in the Americas. What makes Rembrandt such a great artist is his highly developed historical antenna; even in the early stages of his career when he was still so ambitious and aspirant, there is an ambiguity – a shadow – which creeps into his paintings, the expression of his unconscious but infinitely refined attunement to the deeper historical current, the dark underbelly of capitalism itself. Thus he is able to depict the process of historical life in all its contradictions and antipodes, in and through the semblance of joy and melancholy of his individual subjects, fused in the most profound and harmonious realism.

And that provides the unifying theme in this collection, the "angels" and "demons" are all figures whose politics, philosophy or art mediate most profoundly the most significant contradictions within the capitalist order at different stages in its development; these lives all come to channel the deeper, underlying forces at work within the furore of human life in the modern era, graduating them into the most terrible or beautiful self-expression. In learning about them, in encountering their work and their deeds, in absorbing their intelligence and their follies, their triumphs and their tragedies, we are able to glimmer more vividly the shapes and the contours of our own epoch, and perhaps understand a little more about our own role within it.

Chapter One

Victor Hugo: Bard of the Barricades

Victor Hugo was a child of the French Revolution, and perhaps more importantly, he was the scion of the contradictions which were contained within it. He was born in 1802. Several years earlier the forces of the left and the right had battled each other to a standstill as the revolutionary process unfolded, at which point Napoleon Bonaparte's military machine was able to raise itself above them in a brutal *coup d'etat*. Hugo's childhood took place at the time of that dictatorship, a dictatorship curtailed in 1814 – briefly revived in 1815 – and then replaced once and for all by a constitutional monarchy which would sustain until the middle of the century. Hugo's father, Joseph Leopold, was a dyed-in-the-wool Bonapartist, a supporter of the republic which had emerged in 1793. An atheist and a strict military man, he climbed high in the army as the brilliant, vainglorious emperor strutted across the European stage, conquering country after country, until finally his audacious military campaign – having flamed across a whole continent – burnt itself out in the cold, icy swathes of the Russian winter.

Victor Hugo's mother, Sophie Trebuchet, was an ardent Catholic, a royalist who hankered after a more traditional, hierarchical and sentimental vision of the French past; committed to restoration, she was both truculent and bullish, heroic, fiery and fiercely independent. According to the writer himself[16] his parents met when his father was sent to suppress a royalist rebellion his mother had taken part in. A more fitting plot for a tumultuous, romantic novel one could not hope to find. While Hugo's childhood took place against the backdrop of the French Revolution, weaponised according to the resounding clatter and rhythm of Napoleon's armies on the march, his adolescence was enacted against a background of military defeat, counterrevolution and royalist reformation. Such historical polities provided the material for Victor Hugo's early political and aesthetic development, and as his life unfolded those contradictions would receive an ever-changing expression in the political decisions he made and the tenor of the poetry, art and literature he would go on to cultivate.

Between the remote figure of his father, decked out in his military regalia, stern and severe, and the whirlwind-like colour of his mother – the passionate, elemental force of her personality – it was always clear which parent would win the heart and soul of their youngest, most precocious child. Although the family relied very heavily on Joseph Leopold for financial purposes, and though they spent much of Victor's childhood trailing him around on his various military assignations, nevertheless the child's loyalty and adoration was heaped first and foremostly on his mother. Due to extra-marital affairs on both sides, Sophie separated from Joseph, and Victor was, for a time, raised in Paris with his mother where her temperament and politics asserted a powerful influence on his earliest views. His early poetry and fiction reveal a strong religious feeling which is married with a devotion to monarchy. And yet, the conventionality of such politics is shot through with a romantic beauty and pathos which somehow manages to evade the mundane and escape ossifying into the foghorn propaganda of an antiquated conservatism. Instead it is youthful and melancholic; in the same moment both worldly wise and childlike. Consider, for instance, his ode to King Louis XVII, the young son of Louis XVI and Marie Antoinette, who died at the age of 10 in the Temple Tower prison at the height of the revolutionary terror. Two of its most potent stanzas read:

A fair child fleeing from the world's fierce hate,
In his blue eye the shade of sorrow sate,

His golden hair hung all dishevelled down,
On wasted cheeks that told a mournful story,
And angels twined him with the innocent's crown,
The martyr's palm of glory...

Yet far off in dim memory it seems,
With all its horror mingled happy dreams,
Strange cries of glory rocked my sleeping head,
And a glad people watched beside my bed.
One day into mysterious darkness thrown,
I saw the promise of my future close;
I was a little child, left all alone.[17]

Already, in embryo, we encounter the lineaments of the future writer. Firstly, there is the element of pity, so pronounced, in this case directed toward a wretched, lonely child "left all alone" and of course, Hugo's attention to the suffering of children, and also the great, guileless kindness of which they are capable – is one of the hallmarks of his later romantic fiction. The romanticism is also evinced by the connection between the suffering child and the religious divinity which enshrouds him – through the medium of monarchy itself: "And angels twined him with the innocent's crown." There is the sense of nostalgia for a lost epoch; the child is able to escape his immiseration only by slipping into slumber, by shutting out the darkness and the dankness for a few moments with "happy dreams", and in this blissful reverie the young boy hears "strange cries of glory" and sees the ghostly image of a "glad people", benevolent and kind, overlooking him as he sleeps. These, no doubts, represent the what-would-have-been: the crowds and crowds of happy royalists who subsisted in a harmonious and organic unity with the monarchical state and saw in the ruler nothing other than the highest expression of their own aspirations and dreams. Alas, such a blessed state of unity was disrupted by the cold, clinical caveats of the men of reason and their revolutionary pipe-dreams and what lingers in the aftermath is a small child huddled in the darkness of a prison tower. The political sentiments in Hugo's poem are unbearably naive, and do no justice to the brutality and utter corruption of the decadent, crumbling charnel house of a regime the pre-revolution Bourbon monarchy represented. And yet, the poem is very moving, perhaps because it provokes a sense of the child's divine innocence and his longing for a mother who has been snatched away – and because it is able to register these feelings through the interplay of loneliness and dreams, the Manichean flit between the darkness of the child's present and the light-riven idyll of his past. Such verses naturally call to mind the poetry and the romanticism of Blake. Indeed in *King Louis XVII* Hugo uses the religious imagery of the lamb to conjoin the innocence of children with the figure of Christ in precisely the way Blake does – "The virgin souls that to the Lamb are near"[18] – and yet, remarkably enough, it is utterly unfeasible that Hugo would have come across any of Blake's work at this time. What is most remarkable of all, perhaps, is that Hugo wrote these lines when he was just 20 years of age.

So an incredibly precocious talent then, and one which had received early recognition when at 15 he won the poetry contest held by the Academie Francaise and the year following came first in the Academie des Jeux Floraux's contest. Although he eventually studied to become a lawyer, his adolescence reveals all the intellectual exuberance of a Renaissance man – by 14 he was filling notebooks with poetry, working on translations of Virgil, and composing his own plays. By 17, egged on by his mother, Hugo had founded a literary review. By 19 his first book of poems was published – *Odes et poesies diverses* – and for these he won a *pension* from Louis XVIII. Naturally, the awards heaped on him – certainly the royal recognition – were a bi-product of, not only his technical talent and artistic verve, but also his pronounced sympathies for the monarchy and the restoration regime. And yet, even by this point, Hugo's romanticism has a radical edge. Having followed his father through a Europe devastated by war and disruption, Hugo would have witnessed first-hand the suffering of vast swathes of displaced and traumatised people. Like Blake he lived at a period of time in which the huddled masses were more and more subjected to the routines and rigmarole of the new industrial society. And like Blake, his romanticism – its evocation of a more traditional past which allowed the individual to remain in some way spiritually intact – was an aghast and heartfelt protest against the suffering which scoured the present and the relentless mechanical drive of modernity which more and more fashioned a world populated by the scattered and the dispossessed.

At a time when the Louis XVIII regime capped off a process of reaction which was taking place Europe wide – Hugo's fervour for the newly restored monarchy[19] naturally began to wither and fade, especially in light of the high levels of social repression and restructuring such reaction pursued in order to subordinate and discipline the vast armies of labour the industrial project required. A system of punishments had emerged, designed to terrify the citizenry especially with regard to crimes against property – specifically theft. In the first part of the nineteenth century the conviction rate for theft spiralled, significantly higher than the conviction rate for those charged with violent crimes.[20] The newly established constitutional monarchy was carrying out the dictates of the Napoleonic Code and its elevation of the property principle very much in the bourgeois spirit. And this is of importance to Hugo's political development, for it begins to cast doubts in his mind as to the viability of restoration as a solution to the problems of modernity; it is, therefore, part and parcel of the way in which the faith in monarchical authority – inherited from his mother – begins to wane. The constitutional monarchy had continued the revolution's practice of guillotining, and had also made use of earlier medieval barbarisms such as the tradition of branding convicts with hot irons. The young Victor Hugo saw such atrocities carried out against the dissolute, hopeless and impoverished; he witnessed several such executions – and the horror and the sadness of those spectacles remained forever emblazed across his consciousness.

By the time, then, we arrive at Hugo's first major work – *The Last Day of a Condemned Man* – its central conceit involves a prisoner on death row, biding his time, before the blade of the guillotine is to fall. The novel – or novella as it might better be described – provides a lucid critique of the death penalty, full of power and pathos. Dostoyevsky described it as a "masterpiece", and while that is an assessment I don't fully share, nevertheless the work has several outstanding features – features which speak to the aesthetic development of the author at this point. Firstly Hugo expresses his scepticism – nay profound disillusionment – at the revolutionary event: as when the prisoner sees a cap of liberty etched out in the mouldering stone of his cell wall along with the epithet – "Bories, La Republique!" And yet, the story is not written from the purview of some imprisoned prince (as in the case of *Louis XVII*) but now focuses on a man who is so poor he can barely afford his own legal defence. Hugo may not have come over to the side of radicalism or revolution at this point in time, but events – the historical backdrop of his own life – are increasingly driving his sympathies toward the poor and the downtrodden. This is also expressed in a very poignant moment in the novella, a bitter-sweet scene, in which the condemned man of the title is invited by his guard to witness a group of convicts as they are marched into the courtyard in order to be chained, collared and strung together with a series of heavy metal implements. The operation of binding these human beings to these gross mechanical attachments – a metaphor which has a particular resonance at a time of the rise of heavy industry and mechanisation – is described in stark and striking terms, and yet the almost unthinking, inured brutality of the guards alongside the interminable nature of the metal bondage – is thrown into relief by the spiritual sense of solidarity which arises from the men themselves:

> The five gangs joined hands, so as to form an immense circle, and thus ran round and round in the court with a rapidity that the eye could hardly follow. They sung some couplets, in their own idiom, to a melody which was sometimes plaintive, sometimes furious, often interrupted by hoarse cries and broken laughter, like delirious ravings, while the chains, clanking together in cadence, formed an accompaniment to a song more harsh than their own noise. A large trough was now brought in; the guards, striking the convicts to make them discontinue their dance.[21]

The novella already exhibits Hugo's delicate facility for pathos, and the manner in which he is able to call it forth with a few deft sentences, and yet here is a romantic writer who is also able to avoid romanticism's single greatest pitfall – that is to say, sentimentality. To this touching scene and its nod to camaraderie, the writer at once injects a mordant, darker and entirely more brutal amendment. As the prisoners perform their strange dance in the very midst of hell, they catch a glimpse of the condemned man who is watching them from his barred windows:

> Then every eye was turned to the window which I occupied. 'The Condemned! The Condemned!' shouted they, pointing their fingers at me; and their bursts of laughter were redoubled.
>
> I was thunderstruck. I know not where they knew me, or how I was recognized.
>
> 'Good day! Good night!' cried they, with their mocking sneer. One of the youngest, condemned to the Galleys for life, turned his shining, leaden face on me, with a look of

envy, saying, 'He is lucky! He is to be clipped! Good-bye, Comrade!'[22]

The men are, quite literally, possessed of gallows humour, and along with the aspect of solidarity there is also that "mocking sneer", a harder, colder sense of disdain for the cruelty which is endemic to their situation, a form of mockery which verges on the deranged. In this work, a more mature, more worldly voice is making itself heard; the voice of a writer who is very much attuned to the idiosyncrasies of suffering – the way in which people can internalise brutality, rationalise it, transform it into a grim, gleeful humour, even if the targets of that humour are themselves. Alongside an astute psychological description of the repressed prisoners, Hugo begins to cultivate a distinctly modern account of the men in authority, the warders and the priests, who regulate the prison regime. The warders are not particularly sadistic or brutal, but rather their cruelty transcends individual personality, and issues from the fact that each one is a cog in the system, forming a machine which regards the prisoners not so much as flesh-and-blood creations possessed of their own individual personalities but as logistical "things" which have to be pressed into shape in order to make sure the system continues to run smoothly. When the priest comes to visit the prisoner to deliver a final religious consolation, his words leave the condemned man cold. Why? It is not because the prisoner has begun to lose his spiritual faith but rather:

[H]ow did that old man address me? Nothing to be felt, nothing to affect me, nothing to draw forth tears, nothing which sprung from his heart to enter into mine — nothing which was addressed from himself to myself...

...something vague, inaccentuated, applicable to any case and to none in particular: emphatic where it should have been profound, flat where it ought to have been simple; a species of sentimental sermon and theological elegy.[23]

In such descriptions we have an almost forensic diagnosis of modern bureaucracy in which the bureaucrat – religious or otherwise – is abstracted from the object of the bureaucratic process – in this case, the particular prisoner. In the Kantian refrain, the priest sees the prisoner not in terms of an autonomous and unique human personality, not as an end in itself – but merely the means by which a particular logistical function is to be discharged: "He had advanced in years in conducting men to death from his youth, he has grown accustomed to that which makes others shudder. The dungeon and scaffold are every-day matters with him."[24] The dungeon and scaffold are "every-day matters" – the priest has become inured to them because he has been abstracted from the rich and real realities of suffering by the bureaucratic process itself: Is this not the very epitome of what Hannah Arendt would more than a century later diagnose in her pithy but chilling phrase "the banality of evil"? In Hugo's description of the prison system, one feels, there is indeed adumbrated the clinical, detached and remorseless psychology of the type of mass slaughter which the Stalinist Gulag and the Nazi death camps would graduate into a demented apex. And it seems to me that one of the reasons why this novella gained favour with writers like Dostoyevsky is because the spirit that it carries is so distinctly modern and psychologically acute. The novella is framed in terms of an internal monologue, a stream of consciousness almost, which is disjointed and inward and corresponds to the sense of dislocation and trauma of the situation the prisoner is being made to endure. In this way one might say it provides a prelude to modernism. In a similar vein the prisoner himself is never named, he remains wholly anonymous. His crime is hinted at – we think perhaps it is murder. But beyond this he remains almost completely opaque. We have only a few threadbare clues. We know, as already mentioned, that he is poor, that he barely owns enough to be able to cover his own legal expenses. Later we read that another prisoner has referred to the condemned man as a "marquis" but whether this is a hint to his social class or merely an ironic reference to a jacket he happens to be wearing – one cannot say. We also meet his daughter whom, the condemned man recounts, fails to even recognise him. The political and historical background of the condemned man remains inscrutable,[25] we know virtually nothing of his crime, nor do we know anything about the social forces, pressures and relationships which helped create the context for it. Here early modernism elides into early existentialism; indeed Hugo's novella was said to have had a very pronounced influence on Albert Camus and certainly there is a thread of coherence which runs all the way through from *The Last Day of a Condemned Man* to *The Outsider*. Both novels depict a subject which, for the most part, exists as a pure consciousness untrammelled and unformed by historical development, a lonely individuality on the very edge of being, gazing out into the beyond.

The Last Day of a Condemned Man was published in 1829 and by this point much in Hugo's life had changed. In 1821 his mother died. Hugo, it seemed, worshiped his mother to the point of mythologising her. He had been born a very sickly baby, and the prospects of his survival had been slim. For this reason, perhaps, Sophie Trebuchet lavished her youngest child with attention, favouring him over his siblings, determined not only to save his young life, but also to shape it absolutely with the strength and desire of her own aspirations and dreams. As a young man Hugo would write how he had been made "twice the child of my obstinate mother".[26] Although Hugo would inherit his mother's stubbornness, her sheer force of will, and a good deal of her self-indulgence perhaps too – nevertheless in the face of the formidable personality who had forged the very parameters of his word as a child and adolescent, Hugo himself nearly always demurred. As a teenager he had fallen in love with his childhood friend Adele Foucher, but the relationship did not please his mother – who believed that the object of her son's passion was socially beneath him. Hugo acquiesced to his mother's demands, and it was only after Sophie Trebuchet's death in 1821 that he felt able to marry his childhood sweetheart. But if the death of his mother lifted the restraints on the young man's romantic life, perhaps it lifted the restraints on his creative life to some degree also. The colour and hue of ardent monarchism which was so much a part of the work of his first phase is ever more thinly applied during the twenties, and by the time we reach *The Last Day of a Condemned Man* it barely features at all. In fact, the one reference to monarchy in this work strikes a distinctly jarring and critical note. In the thirty-eighth paper the condemned man recognises that it is within the power of the "good" king to restore him to life and liberty at a stroke, and yet, muses the prisoner, this is something which won't be done, for that same king is busy with sycophantic ministers who echo back to him his own "opinions; or else he thinks of the Chase tomorrow, or the Ball for this evening, feeling certain that the Fete will come, and leaving to others the trouble of his pleasures".[27]

In the same year *The Last Day* was published Hugo set to work on *The Hunchback of Notre-Dame*. In this work, which he writes in a frenzy of creative haste, one can see that his political focus – particularly his concern for those who are the impoverished outsiders who subsist as *persona non grata* on the very cusps of conventional society – has sharpened considerably. *The Hunchback* is a novel very much about prejudice. Esmerelda, the beautiful gypsy girl, is painted so lyrically, so tenderly, and what comes out so much – what Hugo is able to evoke so easily and yet with such power – is the childlike sense of innocence she has. Esmerelda is all alone, an outcast, so like a child she has taken the time to refashion her loneliness in the guise of the world of her imagination; here she is secure, for she has the companionship of her beloved goat Djali, who performs with her entertaining the crowds, but is also her confidante and the best friend in whom she confides her deepest secrets. This is very much what children do when they are confronted by a world which is either coldly indifferent or actively hostile – they try to make it beautiful and kind with the magic of their imaginations. Even though she has a woman's body, Esmerelda is a child in the way she speaks – in her thoughts about the world which are both utterly kind and unbearably naive. When asked by a potential suitor about love, her answer is guileless and girlish, more the product of a fairy tale than the world she is situated in: "'Oh! Love' said she – and her voice trembled and her eyes beamed – 'that is to be two and yet but one – a man and woman blended into an angel – it is heaven!'"[28] And yet, the novel describes the black bile with which "society" greets such innocence; Esmerelda is doubly despised: as a gypsy, an outsider yes – but also as an impoverished woman from the underclass. The prejudice, the almost elemental loathing which her figure summons up on the part of the well-to-do (who are by no means immune to her beauty and talents) – speaks to the vicious snobberies of a society which has been constructed along such inhuman, hierarchical lines: a society whose inevitable consequence is the snuffing out of childlike innocence and joy, theatre and song. The hunchback of the title, Quasimodo, represents another broken child; the prejudice and hatred he endures because of his malformed body, means, like Esmerelda, he is compelled to retreat into his own imaginary world, only he is far more embittered, and instead of seeking to delight others, he embraces his isolation and his hatred, communing with the stony statues of saints and monsters within the solitary cathedral walls. Although adults in form, both Esmerelda and Quasimodo are children at heart, and Hugo's depictions of injustice are at their most searing and most authentic when threaded through the spirit of childhood.

The novel is set in fifteenth-century Paris, but once again –

alongside the depictions of the great cathedral creaking under the weight of its Romanesque pillars and gothic gargoyles – the psychology of the characters displays a remarkably modern prescience. I first read *The Hunchback* in my early twenties – at the start of the noughties. The Disney feature film of the same name had been released only a few years earlier and in the centre of London where I worked the version for the stage was advertised everywhere in big bright lights. I had the vague impression of a rip-roaring yarn, a bawdy melodramatic romance adventure set to colourful, carousing ballades. I picked up the book, by accident almost, mainly because it was so cheap and I wanted to kill a few hours during my breaks. I was taken aback – by the beauty of the language for sure – but also by the grimness and starkness which offset my preconceptions of a more saccharine work. The character of Claude Frollo was particularly compelling. In him Hugo provides a description of a certain kind of religious sensibility, an old soul, "a melancholy, grave and serious boy, who studied ardently and learned quickly; he was never boisterous at play".[29] Like Esmerelda and Quasimodo, Hugo looks at Frollo as he is as a child; he shows how the young boy has been "cloistered" away in a strict religious college by a father who is only interested in preparing his son for the priesthood in the conditions of the utmost isolation and discipline. Just like Quasimodo, though for different reasons, the young boy is all alone in the world. Quasimodo responds to his isolation by seeking solace with his statues, the young Frollo achieves the same by burying himself in his books, by committing to the priesthood – and the intellectual and spiritual preparations it demands – absolutely. The serious, austere young boy manages to extrude all desire for emotional warmth and companionship in favour of the cold caveats of canonical law, the science of medicine and the study of languages until "it seemed to the young man that life had but one sole aim: knowledge."[30] Hugo paints here another tragic child, a character who has been warped by the world, and yet nevertheless has many redeeming features. Despite his coldness, he has a sense of duty, and cares for his younger brother when they are both orphaned – and later for Quasimodo. But what is vital, what represents a real step forward in Hugo's own development as a writer, is that Frollo – and his tragic situation – is presented as the necessary consequence of his historical development. In *The Last Day of a Condemned Man* the protagonist has an almost existential character which rebuts any historical input; his is an implacable, lonely and mysterious voice, he represents a timeless archetype of suffering without any real genesis or origin. But when Frollo reaches maturity, when he rises high in the church hierarchy, when his intellectual shrewdness is at its most acute and his sense of piety is most enshrined – it is then when he encounters Esmerelda like a bolt from the blue. He sees the beautiful gypsy girl perform, he sees her sing and dance – melodiously and sensually – and in that moment he is reminded of everything the trajectory of his history has evolved to repress. He is reminded of love, beauty, joy, pleasure, kindness – and in his desire for Esmerelda these things hit him with a particularly erotic intensity which threatens to shatter the edifice of his stability, to crack the carapace of every defence he has formed against the loneliness and isolation which was his childhood lot. As a consequence, summoning up all the religious piety and aloofness he can muster, he responds to this existential crisis by persecuting and deriding Esmerelda as a witch, as an instrument of Satan, as a pure evil for the "evil" she had awoken in him:

> The creature before me was of that preternatural beauty which can only be of heaven or hell. This was no mere girl moulded of our common clay, and faintly lighted within by the flickering ray of a woman's spirit. It was an angel, but of darkness – of flame, not of light. At the moment that I was thinking thus, I saw beside thee a goat, a beast of the

witches, which looked at me laughingly. The midday sun gilded its horns with fire...I had learnt who thou wast – a gypsy, a Bohemian, a gitana, a zingara. How could I doubt the witchcraft?[31]

In the character of Frollo, a religious fundamentalism becomes the palliative to a shattered, lonely childhood; a vigorous moral impulse is warped into the type of pathological puritanism which can brook no challenge to its rigid, ossified view of a well-ordered moral universe. A universe devoid of all colour or joy, but one which can offer absolute security and sanctuary against the pain and vulnerability the individual is exposed to when loving others openly, generously and on equal terms. In providing a masterful description of the kind of religious piety which suppresses that which is most human in a single life, Hugo also anticipates certain key themes in modern psychotherapy; the psyche of the grey, austere priest is surely locked into the most severe form of sexual repression – the vision of Esmerelda, therefore, becomes the catalyst by which the unconscious, elemental impulses of the "id" threaten to break out of the box of the priest's thinly contained sanity once and for all. These impulses then feed into the social prejudices of the epoch, the racism toward gypsies, the misogyny which decries poor, isolated women as "witches"; and all this Hugo shows with a chilling, flowing inevitability which arises from the arc of the priest's development from a child onward. By beginning to master such a historical expose of the individual character Hugo surpasses the generic character of the "condemned man" he called into being only a year or so before – the priest's suffering, and then later, the terrible nature of his crime, are rendered more vivid, because the writer has managed to depict a flesh-and-blood being struggling with the contradictions visited upon him by his own historical past.

The central character of Quasimodo is also a historical creation – not as nuanced as Claude Frollo it is true – but perhaps it doesn't need to be. His lot in life is far less ambiguous; born hideously deformed, he is abandoned by his mother, and then taken under the wing of the sinister priest. The only thing Quasimodo knows about humanity as it exists outside the walls of Notre-Dame is the bile and ridicule he has been treated to by the gawking crowds who gather in the squares and flock to the cathedral. Like those who have known almost nothing but hatred, hatred itself becomes his carapace, his defence; his bitterness and sullen disposition become a wall against a world which has offered him nothing but loathing: "[M]alice was not innate in him. From his very first intercourse with men he had felt, and then had seen, himself repulsed, branded, despised. As he grew up he had found around him nothing but hatred. What wonder he should have caught it! He had contracted it – he had picked up the weapon that had wounded him."[32] And yet behind the "thick obdurate bark" and at "the darksome interior of that opaque being"[33] lies something which is not fully formed, which remains stunted and unarticulated – "a poor creature", a guileless child, lonely and confused. One of the most poignant scenes arrives when the deaf and dumb Quasimodo has been manacled to the "pillory" – a wooden platform which the head and arms of a person are forced into so they are visible to the crowd. In this state Quasimodo is savagely whipped while "the public fury was not less forcibly expressed on their faces than by their words. Besides, the stones that struck him explained the bursts of laughter."[34] In this moment Esmerelda approaches the tormented hunchback, who, "choking with rage and vexation" was in no doubts that the gypsy girl "had come to deal her blow like all the rest". Whereupon:

Without a word, she approached the sufferer, who writhed in a vain effort to escape her; and detaching a gourd from her girdle, she raised it gently to the poor wretch's parched lips.
Then in that eye, hitherto so dry and burning, a big tear

was seen to start, which fell slowly down that misshapen face so long convulsed by despair. It was possibly the first that the unfortunate creature had ever shed.[35]

The scene is so beautiful and sad and wonderful all at the same time. Just as with the priest, Esmerelda's appearance in Quasimodo's life provokes a revelation, but whereas Frollo is repelled by her kindness and beauty, in Quasimodo, the simple pity she has shown him proves so miraculous to his damaged spiritual constitution that he spends the rest of his days devoted to her, and indeed would give his life to preserve her own. Quasimodo is able to respond positively to the kindness and vulnerability of Esmerelda, because, despite everything he has suffered, his sense of humanity and childlike innocence remains intact. Frollo despises Esmerelda absolutely because he has lost his own. When the priest is finally successful in his endeavours – to destroy Esmerelda and thus to destroy the desire which lives in him – Quasimodo finally turns on his austere, cruel master, shoving him from the stony heights of Notre-Dame and to his death below. It is instructive that Quasimodo weeps for the vanquished, tormented priest in the same moment he weeps for the loss of Esmerelda herself – "Oh! All that I have ever loved!"[36] In the very final scene of the novel, some years on, among a pit of bodies there is discovered:

two skeletons, one of which held the other in a singular embrace...One of these skeletons, which was that of a woman, had about it some tattered fragments of a garment that had once been white...The other, which held this one in a close embrace, was a skeleton of a man. It was noticed that the spine was crooked, the head depressed between the shoulders, and that one leg was shorter than the other.[37]

Esmerelda and Quasimodo, two lost children, united in death

once more.

The pathos of *The Hunchback* rests upon its delicate observations of childlike joys, wonders and fears, and the mode by which such overall innocence is subsumed by the cruelty of the world. The heightened poignancy was an expression of a writer who had himself first-hand understood the preciousness of childhood and what its loss entailed. Adele and Victor Hugo had their first child, Leopold, in 1823 but the boy died in his infancy. In the 7 years following the couple would have four more children. As well, *The Hunchback*'s emotional resonance comes from the fact that it locates the anima of its central characters in their historical formation, and this was perhaps because Hugo himself was living in the type of tumultuous times when historical pressures built in order to break through the shell of everyday life; great events rupture the illusion of gentle ebbing continuity that "ordinary" development seems always to presuppose. Indeed Hugo was interrupted in his writing of *The Hunchback* by the outbreak of the 1830 revolution. Hugo himself was pulled along by the heady current of upheaval and change, participating in the "three glorious days" which saw the regime of Charles X overthrown and a more liberal monarchy – under Louis Phillipe – established in its wake. And yet, more radical elements, stimulated by the actions of 1830, sought to drive the revolutionary process to even more radical conclusions, and establish once and for all a republic. Two years following, the death of the general Lamarque – a Napoleonic commander who had been an outspoken critic of restoration and an advocate of radical agricultural reform – sparked another rebellion carried by a group of students who were able to transform the old general's funeral march into a broader political standoff. Rioting eventually culminated in an insurrection by which 3,000 mainly working-class rebels managed to gain control of much of the east and centre of Paris; however the action did not spread and was curtly and brutally repressed. It seems that Hugo, at this time, still held a certain wry sympathy for the regime of Louis Phillipe. Overall, however, he clearly favoured the revolutionaries and their republican principles, but he was at the same time still dealing with his mother's legacy, and was reluctant to fully commit to the republican cause, seeing the nation as a whole (and vicariously himself) as still under ripe and underprepared for such a radical form of government. The rebellious actions of June 1832, therefore, represented "follies drowned in blood", and though "[w]e shall have a republic one day...let us learn to wait...We cannot suffer boors to bespatter our flag with red."[38]

The events of 1830 and 1832 had two central effects on Hugo. On the one hand, Hugo the novelist, poet and artist was made to feel, profoundly and intuitively, the force of historical development, and the power and pathos of the movement from below which united in its remit the dispossessed, the exploited and the despised. His once unshakeable faith in the justice of a benevolent monarch, the legacy of Adele's romantic maternalism, was now virtually extinguished. His writings – he finished the majority of *The Hunchback* in the direct aftermath of the 1830 revolution – were now indelibly marked by a sense of the historical, their characters stamped by the rhythm and tempo of events building toward some great and inevitable crescendo. And yet, at the same time, his conscious political sensibilities had not matured such that he was able to make a decisive break with the form of liberalism which lingered in the wake of the royalist dissolution. Or to say the same thing, he was not prepared to come over to the socialism of the masses, to an investment in the possibility of them winning their own political power and self-determination. Perhaps, as a renowned writer whose economic legacy and privilege were by this time assured, the thought of a fundamental transformation of the given social order from below made him a tad anxious.

In any event, 1832 had – to Victor Hugo – demonstrated that, despite their elemental strengths and passions, the masses were not capable of independent organisation, and their political power had to be mediated by some type of force from above. But given he was no longer prepared to countenance a king, where could such a political ingredient be found? Having spent much of his political life in thrall to his mother's vision of a newly invigorated monarchy, Hugo now moved swiftly into his father's camp. Hugo had always taken his mother's part in her conflicts with his father, and clearly resented the level of economic dependence they, as a family, had on the general while he was growing up.[39] However, one year after his mother's death Hugo and his father reconciled. And when, in the 1830s, Hugo was looking toward some kind of power from above which might reasonably balance the interests of the propertied, more socially conservative elements with the chaotic, turbulent but noble flow of the activity of the masses from below – Hugo found the figure of the gallant Napoleonic general carrying forth the spirit of the French Revolution to be an alluring template. This experience of being caught between two irreconcilable forces – was the *aporia* which gripped liberalism in the nineteenth century more generally, and seeking solace in a military solution which would enforce order from without – was often the liberal response in the face of acute historical convulsions. Such liberal leanings would lead Hugo to the single most shameful episode in his political life when the revolutionary forces from below exploded with new vigour in 1848.

By this point the industrial proletariat as a class had emerged with its own independent political programme – it is no coincidence that Marx's and Engels' *The Manifesto of the Communist Party* was issued just as the revolutionary events began to erupt across Europe. In February 1848 Louis Phillipe was dethroned, and a provisional government was established to inaugurate what would become the short-lived Second Republic. The tension between the Parisian workers, the artisans, small business owners – and the forces of the big urban bourgeoisie alongside the landowning aristocracy and their representatives in the "party of order" was rapidly attaining a critical mass; the fissure developing between the city masses and the rural provinces was barely masked by the thin bandage of liberal suffrage which the reformists had plastered over the top. The Parisian workers had little real or trustworthy representation in the Constituent Assembly, and the new government attempted to erode the reforms the workers had won from the February agitations onward.

In June the government moved to abolish the national workshops which had previously been introduced as a state sponsored concession to guarantee work to the unemployed. In response the Paris workers rose once more *en masse*. Hugo, now something of a celebrity and someone identified with more radical leanings, had been elected to the National Assembly and was pulled into the vortex of these events. Faced with the revolutionary workers mounting the barricades, and the fundamental challenge they represented to the social order, Hugo's own instincts of liberal piety, patriotic deference and respect for the rule of law kicked in – and he travelled to the barricades in order to demand that the workers withdraw. They, however, demurred. At which point Hugo himself was actively involved in the violent military action which crushed their rebellion. His complicity in this event would leave a stain on his conscience which nothing could erase. He described the slaughter of the workers in the horrific, hallucinatory tenor of a nightmare:

> Leaving a barricade, one no longer knows what one has seen...There were corpses lying down and phantoms standing up. The hours were colossal—hours of eternity. One has been living in Death. Shadows have passed. What were they? Hands with blood on them. A short deafening din. An atrocious silence. Open mouths shouting; other mouths, also

open, but soundless...One seems to have touched the sinister perspiration of unknown depths. There is something red under one's fingernails. One remembers nothing.[40]

Once the power of the working class had been annulled, the government – bereft of any radical impetus from below – rapidly shifted rightward in its orientation eventually culminating in an all-out military dictatorship. Victor Hugo, like many other liberals of his generation, had engaged in a dark form of political incantation, hoping to conjure up the spectre of the famous French general who had perished decades before on the island of Saint Helena, seeing in the ghostly Napoleonic archetype a means both to revive France's greatness and to quell the social unrest which more and more registered in the proletarian tremors coming from below. Once, however, such a creation had been called into being, once the grotesque, mirthless figure of the nephew had been conscripted as a stand in for the uncle, once Louis Napoleon was in place and was working to consolidate his power through the military tradition with which his name was synonymous; once he managed to employ increasingly authoritarian means, to muzzle the press and to limit the franchise – like the sorcerer's apprentice, Victor Hugo began to baulk before the rushing waters of the forces he himself had helped unleash. At the very last moment Hugo endeavoured to unite with the left-wing opposition, but by this point, of course, it was too late. Louis Napoleon moved against the National Assembly in December 1851 affecting a brutal military coup. A few barricades appeared on the streets of Paris once again alongside around a thousand insurgents, but the power of the organised working class had already been smashed. Those militants who remained were put down by an army of 30 times their number. Hundreds of members of the National Assembly were arrested. Hugo fled, spending nights in hiding, before being smuggled across the border, which would mark the beginnings of a 19-year exile, one which would take him from Brussels, to Jersey, to Guernsey, and would see him write the major part of his most famous work, *Les Miserables*.

By the time of his exile Hugo had lived through various revolutionary upheavals, and as well as soaking in an aesthetic impression of their ebb and flow, their dramatic power and their noble intentions – in 1848 he had compromised himself before the revolutionary struggle in the most dismal and deplorable fashion. And yet, in the months following the June days, Hugo was brought face-to-face with the consequences of his liberalism; in the words of David Hancock Turner he saw how "once the subaltern have been shot dead, their neighborhoods invaded and triturated and countless others repressed and jailed, there is no social force remaining to fight the forces of looming right-wing reaction."[41] He saw what a society looks like when the progressive and collective agents of social change have been decisively stifled. And I think the shock and pathos of this understanding is what informs so profoundly much of the writing in *Les Miserables*. In 1848 Hugo had denounced the "mob" in the same moment he had supported the use of the most brutal force against it as a necessary measure to maintain law and order. By the time he was writing part five of *Les Miserables* – only a few years on – his perspective was that of the melancholy exile and his sympathies now rested most fundamentally with those at the bottom: "And these words that are intended to be insults – 'beggars', 'rabble', 'mob', 'populace' – indicate alas! that the blame lies with those who rule rather than those who suffer, with the privileged rather than with the deprived."[42] This same section reaches its climax when the hero of the novel, Jean Valjean – an ex-convict who has spent 19 years in chains after having stolen a loaf of bread – rescues Marius, an idealist young man who is fighting heroically while manning the barricades. The context is the rebellion of 1832. And here the barricade emerges for the first time as a literary cypher, a symbol of justice and heroism; something which seems to arise out of the earth itself – the revolutionary struggle of the oppressed given a visible form, materialised in the architecture of the streets. Hugo's writing seems to capture the quintessence of the heroic, heady, haphazard resistance and solidarity which is improvised by the fighters on the ground and expressed in the barricade which embodies it:

> This barricade was frenzied...A huge red flag on it flapped in the wind. Shouts of command could be heard, songs of attack, the rolling of drums, the sobbing of women and lugubrious bursts of laughter from the famished. Enormous and alive it was, and crackles and sparks emitted from it, as from the back of some electric beast. The spirit of revolution clouded this summit from which roared the voice of the people, which is like the voice of God. A strange majesty emanated from this Titanic mound of rubble. It was a heap of detritus and it was Sinai.[43]

Describing the people thronging as one, describing the barricade as a living breathing animal of revolution, one could not find a greater contrast with the description of the formless, lifeless murder ground of the actual barricade Hugo helped pacify during the June days of 1848. But along with the description of the revolution as a collective act, Hugo also peppers his tale with individuals and the pathos of their sacrifice. Coming a few pages later, when the barricade is about to be overrun, in order to allow others to leave, it is decided that several men will stay and sacrifice their lives. Whereupon, Hugo brings us into the small claustrophobic space, still fragrant with gunpowder, where these life and death negotiations are being hammered out. But in a truly tragic reversal the brave fighters are not parlaying for the right to leave, but for the right to be the ones who stay and give their lives for their comrades. If the previous description of the barricade resonated with the floral poetry and rich energy of Hugo's romanticist flourishes, then at once the language is modulated in accordance with the solemnity of the scene; the words become sober and spare, and their heroism resonates in the silence:

> 'It is true,' said one young man to an older one, 'you're the father of a family. Go.'
> 'You'd better go yourself,' replied the older man, 'you have two sisters to provide for.'
> And an extraordinary argument broke out. Each vied to be the one who would not be turned away from the tomb...These great Revolutionary barricades were venues for heroism. The improbable was natural here. These men did not surprise each other.[44]

If Hugo now depicts the radicals on the frontline in glowing heroic colours, his attitude to the forces of "law and order" has grown considerably frostier. In perhaps one of his most abiding and chilling literary creations, he gives us the force of law and order personified in the grey, praying mantis-like figure of the police enforcer who lurks in the shadows – the sinister Javert who mercilessly and relentlessly hunts Jean Valjean after the latter slips his chains and escapes his imprisonment. Of course, Javert's obsessive nature is thrown into relief by the pettiness of Valjean's crime – the theft of a loaf of bread – and all the years of confinement, hard labour and persecution he endures for it. For Javert, Valjean's misery and suffering, his humanity – is occluded by the lifeless abstraction of rule and regulation which form the body of the legal system. For Javert the law represents a timeless objectivity which is above the messy, haphazard, imperfect furore of human life; the law exists as a higher power, a cold omniscient divinity whose watchful eye is capable of boring into the heart of human frailty and corruption through its avatar on earth, its humble servant in the guise of the gimlet-eyed and utterly fanatical police inspector. Javert's devotion to duty is such that "[h]e would have arrested his father for escaping from prison and denounced his mother for contravening the terms from her release from gaol."[45] Like the sinister priest Claude Frollo in *The Hunchback*, Javert represents another chilling, meticulous study in repression. His early childhood was marred by the chaos, insecurity and fear wrought by the poverty visited upon his itinerant, criminal parents: "Javert was born in prison of a fortune-teller whose husband was a convicted felon. As he grew up, he believed that he was on the outside of society…At the same time he was conscious of some underlying inflexibility, steadiness and probity within him, compounded by an inexpressible hatred for that gypsy race to which he belonged. He joined the police."[46] The police force and the force of law become the means by which Javert is able to purify the taint and stigma of his background; the cool baptising waters of a higher objectivity in which he is able to wash away all the traces of his past. And yet, as with Frollo, the mental operation – the repression mechanism – isn't entirely successful. Javert carries the *aporia*, latent inside him: he is bent on suppressing and destroying the very type of people whose poverty and background he once shared. When, having hunted Valjean so mercilessly, and for so long, Javert falls into the hands of his nemesis – Valjean responds by showing him great kindness and setting the police inspector free. At which point, Javert's pristine faith in the law is called violently into question; brought into an inescapable contact with Valjean's great sense of humanity, Javert is unable to continue to rationalise the legal persecution of him. The law sheds its semblance of objectivity, and in that moment reveals itself to Javert as a means by which a very particular social interest is served; i.e. the means by which the most powerful are able to forcibly repress and control the poor and dispossessed. For Javert, once this contradiction

– always pregnant within him – bursts asunder, his whole ideological edifice is irrevocably shattered. The lawman acts – with the brutal clarity typical of him – by shooting himself on the spot.

The violent awakening that Javert experiences must be framed in the context of Hugo's own awakening; how his faith in the "justice" of the law in June 1848 was interminably fragmented by the murderous regime which followed on from it and the humanity and courage on the side of those who continued to resist. In this way *Les Miserables* is a tale of redemption in the broadest sense; intimately bound up with the redemption of the fictionalised convict Jean Valjean – is the redemption of the author who created him and who found himself so profoundly on the wrong side of the barricade. Indeed one might note that Jean Valjean becomes, in some sense, an idealised corrective to many of the author's own shortcomings and corruptions; that the convict is a character wrought from displaced guilt. One of the most striking things about Jean Valjean is that he is profoundly asexual in essence. He shows no erotic or romantic interest in any of the many women he comes into contact with during the decades of time the novel spans. Hugo, however, was highly promiscuous – and his sexual relations seemed to have verged on the exploitative. He used his name and celebrity as a cachet to have as much sex as possible with women from every class, from countesses to chambermaids. One of the key themes of *Les Miserables* is how economically vulnerable young women are sucked into the dark maw of prostitution: "Think of your sisters, those of you who have them. Misery, prostitution, police patrols...that's what they'll be reduced to."[47] Indeed one of its central plotlines involves Jean Valjean saving from prison a destitute woman (Fantine) who has fallen into prostitution. The author of *Les Miserables*, on the other hand, seems to have spent more time visiting women in brothels rather than rescuing them from them. Perhaps Valjean was the person Hugo – in his better moments – aspired to be. For a more tragic riff on the similar theme, one notes how one of the great redemptions of Valjean's life consists in the fact he manages to save and preserve the life of his adopted daughter Cosette – against all the odds. The storyline is powerful and tender, but again one can't help but feel it is imbued with the most poignant sense of wish fulfilment. The author was unable to shield his own daughter, Leopoldine Hugo, from the vicissitudes of the world and she died in a boating accident at just 19 years old. The event devastated Hugo, but Valjean's own character arc is far less tragic, for he dies peacefully with his beloved daughter at his bedside holding his hand. And as already referenced, Valjean saves Marius – the brave youth who is described as the "saviour"[48] of the barricade – the type of character whose real-world counterpart had not been saved by Victor Hugo, but had instead been maligned, repressed and destroyed by him.

But if Valjean has a certain saintly aura this is counterbalanced by the powerful and free-flowing historical description of the miseries which have created him. Indeed Jean Valjean represents yet another step forward in the historical awareness of the writer. Whereas Quasimodo is a carefully depicted historical creation, and is clearly one of "the miserables" in the Hugo sense of the word, the repression Quasimodo experiences in *The Hunchback* is very much grounded in the incidental and arbitrary fact of his physical deformity. But in the case of the convict Jean Valjean, another delicately observed historical creation, his repression is a direct result of his own class background, and thus contains a level of necessity which is drawn from a social world which is explicitly depicted in terms of the conflict which opens up between the powerful at the top and the exploited at the bottom. Valjean:

came from a poor peasant family in Brie. As a child he had not learnt to read...His mother had died of milk fever that was not properly treated. His father, a tree-pruner like himself, was killed falling from a tree. Jean Valjean was left with only a widowed sister older than himself who has seven children, boys and girls. And so his youth was spent doing hard and ill-paid work.[49]

Hugo depicts the relentless processes of a crushing, immiserating poverty which closes down every avenue of opportunity for the exhausted, famished individual, blotting out the light. Finally, with his family on the brink of starvation, Valjean commits his hazardous crime and filches that loaf of bread, whereupon he is arrested, chained and condemned to 5 years of hard labour. His personality becomes increasingly stunted, brutalised by the state, lost in the penal system, "in that cold fog where lone destinies founder",[50] his feelings and emotions dull into a crust of numb indifference: "In that heart where there had been an open wound, there was now a scar."[51] Due to various minor infractions, the punitive state sentences Valjean to 19 years of incarceration in total.

And so this is a novel which is about class. The aesthetic depiction of the repression Valjean endures, forensically unfolded over the period of a lifetime, would be in and of itself enough to justify a heap of laurels bestowed on the author, but *Les Miserables* is more significant still, in as much as the individual destiny of Jean Valjean is set against a far broader class panorama. In *Les Miserables* the city of Paris itself becomes for all intents and purposes two cities: the one – an everyday world of open, sunlit squares and thoroughfares alive with the billowing colours of military parades, decorated by the monuments and statues which consecrate the city's past in the hands of both emperor and kings. And then there is another world, a world within a world; a twilight world of winding gothic alleyways, crooked crumbling *pensions* – the medieval quarters sequined with shadows, the graveyards where the homeless gather; the underground labyrinth of sewer and catacomb through which the city's night-time denizens, the outcasts and the wretched, roam. What *Les Miserables* manages to show so superbly, and with such heart – what raises the novel from a more naturalistic and gritty riff on the theme of exploitation and suffering – is how it is able to depict, with vivid artistry, bawdy humour, rich colour – the lives of a whole cross section of the underclass, from the brave, cheeky street children who live in the husk of decaying monuments, to the poverty-stricken radicals who whisper illicitly through the smoke-filled fug of dilapidated bars; from the nimble chimneysweep to the old, arthritic road worker; from the porters and the prostitutes to the shadowy underworld criminal chiefs and the grave diggers in the church cemetery who they provide with such a steady stream of work. More than anything, I think, *Les Miserables* shows how these people manage to fashion their own politics and their own culture from the struggle for survival they are engaged in, how from the shattered remnants of exploitation and poverty they are able to fashion this quirky, strange subterranean world. As the individual story of Valjean tapers and turns, so the momentum of the broader historical movement also builds, such that the convict's story flows into the struggle of a whole broader group of people – as personal redemption elides seamlessly into universal revolution and all – all the wretched and repressed – explode onto the political stage like a fiery barricade blazing through the darkness. It is this combination of the historical and the romantic which has made *Les Miserables* an anthem for revolution that has sounded the world over.

Eugene Debs, the great American union leader, read the novel many times throughout his life – its searing depiction of poverty and struggle was one he would never relinquish nor forget. Over a century later, the great Venezuelan radical leader Hugo Chavez would cite *Les Miserables* as being his favourite novel and went as far as to say the work sparked his turn toward the politics of socialism: "You want to meet Jean Valjean? Go to Latin America. There are many Jean Valjeans in Latin America."[52] The book was a huge commercial success but also cemented the image of Hugo as a radical writer forever on the side of the oppressed. When, in 1861, Louis Napoleon's armies invaded Mexico they were greeted not only with bullets from the Mexican military, but with pamphlets which jeered: "What are you? Soldiers of a tyrant. The best of France is on our side. You have Napoleon. We have Victor Hugo."[53] How did Hugo, who was no stranger to fame and commercial success, react to this outpouring of honour and adulation on a world scale? Well, he remained in exile, disdaining Louis Napoleon's invitation to return to France and continuing to polemicise against the upstart dictator in print. By this point, of course, Hugo was himself an old man – though that doesn't seem to have dimmed his sexual escapades. He lived in the luxury and warm glow his celebrity and commercial success had assured him. His thinking, like his frame, seems to have grown a little more flabby and loose in this period, and his curiosity on matters of spiritualism and mysticism seems to have crossed over into the credulous and absurd. He found solace in communing with his beloved, long lost daughter Leopoldine, of course, but tragedy would swiftly become farce as soon Hugo was nattering away with the great artists, thinkers and playwrights of the ages like Shakespeare and Plato – both of whom, coincidentally, conceded the nature of Hugo's own genius. And yet this is not the whole story. In 1871 the workers of Paris once again set revolution into motion writing what was to be one of the most poignant and tragic episodes in human history. For a little over 2 months the workers took control of the city of Paris forming the "commune" – the radically democratic system of government in which power flowed from the bottom up. The government troops were to repress the commune in the bloodiest of fashions, killing up to 30,000 unarmed workers in the process. In the aftermath of the massacre Hugo did more than simply denounce the government; he opened up his home in order to give sanctuary to communards fleeing persecution. In the years to follow he became the most vocal and visible advocate for amnesty for those communards who had fled abroad. And in the 1880s, such amnesty was granted. At long last, and near to the very end of his life, Victor Hugo had finally found himself on the right side of the barricades.

Chapter Two

Hugo Chavez in the Light of the Mass Movement

During the Great War and on through the twenties Juan Vicente Gomez was president of Venezuela. He is often remembered as having been a moderniser. It was mostly due to his efforts, advocates say, that Venezuela was able to develop a modern economy and infrastructure. As with most explanations which languish in the realm of first impressions, of immediacy, this is profoundly false. Gomez did preside over the development of a more "advanced", more capitalistic economy but at the same time his presidency coincided with the international realisation of the great economic potential offered by the reserves of oil in Venezuela. This is a critical moment in the Venezuelan historical process. Foreign capital now flooded in and superimposed itself; it brought with it more advanced technology, it developed the materials and tools with which to better tap the oil and transport it. Workers were the ones to facilitate these changes; to build the equipment and work with it; in short to extract the oil, for capital is never a mere sum of money invested, but is instead and always the embodiment of the relation between proletariat and bourgeoisie, sometimes veiled, yet continually transforming and acting.

Juan Vicente Gomez for his part opened up the country to foreign investment; he made sure that the big oil companies were met with open arms and with open arms did he receive the financial rewards their "gratitude" delivered. He amassed a personal fortune over and above the personal fortune he had, as president, already amassed. He was a dictator and his relation to the imperial powers of the First World was summarised by another Venezuelan president, Romulo Betancourt, who would later say of him that he "was something more than a local despot, he was the instrument of foreign control of the Venezuelan economy, the ally and servant of powerful outside interests."[54] As an afterthought Gomez did invest in public works with the colourful and lazy charity that someone swollen with money and self-importance often employs. These small benefits were not realised in and through public education, however. Widespread education is, apparently, rarely conducive to dictatorship. And then a procession of dictators with the brief interruption provided by the election of Romulo Gallegos – swiftly overthrown in a military coup led by Marcos Perez Jimenez, who took power before being overthrown himself in 1958. This "caudillo" liquidated much of the opposition against him before he was eventually vanquished, but, like so many military men before him, he was granted asylum by the government of the United States. He took several hundred million dollars of Venezuela's money for good measure because, as a patriot, he no doubt felt it important to retain some keepsake of the country he so very much loved. Despite the outrage and clamouring for justice on the part of the Venezuelan masses, he eventually retired to Spain where he would be met with warmth and understanding by fellow dictator Francisco Franco. It is always good to have friends.

Romulo Betancourt, who succeeded Perez Jimenez, actually won the presidency on a democratic platform. He did this partly as a result of promises made to lift the standard of living for the majority of the population. But although Betancourt did struggle to make sure the state obtained more of the wealth generated from oil sales very little of this money trickled down to the poor majority. The promises melted away in the stark light of the new relationship he forged with the United States. Betancourt also formed an alliance with the big party of the right – the Social Christian Party of Venezuela (COPEI); an alliance known as the *Punto Fijo* pact. The pact ensured a common economic programme and created a situation of shared power between the two large parties – rather than struggle with one another they were content to divvy out the oil revenues between themselves. They saved their strength for the protests below which inevitably flared and which were violently suppressed. For all this Betancourt is now proudly touted as the "founding father" of Venezuelan democracy.

The *Punto Fijo* pact held for the next few decades. Whichever party was in power the same small elite comprised of politicians, oil bureaucrats and investors absorbed the riches generated from the oil. Every now and again some of that money found its way to fund social programmes for education and health but, as might be expected, this was a rare occurrence. In the 1980s this situation grew ever more desperate; the more the social divide expanded between wealth and poverty, the more frantically did the rich few grab all they could. This was the era of the yuppie and the free market; a time in which the wealthy paraded their riches with all the bravado of a drunk who knocks back more rum in order to postpone the inevitable hangover. As the eighties rolled to an end the economic headache did indeed arrive and as usual it was the people who had paid for everything else, the workers, who were expected to pay for this.

Despite its supposedly nationalised status *Petroleos de Venezuela, S.A* (the state oil company or PDVSA) was a corporation which allowed for the continuation of an acquisitive work ethic, its management comprised from the higher echelons of the old private companies and firmly slotted into the structures of global oil production and investment. So it was that in the late eighties the economy felt very keenly the falling world oil prices. There was already a great deal of distrust on the part of the masses toward the IMF and the imperialist countries and, when Carlos Andres Perez was inaugurated in February 1989, much of his success was based on his overt hostility to the IMF – "a neutron bomb that only kills people"[55] – a hostility he had demonstrated throughout his campaign. Within 2 weeks the president had betrayed this perspective. He committed to the IMF and ratified the Washington economic proposals which saw the few state-provided goods and services liberalised, and government spending restricted; measures which would yet again extract more money from an already desperately poor majority.

Venezuela's capital, Caracas, is beautiful. In the centre stand the great skyscrapers of the business district. Streamlined and pristine some of these are the colour of marble while others are a deep, rich blue; a sapphire colour which is able to imprison the sunlight such that the surface of the building shimmers. As the view pans out you can see all around the shape and contour of great hills. The shacks and skeleton houses of the shanty towns attach themselves to these hills, and there are so very many and they are pressed so tightly together that their situation looks almost perilous. It really does seem like they are clinging on for life. And in effect that is what the poor here have always done; albeit in a time of military dictatorship, or during the more "civilised" and "democratic" governments which still took so much and gave so very little. However, all great historical events know the transition from quantity to quality and on the morning of 27 February 1989 the people from the slums and from the hills could take no more.

The immediate consequence of Perez's deceitful concession to Washington in February was a 100 per cent increase in the price of gasoline. On the morning of the 27th when the population awoke to the new changes the astonishment was widespread. In Caracas, where the informal workforce commuted in from the shanty towns to clean and cook in the houses and offices of the wealthy, the disbelief soon turned to outrage. Many people refused to pay. Rioting and the burning of buses coincided with wider demonstrations as the whole country was engulfed in protest. The response of the "democratic" government was deathly simple. They turned their guns on the population. The first reported fatalities arrived early afternoon when police opened fire on students in a park and the violence intensified after "democratic" president Perez appeared on national television to announce the suspension of constitutional rights and a state of siege. In the largest and poorest barrios, the repression was more extreme and many of those most active in the rebellion were "disappeared". It seems that no one knows just how many people were murdered in those few days – some say 300, others put the number closer to 3,000.[56] We do know that those killed were predominantly poor. Following a logic of self-preservation, the government tried to conceal the true nature of the uprising; it insisted that no more than 257 people had lost their lives; that the *Caracazo* was a limited and opportunistic action on the part of a criminal element and that looting was its main expression. The wonderfully "independent" Venezuelan press, in support of their leaders, carried the same misinformation and tried to further poison the issue with furtive references to the activities of "foreigners" – shady and unnameable orchestraters of chaos lurking from behind the scenes. These racist slurs were conceived of with deliberation on the part of the government and media; it was no doubt calculated that these would be the most expedient means of directing public anger away from themselves. It is worth noting that these were the same papers as those owned by billionaire media moguls such as Gustavo Cisneros; papers which today in Venezuela present themselves as the friend of the masses and the righteous guardians of truth. In the case of the *Caracazo* their lies were corrected in the most simple of ways by the unearthing of a mass grave one year on.

The *Caracazo* marked the beginning of the end for the government. True, they were able to suppress the uprising and hence cling to power. For the moment. But something had changed and profoundly so. A lot of people talk about "Bolivarianism" and how it was cooked up in the barracks among the generals but this is not altogether accurate. The Bolivarian movement, its revolutionary core, was forged on a cold morning one February. The people who could no longer afford the price of a bus fare stood against the forces of international imperialism and the aftershock tore the semblance of Venezuela asunder revealing vividly two very different entities; the poor majority, and the wealthy few who would do the unthinkable in order to sustain. The military experienced a similar polarisation; already many of the soldiers whose ranks were swelled by the poor had refused to fire. It is against this background that a man named Hugo Chavez steps forward.

Hugo Chavez was born in a mud hut in a small village. The first part of his childhood was impoverished and his parents later made the decision to send him to live with his grandmother in the nearby town of Sabaneta where he would receive better opportunities. There he went through school and eventually entered the Venezuelan Academy of Military Sciences as a cadet. Here he was influenced by the philosophies of various left-wing nationalist figures like Salvador Allende, Fidel Castro and Jorge Eliecer Gaitan. He was also affected by the ideas of Marxists such as Ernesto "Che" Guevara and Lenin. These threads of thought, and others, meshed to create a somewhat indistinct fabric which Chavez would christen "Bolivarianism", named after Simon Bolivar; the military leader who had fought successfully against Spanish imperialism 2 centuries before. It would be interesting and important to undertake a more detailed examination of the ideology of Bolivarianism; its inception and the process of development it was subject to; however this cannot be dealt with here. Suffice to say that, at this time, Bolivarianism was the fusion of revolutionary ideals with the military structure which Chavez and comrades were themselves enmeshed in. What emerged was a radicalism which could not but work from the top down. In 1992 this was expressed when Chavez headed a military rebellion against the hated government. The organisers of the rebellion within the army had made attempts to link up with the masses. But they had no experience, no knowledge of how to do it, and in the end the civilian forces they had made contact with abandoned them. Despite the sympathy of the masses, the movement became isolated and it was defeated. So that he could call on his comrades in arms to surrender, the ruling class offered Chavez a minute of time to appear on mainstream television; a minute at the end of which he qualified the defeat with a warning: "Por ahora" – "For now".

Since the *Caracazo* there had been an almost perpetual stream of protests from a population which had experienced such terrible repression and was still subject to the looming dictates of the World Bank, and a president who held his own people in arrogant contempt. Although the 1992 coup led by Chavez was unsuccessful he nevertheless entered public consciousness as a symbol of the brave and heroic struggles being fought against a ruthless and corrupted elite. Within a year Perez had been impeached. Chavez himself was released from prison and in 1998 he stood in the presidential election. His main opponent was ex-beauty queen Irene Saez whose soft features, strawberry blonde hair and lack of a single coherent political idea made her the perfect representative of an elite which, devoid of credibility, now sought to sink itself in the fantastical. Saez might just as well have stepped out from one of the ghastly and saccharine TV novellas which depict wealthy, Western-esque Venezuelans preserved in a bubble of decadence and glamour, Venezuelans living untroubled by the presence of Venezuela. In contrast to this stood Chavez. Chavez had darker, more indigenous looks. His appearance and his street wise language marked him out as a boy from the barrio and his persona was twofold; underpinned by both the softness which comes from a genuine love of the people and the strength which arises from the desire to fight alongside them. In addition, he called George Bush Jr a "donkey". For all of this it was difficult not to like Hugo Chavez. In 1998 the masses of Venezuela liked him very much for they made him president in what was an overwhelming electoral victory.

Despite their complete redundancy it seems as though the wealthy elite were still astounded by Chavez's victory. The United States government was certainly worried by the change. But though Chavez, from the very start of his presidency, initiated various reforms which would help raise the standard of life for the poor in terms of education and healthcare, he did not challenge private property fundamentally and made it clear he wanted to work with the international investors and not against them. Nevertheless the elite, both inside and outside Venezuela, mounted a savage and relentless campaign against him. Their reaction, which seems disproportionate, cannot simply be understood by the immediate threat that Chavez did or did not pose to wealth though, in the last analysis, this was the entrenched issue. In Venezuela the wealthy; the oil and media magnates and emissaries, their affiliates in the government, and their offspring – the next generation of happy-go-lucky students who globetrot on the cusp of adulthood before returning home to take up the mantle; to assume a position managing their parents' business or blaze a path upwards through the higher echelons of government, overseen, of course, by the stern but benevolent gaze of "Pappi"; in short – the whole class itself, via its various sub-stratums, had sustained, largely untroubled, rumbling on through time, controlling the various sections of industry and government and reaping the vast financial rewards which arose from such a state of affairs. They felt good. The election of Chavez changed that.

This same elite has since coined a buzz word with which to label Chavez and the movement which created him; they describe it as "feo" which in Spanish means simply "ugly" yet much more is transmitted by this phrase on their lips. Before 1989 their main contact with the workers who maintained them had been through the comings and goings of domestic servants who cleaned and cooked; a mainly indigenous army whose poverty and the subsequent compulsion to stay employed rendered them almost invisible to their "benefactors". Then again the "benefactors" never troubled themselves to look that hard. But one February the image of these people, exploding in protest, was emblazoned indelibly across their field of vision. That mainly dark-skinned majority, who were "suited" to performing the most menial and dirty tasks discretely and from behind the scenes, were now clamouring for recognition and, to a person whose life was wealthy and free of toil, how could this appear as anything but ugly? For a revolutionary nothing is more beautiful.

In *The Phenomenology of Spirit* Hegel describes the dialectical nature of the relationship between bondsman and lord. To immediacy it seems as though the personality of the lord, freed as it is from the burden of manual labour, has attained true nobility and independence, but the great German philosopher observes that in actual fact something else is true:

[J]ust where the master has effectively achieved lordship, he really finds that something has come about quite different from an independent consciousness. It is not an independent, but rather a dependent consciousness that he has achieved. He is thus not assured of self-existence as his truth; he finds that his truth is rather the unessential consciousness, and the fortuitous unessential action of that consciousness. The truth of the independent consciousness is accordingly the consciousness of the bondsman...By serving he cancels in every particular aspect his dependence on and attachment to natural existence, and by his work removes this existence away...This activity giving shape and form, is at the same time the individual existence, the pure self-existence of that consciousness, which now in the work it does is externalized and passes into the condition of permanence.[57]

The ruling classes despised Chavez because his figure was a visible reminder of those who work so hard and for very little; those whose labour shapes and transforms the world; thereby creating a subsistence for themselves and the vast wealth of a relative few. In the person of Chavez this minority was compelled to confront daily its own lack of substance; its wayward and unworldly nature; human beings rendered narrow and cruel by the arbitrary and parasitical role they assume in the furore of social life. This underpinned the racism and venom they directed toward Chavez, and toward the vast majority of the poor. The state of affairs reached a critical point in April 2002 when seething resentment was translated into explosive action.

In the first part of 2002 Chavez had been struggling to reform the PDVSA in order to garner a greater deal of funding for public education and health. Since 1999 spending on these things had increased but now Chavez sought to introduce a law which would set limits on foreign investment and double the obligatory taxes to be paid by the PDVSA to the government. The management of the PDVSA led a strike in response to these measures which was the beginning of a more aggressive campaign of mobilisations and slander on the part of the ruling class. Chavez responded by introducing the "Bolivarian circles" which straight away saw hundreds of thousands from the poorer elements sign up. This period saw an intensification in struggle – with both sides rattling their sabres and their supporters clashing in demonstrations up and down the country.

It is important to note the role of the mainstream media throughout as they intensified their invective directed at Chavez; they inflamed the situations as they actually occurred; they showed images of Chavez alongside angry mobs and burning buildings; they quite systematically instilled the message, directed at small businesses, shopkeepers, craftsman – the lower middle classes in general – that, under Chavez, all you have would certainly go up in flames. Years later we have a clearer view of what was happening. The ruling class had decided to make its move in advance – that is to say having lost out democratically in the elections and realising this route would be ineffective as a means to be rid of Chavez, they were now determined to remove him physically. On 9 April a strike was called whereby business leaders closed down their enterprises. Two days following a large demonstration of some 200,000 anti-*Chavista* protesters was launched and here things took a disturbing turn. At the same time a pro-*Chavista* march was taking place and though both events had routes organised in advance such that they wouldn't conflict, nevertheless the two groups met and violence erupted. It is now known that the anti-*Chavista* march was purposely re-routed without police consultation (a legal requirement) and this resulted in 20 deaths and over 100 injuries. Here the media stepped in at the opportune moment – they recorded and showed images of *Chavistas* with guns blazing and counterposed this with images of civilians shot and running away. Later with the help of amateur footage it was demonstrated that the square below the shooters was empty and that the Chavez supporters were returning fire having been targeted by snipers positioned above. They were in no way responsible for the wounded people shown on television. But the Venezuelan media did not require the lie to sustain; it wasn't necessary that the contrived footage withstand future examination. The images were needed only in the moment; to create the spark which would ignite the explosive events that followed. While these doctored images were paraded ad infinitum by the Venezuelan media and the mainstream media around the world as "evidence" of *Chavista* brutality, army officers came out and announced the coup. They threatened to bomb the presidential palace and had Hugo Chavez arrested. The elected government was disbanded and the president of Venezuela taken to an island military base where he was detained, charged with the violence which had occurred when the demonstrations clashed two days before; the same violence which the opposition had so meticulously orchestrated.

In the hours which followed, the focus of the world was on Venezuela. The media would report that Chavez had resigned as a consequence of the popular pressure – itself a response to repressive action on the part of the government. They portrayed the *coup d'etat* as a spontaneous event which was utterly unforeseen. Now it is common knowledge that the coup leaders, acting in tandem with the media, had long since prepared the action but it is illuminating to dwell on a small incident with regard to this. Pedro Carmona was the head of the Venezuelan Federation of Chambers of Commerce and therefore one of the leading members of the wealthy elite who so despised Chavez. He was made president of the country following the arrest of Chavez. But what is incredible is that this individual had the traditional presidential sash he would wear at his inauguration in Miraflores on 12 April, woven at a tailor's in Madrid several months before. This astounding fact reveals the depth of contempt that Carmona and the others held for the mass of the population. Carmona and co decided to use their wealth and power furtively, from behind the scenes to remove a leader who carried with him many of the hopes and aspirations of the majority. They didn't for a moment falter or hesitate in their schemes. Carmona was so confident that the coup would succeed and he would be made president that he was able to take care of even the smallest of details months in advance such as the ordering of an item of decorative attire. Where did such excessive confidence come from? The question isn't difficult to answer. Carmona knew the kind of solidarity he would receive from his friends in big business who closed down their enterprises creating economic chaos, he was sure of the support he would get from his friends in the media who created the climate of lies in which the coup would flourish, and he was certain that the rich *en masse* would take to the streets furiously pounding the cooking pans with which their servants prepared their food. When Carmona was made president he straight away introduced a decree dissolving the National Assembly, the Supreme Court and a host of other institutions connected with the democracy. As Carmona announced the demise of each of these bodies the small circle of wealthy middle-aged men gathered around, roared their triumph and slapped each other on the back. Venezuela was to be their playground once more. This had been a true demonstration of solidarity.

But there was one type of solidarity that Carmona and friends had not counted on. While they were celebrating in the Miraflores Palace something else was happening outside. People were beginning to gather. These people were notable for their shabbier clothes and darker skins. Gradually, more and more arrived. They came from the barrios and from the hills and they came without any obvious hurry and yet they kept on coming. The anti-Chavista march a few days before had gathered perhaps some 200,000 people which by anyone's estimation is quite a lot. This was different as 200,000 became 300,000, then 500,000 and then 1,000,000 and still the people kept coming. From the balcony of Miraflores the coup plotters must have beheld the vast human sea. What were they thinking in those moments? Did they hold any hopes that their coup, so carefully planned, could be sustained? Or did they feel a sinking sense of dread before the mighty power they had awoken? Whatever the case the military officers realised very quickly the perilous nature of the situation which confronted them. Simply put they understood that before the gathering storm nothing could stand. They radioed in the order to stand down and the coup collapsed with the plotters fleeing the palace. After 48 hours of imprisonment Hugo Chavez was returned to the presidential palace amid jubilant celebrations.

Now this is another of the critical moments in the history of Bolivarianism and more generally the working-class struggle in Latin America as a whole. The election of Chavez, the laws he sought to implement and the investment he put into social works subsequently; these were radical occurrences for certain but it would be difficult to describe them as revolutionary. However, with the defeat of the 2002 coup something took place which was profoundly revolutionary and that was the appearance of the masses on the world historic stage as protagonists. Their collective action thwarted the coup and altered the course of events decisively. For that short time, history was no longer something which unfolded gradually and enigmatically over centuries; it was no longer that which resided in a faraway realm cloaked by the same sublime invisibility as heaven before earth. History became; revealing itself to be something people could lay their hands on and make their own thereby changing the world.

It is important to describe the dialectical nature of the relationship between Chavez and the masses. The masses emerged decisively in defence of Hugo Chavez precisely because in him they recognised someone representative of their own struggle, a figure that embodied their culture and was able to grasp organically their inner life. In turn Chavez was extremely responsive to the mass movement; each time the poor rose up in solidarity with him, his thought received revolutionary impetus and his endeavours to create better conditions for the masses were further energised. In addition Chavez was both honourable and courageous – characteristics which are important in the arena of political struggle and vital to a political leader of a left-wing bent. But also important, from both the perspective of reality and the analysis of it, is a detailed consideration of the set of social relations which the leader here entered into. Chavez remained firmly slotted into the structures of parliamentarianism. It is the paradox of the Venezuelan revolution that, in defending Chavez and returning him to power, the masses became a force which far surpassed the government they sought to restore. In returning power to Miraflores, a new type of power was itself created. The most revolutionary agency world history knows was gathered in the squares and in the streets outside the palace. For that short period there existed a situation of dual power with the unique historical quirk that rather than oppose each other, the two separate phenomena regarded one another favourably.

Nevertheless such a situation cannot be maintained indefinitely. Chavez thanked the people humbly and asked them to return to their homes. This they did. There was at this time no grassroots party which could convert their revolutionary energy into a sustaining force. There was no organisation which might help ensure that the governance of historical events by the majority might become something typical and everyday. There was no group which could provide a centre around which the workers and peasants might rally; organising on the ground to facilitate collective control of society's economic organs. Might Chavez have provided the leverage by which such a situation be realised? Doubtful. Hugo Chavez contained within himself the paradox which lives at the heart of the Venezuelan revolutionary process. Chavez's great political victories have taken place via parliamentarianism whereas his political fermentation took shape in and through the activity of the masses. Chavez always felt himself (and quite correctly so) to be organically affiliated to the masses but at the same time he sought to apply this sense of things to an arena which is abstracted from the day-to-day activities of the majority. This is in no way a condemnation of Hugo Chavez. It is merely the inevitable result of the two political realms that the personality of the Venezuelan president mediated.

Some might object. What other head of state has ever called for workers in factories to take increasing control in terms of organisation and in some places run the factories for themselves? This Chavez did. However, there is a great deal of complication here. Chavez gave directives for workers in a few factories to take them over and manage them for themselves, which was certainly a radical and positive step. It is often helpful to first dip your toe in the water before swimming. But it should not be heralded as the inauguration of a workers' state. Even if Chavez had demanded that not a few but all factories be put under the control of their workers this would still fall far short of proletarian revolution. And the reason for this is that such a revolution must grow organically from the economic sphere to the political, in conditions of extreme struggle. That is to say that the factory workers, confronted by severe wage repressions, strike with the hope of reversing them. The owners respond by firing those workers and replacing them. The workers seek to counteract this measure by occupying those factories. The owners again retaliate, this time employing the state in defence of private property; they endeavour to use the police or any other body to remove the workers by force, or they stay patient waiting for the workers to become hungry and demoralised. The occupied factories in isolation cannot sustain for these reasons – and so, in great crisis, they must necessarily look forward to the only form of salvation they might hope to obtain; the solidarity which arrives from the groupings in other occupied factories and workplaces. The basis of proletarian revolution is categorised by precisely this; the organic connections which spring up between factories and workplaces; the exchange of information and resources, the only key to their continued survival. And while this process is taking place our modern prince enters the fray decisively. The Marxist party is galvanised for the process of struggle, providing the centre around which all other operations are organised and coordinated and, in this democratic capacity, the party arrives at the point of insurrection.

If a leader simply "hands" power to the workers in the factories the process outlined above hasn't taken place; none of the connections between factories have the chance to fuse and there can't, therefore, exist the network via which the factories and workplaces can communicate their collective intentions to a central government. In other words, though a few or even many workplaces might be occupied, the big political directives would necessarily be formed in and issue forth from the concentrated power holed up in Miraflores. There could be no truly organic interplay between the government and the workers no matter what Chavez's best intentions might be. In connection with this Marx's statement that "the emancipation of the working class must be conquered by the working classes themselves"[58] resonates with a telling power.

Chavez did not understand this. He could not. He recognised the power of the workers, but in an abstract and one-sided way. He saw that they were the basis of his government's power and realised very well his own moral responsibility to act in the interests of the workers and peasants as the head of the republic. But in the period of Chavez's leadership the director of the revolution was always a government which endeavoured to act in the best interests of the masses rather than a party which emerged organically in and through the day-to-day activity of the class to assume the position of vanguard; a vanguard which absorbs organically every convulsion in the working-class movement such that it is able to filter and concentrate them into sustained revolutionary action.

Chavez's situation was made more precarious because of the people and mechanisms surrounding him. Without the sustained and continued stream of working-class activity filtering its life blood, his government couldn't but become isolated. The elements which joined the party from the workers and other layers of society were often quickly detached. In their day-to-day activities within the party they were exposed to a whole host of privileges, propelled into a new social stratum and the connections and relationships which would go on to form the basis of a new bureaucracy.

For this reason the *Chavista* government has always had an extremely contradictory character; on the one hand it is compelled to act favourably toward the workers and peasants whose votes brought it to power, while on the other the bureaucratic elements in the party resist extreme concessions to the poor precisely because such things threaten to undermine their own newly won gains. When the more radical elements of the party fought to win the referendum of December 2007 which would have granted a number of radical concessions to the working masses, they were not merely battling the relentless efforts of the ruling class to thwart the measures, they were as well fighting those within the party who had formed a dead weight, slowing and stilling the dissemination of information expressing the radical content of the reform, preventing it from effectively reaching a mass audience. If Chavez had won the reform the same elements would again have provided an anchor; as the directives from central government travelled down through the bureaucracy, the new measures would have been blunted and rendered as innocuous as might be.

The defeat of Chavez in that referendum was often regarded as a result of the fact that the Venezuelan revolutionary process had not sufficiently advanced; that the masses were tired and dissatisfied with the level of actual change which Venezuelan society had experienced and yearned for more radical measures. This was undoubtedly true. Some socialists argued at the time that the *Chavista* government should have acted in a more radical, more revolutionary, manner and thus satiated mass expectation. But one gets the impression that it wasn't from a lack of trying. The stilted development of the Venezuelan Revolution in this period was not due to the fact that Chavez and ministers didn't act radically enough but moreover because the revolutionary capacity of the government was limited by its objective position. The government then, as now, remained in a type of limbo; its position secured by a great revolutionary movement, while at the same time operating in a realm abstracted from it.

Of course this, in itself, was no reason to abandon a government which had become a beacon of hope to workers around the world. Vladimir Lenin wrote both incisively and extensively on the question of parliamentarianism; how important it is that the working-class struggle be extended to this arena in order to fight for real gains which improve the lives of people and, furthermore, give a boost in confidence to the mass movement. But what is also crucially important in Lenin's analysis is the notion that by participating actively the working class come to realise the limitations of the ballot box. The defeat of the referendum wasn't simply an expression of the desire for more radical action on the part of the government because the referendum which Chavez held included some of the most radical measures yet. The defeat of the referendum indicated that a large proportion of the masses had learnt in practice the vital lesson that the most revolutionary of transformations cannot take place in and through the parliament despite the best intentions of president or party. Though the loss in the referendum at this point was a defeat for the workers and peasants of Venezuela it was also a cloud which did have a silver lining. Chavez, by accepting the results graciously in defeat, refuted in practice all the slurs which were made against him to the effect that he was a dictator waiting in the wings to seize power the moment events took a course he didn't approve. But most importantly the referendum defeat demonstrated to the people the limits of the purely parliamentary party.

In 2006, however, Chavez established a new political organisation – the PSUV (The United Socialist Party of Venezuela). In so doing, he united the different parties and elements favourable to Bolivarianism under the single banner – and here it has to be remembered that such a project was always in danger of creating an artificial unity; one can be favourable to Bolivarianism for the reason that it is a movement which has raised the lives of the poor, or one can be favourable to it because in the current political climate of Venezuela aligning yourself with *Chavismo* is an effective way of getting ahead. At the time of its creation, both tendencies found expression in the organisation and there were many clashes. Those who were more sharply critical of the PSUV suggested that the party was created by the bureaucratic elements which surround the Venezuelan president at the highest levels of government and this was reflected by the fact that persons like Cabello, a wealthy businessman, obtained prominent positions in the organising committee of the new party. From the outset the character of the PSUV was ambiguous; it evolved into an organisation which united a motley mix of genuine activists, bureaucrats and even some prominent capitalists.

In that period, Chavez himself was criticised for condemning parties that didn't join the body as "counter revolutionary" and therefore using the PSUV to further develop the concentration of power in Miraflores. But Chavez, who always mirrored the contradictions which exist at the heart of the Venezuelan revolutionary process, at the same time appeared before the Venezuelan masses and with characteristic flamboyance urged everybody to join the party. The masses heeded his call. A year after its inception, the PSUV had 5.8 million members. And that was most important. Whatever the basis of its beginnings, the PSUV was very swiftly graduated into a mass organisation, perhaps the largest of its type in the world. Not only that but it brought together many of those who passed through the experiences of 2002; the coup defeat and the oil lockout; experiences which had revolutionised the consciousness of the masses by acting as a vast mirror revealing vividly and truly the nature of their own social power.

Chavez passed from the scene in 2013, having fallen ill with cancer, and the years since have not been kind to the Bolivarian revolutionary process. From 2013 onward, the price of oil plummeted; in 2013 it stood at around 100 US$ per barrel, by

2016 it was down to a low average of 35 US$ a barrel. Oil had for decades been the mainstay of the Venezuelan economy constituting 95 per cent of Venezuela's external income as of 2016.[59] From 2012 onwards the fall of GDP reflected the oil losses: in 2014, GDP growth was – 3.98, in 2015 that figure was – 6.2, and in 2016 it was – 16.5.[60] Such objective developments were compounded by the government who resorted to printing money in order to cover the deficit, thus creating hyperinflation and a situation in which the American dollar has significantly more purchase in the economy than the indigenous currency, the bolivar. At which point, the standard practice of allocating dollars to importers at preferential rates in order to stimulate the economy became an impetus to the wealth of the bureaucracy, as importers – in league with government officials – began to use their dollars instead to enrich themselves by investing on the black market. Billions of dollars were syphoned off in such a fashion, it became the equivalent of a black hole, nestled at the heart of the economy, sucking in funds.[61]

And the strength of the burgeoning bureaucracy has increasingly found expression in the politics of the *Chavista* leadership itself. Concessions to the private sector are ever more common, with state regulated prices being replaced by "agreed prices", and the current president, Nicolas Maduro, making overtures to big business interests, opening up the country to international mining super corporations through initiatives like the Arco Mineral Project, for example. At the same time, the hardcore element of the right has continued its war of attrition against the Venezuelan economy, seeking to destabilise the government by sabotaging production, and also engaging in sporadic terrorist atrocities launched against radical campaigners such as Sabino Romero, murdered for taking the part of the indigenous peoples in the struggle for a more equitable distribution of land.

Of course, it is the poor majority more generally who

have suffered. Who have seen many of the gains made under Chavez's stewardship slip away, and a long winter of economic crisis set in, one which has seen many unable to keep up with the spiralling prices of food and other essential goods. In 2017 it was estimated that "81 percent of Venezuelan households are now living in income poverty, up from 75.6 percent in 2015", and that same survey pointed toward increased malnutrition with around 9.6 million Venezuelans eating two or less meals a day.[62] Such immiseration has led to an outbreak of anti-government protests, alongside rioting and looting in poor neighbourhoods which have traditionally been *Chavista* strongholds. Perhaps because the spectre of Chavez looms so large in the popular consciousness, because his memory is held in such warm esteem by all those people who gave their lives' blood to fight with him; perhaps it is for this reason that the current government, and the privileged layer of bureaucrats who have formed a power bloc at the top of the PSUV, have become ever more complacent. Even as the right-wing elements move in to silence the voice of Bolivarian revolution once and for all, even as the tendrils of corruption and crookedness sink deeper into the Party structures, it seems as though the leadership believe they can count on the support of the Bolivarian masses indefinitely. In 2015, for the first time in nearly 2 decades the opposition won two-thirds of the seats in the National Assembly. Not because the right was widely popular, but because more and more long-time *Chavistas* had chosen to abstain. Perhaps this is an augury of things to come, a message to the government warning them that the very social agency which underwrites their authority, which has made them out of the material of the mighty mass movement, also has the power to break them. That is something which the foxy, courageous, committed and kind-hearted founder of Bolivarianism always understood.

Chapter Three

Christopher Hitchens: Pathology of an Imperialist Ideologue

In November 2011 the journalist and author Christopher Hitchens succumbed to cancer. The occasion provoked an outpouring of encomia on the part of the world's mainstream press. At the same time weaker voices – mainly from smaller alternative organisations – endeavoured to affect a shift in focus: from the lachrymose lament for a writer who spent much of his life in the media spotlight – to the anonymous hundreds of thousands rendered still and cold by the wars in the Middle East the same writer so eloquently helped to prosecute. This chapter provides an examination of some of the central political themes and methodology which underpin the essays Hitchens wrote in that period; the period post 11 September where the world seemed to grow inexorably darker, overshadowed as it was by the sinister Orwellian abstraction – "War on Terror" – and its real-world materialisations. Hitchens didn't start out this way, of course. Once upon a time, he was a member of the Trotskyist group the International Socialists in Great Britain, was arrested taking part in militant demonstrations in the late sixties, and wrote a great many penetrating articles with a radical left bent. What makes his "damascene" conversion to the politics of power worthy of consideration? After all, the tawdry graduation from young and ostensibly left-wing radical to belligerent, seasoned conservative trumpeting the status quo – is hardly a unique one. For over a decade now, voices on the left have criticised Hitchens for selling out, for cynically prostituting his politics and becoming a flag-waver for the wars in Iraq and Afghanistan. The allure of money and privilege no doubt played its part. And yet, Hitchens wasn't lacking in either before he became the left's most notorious *enfant terrible.*

Rather it seems to me that – post 9-11 – the instinctive conservatism which had been part and parcel of Hitchens' political make-up throughout, now inexorably asserted itself; he was compelled to reconfigure those Marxist elements in his early political education, fusing them with a violent, atavistic reactionarism, in order to provide the most up-to-date defence of twenty-first century US imperialism. And it is the means by which Hitchens was able to combine such antithetical polarisations – Marxism and imperialism, freedom and oppression, an Enlightenment style rationalism along with virulent anti-Islamic forms of racism; the means by which he attempted this synthesis at the most fundamental theoretical level – that are most fascinating and worthy of consideration. From the standpoint of pure intellectual curiosity, for sure, but also for more practical purposes too; the toxic brand of alchemy which Hitchens so effectively practised – and which creates revolution from reaction and reaction from revolution – is a potent political formula. And it has often resonated with certain sections of the left. In 2006, for instance, a group of left-wing academics – including some who explicitly identify as Marxist such as the academic Norman Geras – signed "The Euston Manifesto". This declaration broadly asserted that the left as a whole had been over-critical of "Western" governments – specifically with regard to the issue of military deployment in Iraq, and far too tolerant of the forces which opposed the invasion.

Any study of Hitchens should concede from the outset that its subject was an extremely gifted individual. Hitchens had a wonderful facility with words. His literary flair surpasses that of his idol Orwell, in my view, in terms of its fluidity and grace. These qualities are accentuated by a mordant, dark humour, and a bewildering ability to draw on the most obscure but apposite quotation from classical German philosophy, for instance, or the provision of some telling epigram from one of the leading lights of the Enlightenment that provided Hitchens with so vivid an inspiration. And it would be churlish not to add, even in his later years, the increasingly rotund figure of this patrician journalist was in possession of a certain stoutly courage. One of his essays involves a rather disconcerting and claustrophobic meditation on the author's first-hand experience of being "water-boarded", ostensibly as a means of research – to gauge whether the procedure constitutes a form of torture (it does), and to decide whether illicit, covert sections of the US military are justified in their recourse to it (they aren't).

As an investigative journalist Hitchens would also travel to many of the war-torn countries he was keen to analyse, often at considerable personal risk. In the centre of Beirut he spies a symbol which resembles a swastika, one which he scrawls across with a bright felt pen – "call me old fashioned if you will but I have always taken the view that swastika symbols exist for one purpose only – to be defaced."[63] This spontaneous act of courage at once exposes Hitchens to the violent attentions of a thuggish group of party sympathisers, and the journalist and his companions are lucky to make it away in one piece.

However this singular act of bravado manages to obfuscate what is a far from minor detail. The party whose symbol Hitchens interfered with – The Syrian Social Nationalist Party – was not a fascist one. Granted it had, and does have, some deeply unpleasant elements within its ideological spectrum; a predilection for a racial nationalism which the founder hoped to culminate in a "Greater Syria", and a propensity toward anti-Semitism among some of its elements. At the same time it has a fundamentally different *modus operandi* to fascist regimes. The fascist party of the classical type grew from the reaction to a revolutionary situation and the concomitant need to neutralise it. German fascism, for instance, developed out of the revolutionary situation of November 1918 which saw proletarian unrest spread to the major cities; the *Freikorps* (the antecedents of the Nazis) were formed from the shock troops responsible for assassinating key members of the revolutionary leadership and helping terminate the rebellions. One might add that the movements headed by Mussolini, Franco and Pinochet followed a similar trajectory. But the Syrian Social Nationalist Party did not emerge as a mechanism to abrogate internal working-class dissent; rather it developed as a means by which resistance to French – and then later Israeli – colonialism might be channelled; it had a specific and distinct basis that also implied a complex of progressive social tendencies which genuinely fascist regimes lacked.

In one way Hitchens repeats the mistake of the shrill and youthful student progressive who is inclined, almost reflexively, to denounce any organisation or regime with right-wing, racist, or authoritarian leanings as "fascist". But whereas our hypothetical student might plead naivety, Hitchens – who was weaned on the esoteric paraphernalia of a Trotskyist idiom designed to admit all sorts of minutiae and difference in the socio-historical classification between various state forms – cannot claim ignorance here. So why does the word "fascist" – in Hitchens' speak – so often become little more than an emotive pejorative lacking in sociological seriousness?

The reason relates to his carefully constructed worldview and the role the concept of "Islamofascism" plays within it. Islamofascism provides the theoretical linchpin of Hitchens' perspective; it permits the amalgamation of a series of regimes, parties and organisations which often promote extreme forms of Islamic ideology – but tends to disregard the socio-historical conditions in which such entities were shaped and the power relations which surround them. Hezbollah, for example, is regarded by Hitchens in much the same way as it is viewed by mainstream politicians in the West – as a rogue terrorist organisation with a rabid almost Bin-Ladenist type agenda – an organisation which is at the same time somehow alien to Lebanese society; for it has been projected outward by the subversive influence of the Iranian state – "part of the shadow thrown on Lebanon by Iran, is Hezbollah."[64]

But such a perspective obliterates the historical realities for it fails to concern itself with the manner in which Hezbollah emerged – essentially a widespread resistance movement which came out of the 1982 war with Israel and the latter's 18-year occupation of Southern Lebanon. The resistance involved not only military activity but also the development of a far reaching social welfare programme which underpinned hospitals, schools and agricultural centres; the vast support Hezbollah enjoys in Lebanon translated into a series of electoral victories – in 1992, for example, it won all 12 of the seats which were on its electoral list.

In Hitchens' assessment, Bin-Ladenism and the atrocities of 11 September and Hezbollah, are two strains of the same phenomenon; i.e. the snarling visage of Islamofascism. That each was cultivated in a radically different set of social conditions, that one is Sunni and the other Shiite is beside the point – indeed it serves the thrust of Hitchens' argument to remain purposefully oblivious to this. The arming and training of Bin-Laden's militias by successive US governments as a counterweight to Russian hegemony, and the systematic military interventions by the US in the Middle East in order to secure its geopolitical interests; these factors went a good way to preparing the ground for the creation of what would later loosely be termed "al Qaeda" – but the endeavour to deploy historical analysis as a means to understand such phenomenon is, by Hitchens, invariably transmuted into a ditzy liberal attempt to justify the bloodthirsty Bin-Ladenist agenda.

This is par for the course. For Hitchens' worldview to retain its coherency, it requires the annihilation of the living historical narrative. It is not important that Bin-Laden was once a creature of the US government cultivated as part of an ongoing series of imperial interventions in the region; what is significant is the savage irrationality inherent to "Islamofascism". The lack of any genuine historical analysis in his essays from this period means that the socio-historical relationships between nations and classes are increasingly subject to crude ahistorical personifications; consequently Hitchens becomes a master polemicist in the language of "us" and "them".

Consider, for instance, his analysis of the relationship between the US and Pakistan developed in several of the essays from this time. For Hitchens, it is not the case that elements of the ruling class in the United States through the agencies of state foreign policy have devoted vast resources to ensure that the governments which emerge in Pakistan maintain a line favourable to US hegemony, helping to preserve its economic interests in the region. No, such historicity is displaced by the astonishing realisation that the finance which is streamed into the country actually comes from a group of well-meaning but misplaced "rich dumb Americans who foot the bill".[65] A coherent socio-historical analysis which locates an objective relation between the ruling elites in Washington and the higher echelons of political power in Pakistan that the former seek to infiltrate as part of an ongoing imperial project – is progressively eroded in favour of a haphazard, almost colloquial association between those "rich dumb Americans" and the sinister foreigners who abuse their personal largesse.

Indeed the various forms of antagonism toward the imperial power the US exerts in the country is, by Hitchens, rendered bizarre and absurd by the juvenile incoherence of the question he places at the heart of his investigation: "Why do they hate us?"[66] By anyone's estimation such a question is surely nonsensical – the "they" refers to a country of over 180 million split into vast territories with exceptional ethnic and linguistic diversity and a multi-faceted economy which has pronounced agricultural and semi-feudal forms that have themselves combined and merged with a rapid industrial development; a development which has been achieved, in part, by a succession of top-down military dictatorships but also federal democracies. The constant kaleidoscopic shifting in political forms is a product of the cataclysmic instability in the country produced by the pre-existing contradictions of partition, internal regional and class divisions and the territorial tensions with other countries which exacerbate these. For this, Pakistan's ruling classes inevitably have a conflicted and contrary relationship to all these elements – and, depending on the confluence of circumstance and agency, maintain both a hostile and conciliatory relationship to Washington itself. But again such banal and laborious considerations fade away, for Hitchens has hit upon the answer; he has understood – *why they hate us*. "They hate us," he says, "because they owe us, and are dependent upon us."[67]

And so, any resistance to US forces on the part of sections of a population which has experienced United States military incursions and where US governments have helped finance dictatorships – is now transformed into a grudging resentment by a country whose social contradictions and international relations have been obliterated by a crude and illegitimate personification which redraws Pakistan in terms of some surly, swarthy caricature – "if Pakistan were a person, he (and it would have to be a he) would have to be completely humourless, paranoid, insecure, eager to take offence, and suffering from self-righteousness, self-pity, and self-hatred."[68] This kind of analysis is astounding from one who claims to be a Marxist. Because, at least nominally, Hitchens did still claim to be a Marxist in the twilight of his life, he was compelled to try and reinterpret the US Imperialist ventures post 9-11 as developments which could, in Marxist terms, be described as "progressive". How did he even attempt such a seemingly impossible exercise in theoretical contortionism? He first went back to Marx's own writings on India citing a couple of sentences in which Marx writes: "England, it is true, in causing a social revolution in Hindustan was actuated only by the vilest interests...but that is not the question. The question is, can mankind fulfil its destiny without a fundamental revolution in the social state of Asia?"[69]

Hitchens was thereby able to argue that Karl Marx thought that "the British had brought modernity to India in the form of printing presses, railways, the telegraph, and steamship contact with other cultures." From this Hitchens concluded, "Marx...felt that the encounter between England and India was fertile and dynamic and revolutionary."[70]

Leaving aside the highly dubious, neutered use of the word "encounter" to describe British imperialism in India, Hitchens has traduced Marx's analysis here, transforming it into a lifeless technological determinism. One country brings to bear – albeit in a bloody manner – the forms of a more sophisticated technology on another and facilitates the latter's modernisation thereby. In actual fact Marx's account of India is far more qualified than Hitchens suggests – in the same article Marx wrote that, "England has broken down the entire framework of Indian society, without any symptoms of reconstitution yet appearing."[71] This qualification allows a little light in, allows us to see just how empty Hitchens' interpretation of Marx here actually is – for Marx is not simply concerned with modernisation in "the form of printing presses, railways, the telegraph and steamship contact with other cultures". Rather he is concerned with "the framework of Indian society" and the possibilities of "reconstitution".

What British imperialism carried with it, was not simply advanced technology but also advanced socio-economic forms. Marx's logic seems to have been that India would inevitably succumb to one form of imperialism or another, but the British strain would offer the possibility of a thorough-going capitalist transformation of Indian society in terms of its social organisation. The adjunct to this, and it is a most vital caveat, is that the development of widespread capitalist social relations across India would also, of necessity, facilitate the creation of a proletariat of the modern type – i.e. the social agency which, according to Marx, had the power to overthrow capitalism – and, consequently, destroy the very form which carried it – i.e. British imperialism. Thus an appreciation of any "progressive" elements of British imperialism on Marx's part was simultaneously bound up with the overarching requirement of its destruction (Hitchens' analysis of Iraq is not, for the uninitiated, bound up with the destruction of American imperialism).

It's also worth noting that Marx's early comments on India were based on a relative paucity of factual information about imperialism's actual impact on India. Aijaz Ahman suggests, in his book *In Theory*, that "the image of the so-called self-sufficient Indian village community that we find in Marx was lifted, almost verbatim, out of Hegel"[72] because of the limited information available – and also the fact that company rule in India was still a relatively new phenomenon (dated from 1757 onwards) whose consequences were far from manifest. More importantly, perhaps, Ahman argues that once "the hope of brisk industrialization under colonialism turned out to be so misplaced...Marx himself seems to have abandoned it in later years."[73]

But Hitchens does not examine any of these complexities or theoretical nuances. Once again his misreading cannot be chalked up to naivety or lack of knowledge. It cannot be dismissed in this way because it fulfils a very precise ideological function. It dissolves the role of class, and more specifically, it annuls the function of social revolution therein. Hitchens' analysis deliberately tries to show that India's revolution was not dependent on the social development of an oppressed class; rather it was achieved by the enforced technological modernisation which a colonial power subjected it to. It then becomes clear how Hitchens managed to claim Marxist credentials even as he supported the US decimations of Iraq and Afghanistan, for "the war on terror" – under this particular variant of "Marxism" – could then be described in terms of revolutionary progress.

On Afghanistan for instance – "one can so easily fall for a place where everybody thinks about sex, where bombing has blasted a society out of the Stone Age, and where opium is the religion of the people."[74] Just take a few moments to reflect on that second clause, to register its sinister militaristic tenor – "where bombing has blasted a society out of the Stone Age" – for this was the way Hitchens, in his later years, understood human emancipation to be unfolded – through the smoke and rubble and smouldering ruins imperial power leaves in its wake.

And so one can see that any anatomisation of Hitchens' methodology reveals two underlying and related tendencies. On the one hand certain forms of historical development are dissolved in a generic category – "Islamofascism" – in particular with regard to those countries in the Middle East and surrounding areas – which have been, or continue to be, progressively destabilised by US, British and other strains of modern imperialism. Simultaneously colonial power, at least its US variant, is comprehended in equally ahistorical terms – not as something which is driven forward by specific class interests compounded by the imperatives of geopolitical competition on the international stage but rather something which has been abstracted and personified: on the fewer and fewer occasions when Hitchens tackles the bloody events of US imperialism past which once he denounced from the purview of a radical progressive, he is now compelled to articulate them in almost exclusively intrapersonal terms. The horrific legacy of Vietnam, for instance, is chalked up to the "real monsters such as Robert McNamara and Henry Kissinger, who calmly gave the orders and the instructions"[75]. In one way this is inevitable. Having developed the theoretical rationale which allows him to perceive American imperialism as an essentially progressive force,

Hitchens cannot but regard the Vietnams and Irans as sinister but incidental aberrations; the productions of corrupt individuals – rabid war-mongers like Kissinger – rather than the expressions of a moribund and systematic form of capitalist exploitation that has attained global proportions.

And if it came to pass that Hitchens understood capitalist power in this way, as something declassed and individualised, so too did he conceptualise any genuinely radical response to it. In an article entitled "Hugo Boss" Hitchens provides us with a tawdry deprecation of the Venezuelan leader Hugo Chavez – an account which combines tittle-tattle and spite to evoke an invidious and toxic vision. Chavez has "an idiotic weakness for spells and incantations",[76] Hitchens claims, though nowhere does he provide evidence for this – yet he continues nevertheless, deliberately and maliciously graduating the calumny. We are informed that Chavez has "many of the symptoms of paranoia and megalomania"[77] and by way of a comic aside – "Chavez, in other words, is very close to the climactic moment when he will announce that he is a poached egg."[78] Hitchens utilises a very specific lexicon here, reeling out terms like "the boss" and "Venezuela's capo" to supplement a sense of a deranged mind with the notion of a criminal tyrant – thus giving to Chavez's political role a particularly fateful and ominous aura. But, from within the miasma of personal impression and spiteful insinuation one is hard-pressed to find a single salient and telling fact. We are not told, for instance, of the 17 elections and referenda successes that the late Venezuelan president enjoyed, the majority of which took the form of electoral landslides and made Chavez, in the words of British politician George Galloway – "The most elected leader in the modern era".[79]

More than this, once again we discover an absence, a void, the lack of any comprehensive historicism. Hitchens does not reference the Venezuela pre-Chavez; a place in which a small light-skinned elite exploited the vast oil reserves in conjunction with Washington, forcing the majority of the darker mixed and indigenous to languish in almost apartheid-like conditions of poverty and exploitation. Hitchens does not reference the *Caracazo* of 1989 – the massacre by government troops which took the lives of thousands of the Venezuelan poor and, in many ways, provided the impetus for Chavez's Bolivarian movement. And Hitchens neglects to refer to the coup of 2002 in which Chavez was illegally removed from power by the Venezuelan elite in an operation backed by the CIA – an operation thwarted by the intervention of the masses, as they thronged from the barrios and the hills, closing in on the Miraflores Palace and compelling the return of their democratically elected president.

All of this living history, rendered vivid by blood and suffering, is by Hitchens simply washed away, in favour of a haughty character assassination directed at Chavez which is both unprincipled and false. The elegance of Hitchens' prose and the beauty of his rhetorical flourishes do not manage to belie the fact that this is primitive politics; *ad homonym*, gutter sniping of the lowest order, but it is worth noting the edge of sarcastic bitterness which creeps into Hitchens' writings whenever he deals with a genuine proponent of social emancipation.

And in one way this makes perfect sense. What becomes clear on reading his autobiographical memoir *Hitch 22* is that throughout his life Hitchens was keeping two sets of books. On the one hand – as a bright young student inhaling the intoxicating aromas of the late sixties, the heady atmosphere of rebellion and freedom which reached its zenith in May 1968 – Hitchens developed many radical sensibilities. At the same time he was inexorably drawn to the glittering glamour of the student elite and the establishment more broadly; the gorgeous, seductive, twilight world of champagne sparkling soirees and the subtle, flirtatious attentions of its denizens who permitted him "to sing for my supper".[80] The need to have it both ways, so to say – to be able to indulge the exhilarating frisson and enjoy the moral vitality which are the remits of the freedom fighter, while simultaneously partaking in the silky confidences of the most famous and powerful; this was the central, elemental contradiction which fissured across Hitchens' existence – and his stance on Iraq and Afghanistan post 11 September would provide for its erstwhile, though ultimately artificial, resolution.

For by tinkering with Marxism, blunting its class dynamic and its revolutionary edge, and transfiguring it into a form of technological determinism used to fortify American imperialism in Mesopotamia with a veneer of progressivism – it was this contradiction which Hitchens, intuitively and semi-consciously, was seeking to address. He was able to replace fundamental socio-economic conflict and exploitation – both nationally and internationally – something that had culminated in an imperialism of global dimensions; Hitchens was able to replace such concrete social categories with an ahistorical conflict between generic ideological forms – the spread of Islamofascism to be countered by the flowering of a second resplendent Enlightenment; one to be carried by American bombs and the rousing words of one Christopher Hitchens – who had assumed the mantle and provided the movement with its own twenty-first century Paine. In this way Hitchens could manifest as the revolutionary of reactionaries; the figure who channelled the intransigence of rebellion in and through the prosaic but lethal operations of global empire. Ironically for the ultra-anti-theist Hitchens, the methodological constructions he provided contain a quasi-religious power; that is to say they make possible a miraculous transubstantiation whereby oppression becomes freedom and the colonialist steps forward as liberator.

But the fantasy of his own intellectual creation was consistently perforated by the historical realities. By the implosions of Iraq and Afghanistan, and the strengthening of Islamic terrorism rather than its diminishment. By the Arab Spring which perfumed across much of North Africa displacing several pro-American dictatorships – something which Hitchens would, at the last moment, try to ally himself with – though he had long since forgone any commitment to the concept of revolution from below (unless it worked in conjunction with "Western Civilisation" i.e. American imperialism). Those who articulated their radical criticism of American foreign policy and their solidarity with the victims of it were despised by Hitchens with unadulterated vitriol as "demagogic" and "dangerous" and, for those like Chavez, who represented the highest forms of social struggle and revolutionary overcoming, the sheer potency of his bile was almost without limit. For such struggles, however far away, still manage to resonate; even, perhaps, across the burble of well-mannered conversation and vapours of fine wine which pervade the most exclusive establishments in Washington Hitchens so dutifully frequented; even as he once more sang out so eloquently for his supper in the midst of the nation's most well-to-do.

Chapter Four

All Around are Familiar Faces: Rembrandt and the Portrait of Modernity

In the sixteenth century it was across the network of burgeoning towns, canal riven planes and bustling sea ports of the Low Countries where the winds of change were most profoundly felt. A marked urbanisation, an exponential growth in the size of cities and the seaside hubs of trade, had allowed for increased concentrations of artisans, investors, businessmen, small tradesmen, fisherman and waged labourers. Across these sections rippled the ideas of a modern and popular reformation. A new kind of political agenda which sought out individual liberties, and the destruction of the taxes and tariffs which inhibited trade and which had been visited upon the population by the gargantuan, grotesque feudal empire whose power was projected out from Habsburg Spain. The new breed of Dutch burgher more and more found himself and his economic interests pressed into irreconcilable contradiction against this mighty behemoth of empire, and in 1566, the pressure reached its zenith, and the damn burst asunder.

Energised by a bout of iconoclasm which saw Calvinists strike out against the religious images and totems of the Catholic orthodoxy, the high bourgeoisie and some members of the indigenous nobility used this weaponised Protestantism as a focal point for a revolutionary movement which was cultivated in both national and class terms during the Dutch Revolt. The Spanish Empire was a glittering monolith; draped in blood, loot and silver from the New World, it might well have crushed the audacious burghers, the stadholders, the fiery Calvinist preachers, the roaming merchants, the intrepid seamen and soldiers – before their movement was ever able to coalesce. The

84

Habsburg power, however, had its hands full. It was involved in an almost perpetual series of skirmishes and wars which ranged from the conflict with Protestant England, to the battles with the Catholic Valois dynasty who were seated on the French throne, to the eastern reaches of Europe and North Africa where the Ottomans were the masters of the Levant and much of the Mediterranean Sea.

In addition to fighting on several flanks, the Spanish Empire was also top-heavy, archaic and inflexible. The resistance fighters in the Netherlands, especially to the North, were aided by the topography of the land, the open floodplains, the deep woods, the canals, the estuaries and sea. The Dutch Revolt began to take on the character of a guerrilla war in which the fighters, the "beggars" as they were known, ran the empire's troops ragged and struck out suddenly and ruthlessly against any collaborators. Such erratic, unpredictable waspish-like attacks were maintained over decades of struggle and supplemented by sporadic but powerful uprisings which seemed to come out of the blue and engulf whole cities. After the years of invasion, bombardment and resistance, the Southern territories eventually slipped back into Spanish hands, but the North broke away decisively, establishing itself as a republic and in 1609 signing an armistice with Spain which included its right to trade with Spanish territories. The upshot of this was the consolidation of a merchant oligarchy in the North which took the reins of state and which facilitated a revolution in production on the land. This, in turn, would help revitalise industry including textiles and ship-building, and thereby provide the impetus for the creation of a world empire; an empire which would send commodities and riches flooding back into the major cities like Amsterdam, Leiden and Gent.

These wealth-saturated cities, alleviated from the archaic pressures of feudal power and Catholic inquisition, became the havens of free thinkers and exiled intellectuals from all over

Europe. At the same time the new economic model – unfettered by feudal constraint – drained away aristocratic privilege and sanctified the economic middle; alongside the bigger industrialists and oligarchs – the class of merchants, artisans, side street businesses and petty traders held sway. The spoils of empire as well as a spirit of internationalism and economic individualism were crystallised in the cultural and ideological creations of a breakaway bourgeoisie which stood at the dawn of a new epoch. It was into this context – into the bustle of the large, open northern cityscapes which had been enlivened by new freedoms and the sweeping sea breeze – that the young Rembrandt was born.

He was born in Leiden in 1606. His father in many ways epitomised the new man of the epoch, for he was a "self-made man", a mill owner – and his mother was the daughter of a baker. She was also a Roman Catholic while Rembrandt's father, more typically, was a devotee of the Dutch Reformed Church, so together they exemplified the emancipatory spirit of the new middle classes and a sense of religious toleration. The child was enrolled at the University of Leiden at 13 years of age – probably because his father envisaged his son's future in terms of some lucrative and practical trade. Nevertheless the young Rembrandt left the university after only a few months in order to follow his passion for painting. He went on to be apprenticed to the painter Jacob Isaacsz van Swanenburgh who had studied in Italy and whose art was imbued with the classical perfection of the high Renaissance alongside the dark, dramatic power of the Baroque, influences which the young student would greedily imbibe. Rembrandt, then, was brought up in an atmosphere of Protestant individualism which guaranteed to the boy an almost unheard of amount of freedom; he inherited from his burgher parents a sense of ambition and a healthy longing for the material benefits of commercial endeavour. At the same time, these instincts were subordinated to a precocious devotion to art which began to flower almost at once, watered by some of the leading lights and most profound influences of the era.

Having apprenticed for 3 years, Rembrandt then went on to work with the artist Pieter Lastman in Amsterdam. They say that genius begins with emulation, and many of Rembrandt's earliest works were attempts to mimic the style of Lastman, particularly his teacher's ability to imbue his paintings with a sense of movement, heightened conflict and dramatic life. Like Lastman, Rembrandt's early period tends to focus on biblical, mythological or historical scenes, and one of his earliest known works, *The Stoning of St Stephen* (1625), is an effort on Rembrandt's part to capture the dramatic credentials of his mentor. Perhaps the painting is not as technically accomplished as the work Rembrandt is drawing from, but already, it exhibits certain innovative and superior qualities – as well as a sophisticated familiarity with aesthetic traditions and the ability to blend them seamlessly. The shadowy turrets of a cobbled castle on a hill in the distance are classically Renaissance and deeply atmospheric but in the forefront the dramatic conflict between the martyr and those who are stoning him is emphasised by the type of *chiaroscuro* redolent of someone like Caravaggio; the stark dialogue between shadow and light. On one side there is a single executioner wreathed in shadow, flanked by an ominous horse bound figure – both of whom loom over the kneeling figure of the Christian saint. But the martyr himself is bathed in light – his face turned upwards to the heavens, his expression frozen in a lucent, rapturous glow in the very moment when the curtain is about to fall.

The ease by which the artist synthesises such motifs is also complemented by the strikingly original depiction of those in the light who are gathered round. The faces of the men at the centre of the work lack the semblance of holy tranquillity or divine, muted suffering which so often categorised the religious figures of the Renaissance. Rather, many look a little shop-worn and wrinkled; the unruly streaks of dirty blonde hair and full bulbous noses, the somewhat more stolid and stocky frames, speak to the physical characteristics of the Dutch market people, the petty traders and merchants who flocked into Amsterdam's large open squares. There is a kind of plebeian exuberance which emanates from the people in the light – as opposed to those in the shadows who have the swarthy, elegant features, the draped robes and sleek flowing beards of Middle Eastern kings. It is an unusual and somewhat incongruous painting, for the people who are most alive, who are most contemporary – those bulbous Dutch burghers – are also the ones rallying around with their own stones, in a kind of frenzied desperation, hungry to hasten the drama toward the moment of murder. And from the centre of the pack, a smaller face looks out – not at the prostrate saint, nor at the gathered assassins – but out toward us, the audience ourselves – his forehead wrinkled, his face lined in a momentary frown of uneasy surprise as he catches our eye – he is within the mob, and yet he is not quite part of it, for the lines of his expression denote a profound ambiguity as events spin onward with a whirlwind-like inevitability. The figure thus captured is, of course, the young Rembrandt himself.

The act of insinuating himself into the painting marks Rembrandt's first self-portrait, and although these weren't unknown in the Italian Renaissance – think Titian's *Portrait of a Man* for example – nevertheless, the genre was incentivised by the Reformation. It very much expressed the Protestant individualism which Rembrandt was in the sway of, and which had been adumbrated by his German predecessor Albrecht Durer who himself was master of the self-portrait. In the later part of the 1620s Rembrandt begins a close collaboration with the artist Jan Lievens, which is important for Lievens too was an exponent of portraiture and the self-portrait. In his company, Rembrandt begins to shift focus somewhat. Like Rembrandt, Lievens fell under the influence of the *Caravaggisti*, utilising the stark interplay between light and dark, being and nothingness. At the same time, the portrait becomes the more predominant genre; hence the drama is increasingly displaced from the outer exhibition of physical movement evinced during some biblical or historical conflict – to the inner emotion which is exhibited by a single subject in repose. It seems that Lievens was more technically innovative at this stage than Rembrandt, but the latter was already organically more expressive, already demonstrating that sublime facility for inner emotion which was to become the mainstay of some of his greatest works.

The shift away from the more classical model of the Renaissance or the Baroque can't simply be understood by these personal and professional relationships in isolation, but was very much the product of the new epoch. The rise of a class of new men – the moneyed bourgeoisie – whose exuberant political freedoms were built on the merchant's increasing control over peasant production in the countryside and this had facilitated an upswing in industrial production in the burgeoning cities, which – in turn – would come to power a whole empire. These early entrepreneurs, these "self-made" men, wanted to memorialise their stratospheric successes, not in terms of the portraits of old – aristocrats garbed in heroic uniforms or finery, mounted on great steeds or stood before magnificent castles – but in terms of more personal, particular characteristics – their inward, idiosyncratic qualities rather than their outward titles. At times, of course, they wanted to be depicted in their finery in order to display their commercial success, though this was often downplayed in favour of the dour, darkened elegance of a Calvinist ascetic. But more than anything they wanted to be individualised according to the heightened sense of self which had emerged out of the Reformation and was part and parcel of a developing capitalism, the feeling that it was not so much one's breeding, but one's individuality, which became the sacred principle on which enlightenment and economic advance was premised. Rembrandt – developing in this *milieu* of creative freedom and economic expectation, feeling his own burgeoning individuality stir in the midst of all the vibrant activity, colour and change of Amsterdam itself – was particularly attuned to this new aesthetic sensibility, and this is a period in which he becomes very swiftly renowned for his portraits of the great and the good of Dutch society. These are portraits which above all reflect the optimism and inner certainty of a class which holds in its hands the future as palpably as the merchant grips the log book which outline his transactions and profits. To put it in the modern refrain, the future was bright, and it was most definitely orange.

In the 1630s Rembrandt paints many of these portraits, earning large sums of money and a great deal of renown. He makes powerful connections and is indeed commissioned by Constantin Huyghens, the secretary to the Stadtholder – Prince Frederick Henry of Orange. It is in this time of opulent success that Rembrandt marries into high society – he weds Saskia van Uylenborgh, daughter of a wealthy burgomaster. Saskia's presence provided a powerful impulse to Rembrandt's art, for he used her as a model in a number of his religious and mythological paintings of the period. In the picture *The Prodigal Son in the Brothel* Rembrandt not only embodies his passion for Saskia, but he also blends it with the feeling, optimism and lavishness of the epoch more broadly. The surroundings of the scene are salubrious; a table topped with the finest food, specifically a rare, exotic bird – shipped in from the Dutch East Indies, perhaps? The fabric of the cloth which covers the table is equally lavish, embossed with a deep hued, tortoise shell mosaic of dark, textured green. In the far right corner, a voluptuous, velveteen curtain flows downward, billowing in the mahogany gloom. In the centre is sat Rembrandt himself. A sword is holstered to his side, the swirling gold whorls of its handle glittering in shadow, his shirt a plume of blood orange which flows across his outstretched arm, an arm which curls around the full curvaceous figure of Saskia who is perched provocatively on his lap. In the other arm, Rembrandt holds aloft a ridiculously long flute of champagne, and his eyes are unfocussed, wavering with drunken glee.

In one way the picture is cheeky, almost vulgar. It is a very pronounced celebration of wealth and illuminates the psyche of the young artist himself by its array of rich flowing colour, and the meticulous attention to the textures of the objects of wealth which adorn the room. In some ways, the object *par excellence* is Saskia herself. The whole painting exudes the gaudy triumphalism of the *nouveau riche* – the young man, the miller's son, is announcing to the world that he has made it; through his creative endeavours, he has raised himself up and won his place in the elite – he has the clothes, he has the money, and now he has the girl! And yet, just as with *The Stoning of St Stephen*, an element of ambiguity extrudes itself into the scene. While Saskia is to be displayed alongside the wealth of other objects, her eyes contain in their gaze a type of cool independence; a withering almost ironic awareness, an unspoken understanding she shares with the audience about the slightly ridiculous nature of her drunken husband. Her lips contain the beginnings of a wry smile. Rembrandt, on the other hand, appears blithely unaware, his whole expression raised in that glow of bleary, drunken self-satisfaction. This contrast: the delicious mystery of Saskia's unborn smile, the coolness in her eyes – with the slightly ridiculous figure of Rembrandt himself, his drunken giggle and the theatrical, tumescent sword sticking out from his side – such a contrast allows a sense of ambiguity and distance to be smuggled into the scene. Yes, it is certainly a celebration of wealth and commercial success, but at the same time there is the unstated acknowledgement that these things are perhaps a little more frivolous, a little more transitory, than the artist – who is swept up in the moment of his greatest triumph – is ever able to acknowledge.

Perhaps the most famous and iconic picture from Rembrandt's youthful period is *The Anatomy Lesson of Dr Nicolaes Tulp*. If *The Prodigal Son in the Brothel* commemorates the purchasing power of an emancipated bourgeoisie, and contains an element of giddy triumphalism which verges on the vulgar, *The Anatomy Lesson of Dr Nicolaes Tulp* provides us not so much with a paean to bourgeois commerce, but rather bourgeois science. Representing Rembrandt's first major commission in Amsterdam, this oil painting depicts the dissection of the body of an executed criminal being carried out by one Dr Nicolaes Tulp, who has opened up the left arm of the cadaver and is highlighting the tendons which he is holding between the blades of a pair of surgical scissors. Gathered round are various doctors, who are leaning in to better hear the discourse Dr Tulp is delivering. To the right a large, open book has been propped up. At first glance, there is no ambiguity in this painting. It is quite simply a celebration of enlightenment, of a science which has been freed from the fetters of the Inquisition and medieval Catholicism. It is the quintessential depiction of a humanism which, quite literally, places the inner workings of the individual at the centre of its universe. As such it is almost universally celebrated as a picture which positively heralds an age of secularism and science. And yet. Look again. There is another, deeper layer. When one looks at the doctors who are gathered around, one notices something about their postures. Several seem to be craning forward, their necks unnaturally elongated, their heads garishly protruding out from their bodies. There is something distinctly birdlike in the way they hover around the corpse. And the body itself. So unceremoniously denuded of its protection and privacy, the skin of that bare arm so clinically peeled away, the obscene blushing red and yellowing tissue exposed so rudely to the hungry gazes of those leaning in. In fact, when one looks at this painting, one struggles to avoid the quite sinister impression – the scientists are not men at all for they have the very distinct aspect of vultures.

There is a further detail which renders the painting even more macabre. The faces of those doctors who are leaning in as the lesson commences are of a very similar type. The majority of them have long, beaky noses, they all have beards, and the colouring of their hair tends toward a greying ginger. Just like many of Rembrandt's other paintings, these people are recognisably the Dutch people of the day – indeed, the faces are of actual doctors who paid significant sums to be included in the picture. But what is most striking is the face of the corpse. True, the faces of the men observing are bathed in light, and tinged with pink, while the face of the corpse is wreathed in pale grey shadow; it is clear that the man on the table is a lifeless lumpen mass, an inanimate object, whereas the people gathered around are full of life, their eyes shining with an ambitious hunger for knowledge. And yet. Look again. The face of the man on the table is a *dead* ringer for the faces of the living. It has the same pronounced nose. It has the same style of beard. One imagines it was of the same age when it slipped into its eternal sleep. *Media vita in morte sumus,*[81] observes Martin Luther beautifully, mordantly – in the midst of life, we are in death. The face of the man on the table represents the inexorable, unalterable destiny each and every man in that room is hurtling toward, and yet they seem blithely unaware of their trajectory. None of them are looking into the dead man's face. They see him only in terms of an object like any other, to be appropriated, to be carved up; as a means to enhance their own material and intellectual powers. They see him thus even as the shadows in the room – the long charcoal hues of darkness – creep ever closer, gradually encroaching on the small periphery of light which encircles their faces.

A common account of Rembrandt runs something like this: technically precocious, deeply imaginative and at the height of his powers – the artist was to experience a series of tragedies, at which point his work turned inward, became increasingly darker and desolate, meditative and brooding. However it is also true that present even in some of these significant early works is already a strong element of ambiguity and darkness, perversity almost. The doctors in the anatomy lesson are important men, and the painting Rembrandt's first major commission; they were men of the class to which Rembrandt aspired, he probably regarded them with genuine admiration, and yet there is something in the unconscious of his aesthetic which drives him toward the sense that there is something creepy, almost grotesque in the whole arrangement – that even in its moment of most resplendent triumph, its scientific mastery over the world, the Dutch bourgeoisie already contains in itself the germ of negation, of decay, of decadence and death. "All that comes into being is worthy of perishing,"[82] says Goethe. That the great artist is particularly attuned to this fact; that he or she detects in the epoch the seeds of its own decay is noteworthy but not, perhaps, surprising.

One is reminded of Aeschylus' play *The Persians*. The great tragedian wrote his play at the start of the classical age of the Athenian polis. Ostensibly the play is about the history and decline of the Persian Empire, the most powerful of its period, and how its hubris caused it to overstretch itself by attacking Ancient Greece, suffering a defeat which culminated in the decimation of its navy at the battle of Salamis. But although *it does* tell the tale of the once mighty Persian Empire, you can't help but feel that Aeschylus is really addressing what he sees around him, the Athenian polis of his own day which had broken away from the imperial clasp, and was surging ahead in the process of forging its own empire. It is as though even in the moment of Athens' greatest victory the playwright detects the shadow of its own historical decline; the play acts as a warning, a bleak lament on the interminable power of history which has in its capacity the ability to reduce even the most glittering, resplendent and mighty of empires to little more than a husk sinking in the sands of time. As another poet, more than 2 millennia later, would lament – "on the pedestal these words appear: 'My name is Ozymandias, king of kings: Look on my works, ye Mighty, and despair!'...Round the decay, of that colossal wreck, boundless and bare, the lone and level sands stretch far away."[83]

It is this type of sensibility which makes Rembrandt such a great figure. For sure, Rembrandt looked around him and like a loyal child of the bourgeois epoch, a scion of the new commercial class, he was dazzled by the economic prowess and military success of the young republic as it boldly and rapidly stormed the furthest reaches of the world. The young Rembrandt hungered after the economic rewards and the social status which would come from becoming a card-carrying member of the United Provinces elite. At the same time though, that restless aesthetic awareness which is somehow irrepressible, and which causes one to be alive to the processes and contradictions which are at work, invisibly but inevitably, beneath the surface of the social world – in Rembrandt, this almost unconscious instinct was highly pronounced and would never relinquish its grip on his art, even in the face of his ambition and the need for validation from the most powerful layers. The engine of empire was an awesome, powerful machine. Alongside the never-ending circulation of capital and commodities it generated from the far corners of Asia to the New World, alongside the modern capitalistic model of fusing domestic economic interest and shareholders with the imperial project abroad in the form of the first joint stock companies – the Dutch paradigm also provided an impetus to slavery, and the destruction of entire communities through the wholesale violence required to extract surplus, coerce labour and protect the burgeoning imperial monopoly. The level of exploitation directed against children climbed, including the increased use of them as slaves in an impersonalised slave system which opened up in the Banda Islands in the Far East whereby a corporation, the Dutch East India Company, replaced the private individual in the role of slave owner.

In certain areas, then, a slave owning system was increasingly being refashioned according to the prerogatives of international capital as it preyed on the dispossessed, while at the same time on the domestic front, in the United Provinces themselves, a project of ongoing social engineering was taking place which was almost as brutal. A process of primitive accumulation whereby peasants had increasingly been expropriated from the land and their own means of production thus forming the raw human material to be syphoned into the cities and recast according to the structures of wage labour – was complemented by the thousands of people who had been made destitute by the decades of war with the Habsburgs. In the aftermath of such vast social upheaval a large class of beggars developed on the periphery of the expanding cities, alongside the workers whose narrow, cramped hovels were expanding like barracks and swelling the slums. Such groups were subject to the ruthless, often murderous measures of social discipline – flogging, branding, mutilation, a variety of forms of execution – that burgeoning Dutch capitalism required in order to maintain its strict, orderly Protestant work ethic and ensure capital expansion remained untrammelled.

Slavery, repression, persecution of the poverty-stricken and the dispossessed – these were the dark compromises the revolutionary bourgeoisie wrought in order to inaugurate its epoch; in the very moment it was raising the individual up and proclaiming him sacred in terms of a whole host of new political and economic freedoms, it was at the same time nailing his real-world counterpart to the cross – in his guise as slave, pauper or proto-proletarian. Rembrandt was a revolutionary painter in this way. For he channelled this dualism in an art which attains a new depth of individuality and interiority, illuminating the flickering shadows of the soul, while at the same time possessing the kind of aesthetic integrity which was able to express the suffering of an age, allowing it to bleed into the backdrop of his paintings. His delicate sketches of beggars, for example, are like nothing quite seen before. His *Ragged Peasant With His Hands Behind His Back* of 1632 is a beautifully etched drawing of a destitute peasant whose flinty face has all the wisdom and experience of parched stone, while his black sickle like eyes seem to gaze into the forever. It is amazing that someone can carry such stoicism with just a few delicately strewn dark lines – and it is unlike its forerunners in this tradition for it does not depict the homeless as grotesque or alien, but involves a profound identification with the subject which leaves in its wake only a deep and gentle pathos. Such identification was exhibited most directly in the 1630 etching *Beggar Seated on a Bank*. Here we see a young man in tattered rags, sat on the edge of a bank, looking out at the world with a gaze of baffled anger, as though he can't quite comprehend the series of steps in his life which have led him to this. It is an image both of suffering and humanity. And the face of the young man, the face of the beggar, is none other than Rembrandt's himself.

In his painting *Two Negroes* Rembrandt provides a subversive critique of the slave trade by the simple gesture of investing his two black subjects with humanity. William Bosman, a slaver in the service of the Dutch West India Company, wrote of the blacks he sold that they were "all without exception, Crafty, Villainous, and Fraudulent".[84] The virulent racism here works in tandem with mercantile capital and the logic of the commodity form in its aspect as exchange value: the human being is reduced to a generic object, one of many, to be shipped out in order to realise its value on the world market. The particularity, the richness and diversity of the individual personality is dissolved into the uniform and abstract aspect of a single commodity – a body which has the capacity to work. The racist line – "they are all the same" – dovetails perfectly with the economic logic exhibited inherent to this. Rembrandt shatters it irrevocably by illuminating the individuality and richness of the human personality which underpins the slave as commodity. It is no coincidence that his painting features two black subjects, for he is purposely differentiating them, revealing them as unique and contrasting individuals. The man on the right looks slumped and exhausted, his eyes are wreathed in shadow, and his downturned face is softened by a thoughtful melancholy. He rests his head on his companion's shoulder for solace. The other man, however, has an upturned gaze, his full eyes are tinted with a hint of green and gold, and a ribbon of light has fallen across them, as he looks into the middle distance with an expression of curiosity and even wonder. The painting is intimate, touching, and the mood of these men, and the friendship which has allowed them to endure, is made redolent by Rembrandt by the warm, rich, gentle orange and brown hues of the backdrop. One feels both pity for the men and a delight in their humanity and affection; the painting provides the most delicate and touching rejoinder to the unnatural warping of human relations which the conditions of servitude and slavery provoke.

Despite the fact, then, that Rembrandt was himself a particle of the Dutch bourgeoisie, despite the fact he introduced a more capitalistic model into his own working practices[85] – nevertheless Rembrandt was unable to turn a blind eye to the dark underbelly of Dutch capitalism and the inhumanity of much of its practice, for his aesthetic intuition was simply too relentless, too deep roaming. Joachim von Sandrart, a contemporary of the Dutch master, was compelled to observe that Rembrandt "did not at all know how to keep his station, and always associated with the lower orders".[86] It was his attunement to pathos; the pathos of "the lower orders" – of the people who had been unvoiced by Dutch capitalism, who had been dispossessed, exploited and broken – which gave light to the inner life of the figures and faces he depicted in a fundamentally new way. Even in his religious art, this pathos, this inner life, is revealed in a way which demarks the works from anything which came before.

Consider, for instance, his rendering of the abduction of

Ganymede. This scene from ancient Greek mythology had featured in many a Renaissance painting, the effort of the late-Renaissance master Domenico Cresti might be considered typical. Here Zeus, in the guise of an eagle, abducts a beautiful youth (Ganymede) whom he intends to ravish. Cresti depicts the young man, being borne aloft on the eagle's back, his face set in an expression of helpless rapture; his glorious pink cloak billowing up against the ethereal blue of the sky, revealing his youthful, perfectly sculptured naked body, his legs ever so slightly parted. That there is a strong element of homoeroticism to the picture seems undeniable, it is a study in mysterious, inevitable, uplifting desire. Now the Rembrandt version. Here nearly all the light has been drained from the sky, sucked away by an amorphous, churning black mass of cloud. The landscape below is drowned in shadow. Ganymede is no longer the serene, resigned youth of the Renaissance depiction but rather a blubbery, overlarge, awkward child. The child's face is screwed up in a look of horror and abject mortification, his puckered, open mouth is a black gaping wound seared into his face. His clothes have been wrenched up violently, his belly, bottom and legs have been pressed downward by the force of gravity in a white wobbling mass of vulnerable, naked flesh. The eagle has its beak deeply embedded in the feeble figure. And the child is pissing himself in terror. This is not ravishment. It is rape. Power can be uplifting, it can be all encompassing, it can be glorious, it can be divine, says the Renaissance. Indeed, replies Rembrandt, without missing a beat, but it can also be sordid, dehumanising and devastating. The artist's sympathies in this picture are, once again, so unequivocally in sync with the rhythm and inner lives of the oppressed.

This is important because we have to understand that even in his early work – and his Ganymede and the beggar sketches come from this period – even here one is aware that beyond his celebrations of the new epoch Rembrandt is as well the foremost chronicler of its darkness; the antinomy of the bourgeois revolution – its dual guise of liberation and oppression – was an antinomy which had by history been grafted onto the aesthetic psyche of the artist himself as he fought to come to terms with the world around him. When art historians describe the early Rembrandt as a cheerful, vibrant virtuoso whose optimistic art was blessed with success, and it was only when he fell on hard times, that his paintings would slip into sadness and interiority – would begin to plumb the dark night of the soul – such an explanation is facile because it severs the individual from the broader historical context. Any number of artists encounter tragedies in their lives but few end up painting like the late Rembrandt. There is a difference between the early Rembrandt and the later works, it is true his art becomes darker and more introverted in its twilight phase, but this was only ever the accentuation of a tendency which was already present in the work in the first place; the aesthetic awareness of the contradictions of liberation and suffering which were latent in the historical dynamic of bourgeois progress itself.

Indeed, having been raised up by the new epoch, it would then go on to take everything from him. In the later part of the 1630s two of the couple's babies passed away. In 1640 another child, Cornelia, died after only having lived a month. In 1642 Saskia died, probably from tuberculosis. Only Titus, the fourth child, would survive into adulthood. These relentless individual tragedies have to be set against the broader pattern of the epoch; the rapacious, dynamic expanding economy which was the fulcrum for a global empire – was also inherently volatile and unstable, subject to blind market forces and compulsions, in sway to the kind of economic contradictions which opened up between the intensity of labour exploitation and the possibilities of mass consumption. Indeed, such contradictions reached a zenith when, in 1636-37, the Dutch economy imploded having developed the first economic "bubble" in history, the first authentic capitalist crisis which was centred around the commodity of tulip bulbs and which saw prices artificially inflated in a feeding frenzy of speculation before the market suddenly collapsed. Many wealthy investors lost their fortunes, along with a host of smaller entities like cobblers, carpenters, brick layers and woodcutters who had staked their life savings on the capitalist dream. Fellow painters such as Jan van Goven were ruined, and Jeffery Cotterall, in his book on the history of Amsterdam, argues "it was remarkable that Rembrandt was not involved."[87] And yet, Rembrandt was not to remain untouched by the intemperate moods and cycles of the Dutch economy. Alongside the series of devastating deaths of family members, his economic situation became ever more precarious. The commissions began to dry up. His art became less fashionable. He was compelled to declare bankruptcy in 1656 and eventually sell his luxury house before settling in more modest dwellings. He had to sell almost everything he owned. He lived long enough to outlive his partner, Hendrickje Stoffels, who had once been his maid. She died in 1663. He lived just long enough to outlive his son Titus who died in 1668. Rembrandt died a year later. He was buried as a pauper in an unmarked grave. The late period of his art is usually dated from around 1651 to the time of his death, though, once again, it is to a somewhat earlier picture we now turn.

The Slaughtered Ox[88] is from 1643, and just as the title suggests, the painting displays the cadaver of an ox, one which has been hung from a solid, wooden, scaffold like contraption in a cellar. Toward the left-hand corner at the bottom, there is a woman kneeling over, working in the background. But she is hardly visible in a gentle gloom which muffles and softens the definition of the cellar – its shapes and the shadows, the murky impression of a wall at the back, the muted outline of the slabs of the floor. To the centre of the painting is the carcass of the ox which has been flayed, gutted and hung. The paradox lies in the fact that while it is the ox which is well and truly lifeless, its full flowing, moist flesh, its glistening sinews, its swirling white pockets of fat – seem to shine in the gloom, radiating a ghostly orange luminesce which acts as an irresistible beacon to the eye. Even though this is a picture of flayed flesh and dead animal matter, the carcass seems to glow with a spectral, inviolable life. On the other hand, it is the woman at the back – who is alive, who is in motion, who is both living and breathing – it is she who seems most distant, most impenetrable.

Again this is (quite literally) a painting about interiority, and again it is revolutionary in the true Rembrandt sense. It was painted at the time of some of his most devastating personal bereavements, and certainly the sense of something which has been so viscerally dismembered provides us with the awareness that existence itself is the supreme, most artful, most relentless butcherer of all. But to this ontological viscerality, there is added a classically Rembrandt-esque sense of pathos. The woman on her knees at the edge of the scene, the human being working away in the background, going about her day-to-day routine, seems impervious, implacable, unaffected in her outer semblance – and yet, the ox provides the observer with the more profound truth; for are we not all, on the inside, in a state of torn, flayed, conflicted helplessness which comes from love and the inevitability of loss? In the picture the ox has been raised up, its top two limbs stretched out horizontally across a wooden bar, and one is unable to escape the sense that what is really taking place here is something more than the perfuncionary slaughter of an animal, that one is being made witness to some kind of... crucifixion. And perhaps that is the artist's ultimate point. Perhaps, through the very unlikely medium of a dead piece of meat, Rembrandt is making us aware that, ultimately, this is our destiny – that, each day, life crucifies us that little bit more and that little more slowly, through the sense of loss and suffering we must inevitably accumulate.

Perhaps, along with *The Night Watch*,[89] Rembrandt is most well-known for the self-portraits he did in his later years. This was a time in which he would lose virtually everything: his partners, all his children, his fortune and his funding, and much of the acclaim and respect in which he was once held. The summer of his life had trailed off into a melancholy autumn before at last slipping into the bleakest of winters. The self-portraits from this period are quite remarkable, perhaps because they are enshrined by that wintery sense of loneliness, of isolation – and for this reason, their depth, their interiority, is all the more pronounced, even by the standards of the master. One of the most poignant examples from the period is *Self-Portrait as the Apostle Paul of 1661* which was painted the year after he was compelled to sell his house and his etching press and the Amsterdam Painters' Guild had successfully fought to make it illegal for him to continue trading as a painter in his own name. The painting is a self-portrait but at the same time Rembrandt is reimagining himself in the guise of the saint. To what end? A recent cleaning of the painting has revealed the faint image of a wall that was hidden behind the layers of accumulated dirt and varnish and which indicates that in this scene the saint has been imprisoned.[90] Along with the sword handle which is protruding from the inside of one jacket lapel, this suggests that the painter's theme is one of martyrdom.

And yet. The painting, and in particular the face, is neither dramatic nor grandiose. The painting lacks entirely the overt sense of melodrama which is so often synonymous with depictions of religious suffering. In fact, the posture of the saint/Rembrandt is in repose, an open book rested casually on the lap. Rembrandt looks at us as though he has just sensed our presence, has just turned his face up, interrupting his reading. At first glance the face itself is quite ordinary, the skin a complex of dappled yellow, pink and brown, the forehead fissured with wrinkles, the cheeks flabby and jowly, the flesh beginning to drip and droop downward like candle wax. It is a muted study in old age and entropy, the rich wearying flesh is illuminated by a single beam which falls from the top corner. Time's remorseless, unblinking light revealing every crevice, every cranny, of a face which has been etched by experience. Beyond this light a blackness abides which is sleek and dark and eternal. Rembrandt is on the very edge of this blackness. The artist would perish before the end of the decade and this picture is a prelude to the night which is about to fall, and yet the rich dark of those full eyes is both melancholy and serene, and his eyebrows are raised almost quizzically. It is the expression of one who has lived and is aware that his existence has entered its final freefall – and yet at the same time that face is still curious, still so capable of wonder. It is achingly intimate and yet it is also fundamentally ordinary, speaking to the gentle, everyday defiance of the human condition set against the ravages of time.

In what was his last major commission and also his last secular historical depiction, Rembrandt's *The Conspiracy of Claudius Civilis* was also (originally) the largest canvass the painter had ever prepared. It was commissioned by the Amsterdam city council for the town hall, so it was a prestigious windfall which arrived at a time when Rembrandt's career and financial situation were in the most desperate straits. Rembrandt was commissioned to depict an episode from the Batavian rebellion which saw a small Germanic tribe (the Batavi) mount a heroic revolt against the Roman Empire in AD 69, temporarily driving Roman garrisons from a territory centred around the Rhine. The rebellion was important in the type of history and mythology which came to inform the ideology of Dutch nationalism unleashed by the Dutch Revolt – for the Dutch bourgeoisie saw in the figure of Gaius Julius Civilis – the leader of the rebellion – a heroic precursor to their own struggles against the Spanish Habsburgs. For this reason, Rembrandt would have been under considerable pressure to strike a triumphalist tone which presented the centuries-dead leader and his co-conspirators in the more modern guise of intrepid revolutionaries seeking through their struggles to raise the possibilities of a new world. But one look at the painting shows that Rembrandt has achieved almost anything but this.

The painting, which has been cut down from its original size, is still of massive dimensions – metres high, metres wide – and it draws the eye in the way of flickering flames in deep, dark night. The scene depicts the conspirators sat around a vast table, they are reaching out toward the centre with their swords, touching the blades, thereby consummating an oath. The periphery of the scene is hewn with rich, dark, reddish-browns, and as the movement flows toward the centre, the figures of the conspirators are illuminated by a ribbon of shimmering golden-white light. The figure of Claudius Civilis dominates the scene, his gossamer robes glitter pale gold, his thick, broad sword is held up, a massive multi-layered crown is perched on his head. Finally, he is looking out at the viewer through one implacable, fateful eye, for the other is missing – and in its place merely a puckered black socket webbed with skin. Many of the figures gathered round the table have features which have been rendered ethereal and translucent by the ghostly light such that the darker, muddier, reddish tones of the background can be glimpsed through the thin, vague fabric of their bodies. They appear as phantoms rather than men. The Dutch burgomasters must have been astounded and outraged by this painting; the domineering figure in the centre is donned in a very un-republican like crown. But more than this, the image has a ghastly, decadent quality; it is another "Ozymandias", another warning, another revelation, another haunting lament on the inevitability of historical decline; a beautiful, grotesque dirge. In the moment when every practical instinct should have compelled Rembrandt to crack on with a more commercial endeavour which would have appealed to the sensibilities of his wealthy and connected patrons, in the very moment when he should have laboured to create a piece which might have hauled him out of the destitution and hopelessness with which he was faced, the artist does anything but. Instead he produces a work of art which seems to crackle with the ghostly fire of the past, with historical ominousness and historical power. The painting is, of course, rejected.

Barely a year after *The Conspiracy of Claudius Civilis* was finished, Rembrandt lost his partner Hendrickje Stoffels. Rembrandt had throughout both a complex and tragic relationship with the women in his life which was at times both tender and unsavoury. His studies of his wife Saskia van Uylenborgh are almost always romantic and delicate, sometimes playful and mischievous, sometimes filled with longing and regret. They run the gamut of any romantic relationship; that first period of exhilarated intoxication which is exhibited in *The Prodigal Son in the Brothel* right through to the time of Saskia's final illness where his depictions of her seem to fade and grow faint, like the life of his subject itself – a beloved partner, too frail to get out of bed, blinking out at the world from under the covers, immortalised in a series of delicate pencil sketchings. The relationship which followed with Geertje Dircx had altogether darker undertones. She had been nurse to his son Titus before she and Rembrandt had become romantically involved, only the relationship soured and she sued the artist for "breach of promise" – a euphemism for a seduction carried out under a promise of marriage which is subsequently not kept. In a response which can really only be read as vindictive, cruel and oppressive, Rembrandt took measures to see that Dircx was committed to an asylum or poorhouse. It is difficult to reconcile such behaviour with the various paintings Rembrandt does of women throughout his lifetime, because many of these are so finally attuned to female pathos, suffering and oppression; they are so deeply empathetic. It is difficult to reconcile this with Rembrandt's behaviour toward Dircx but not impossible, perhaps. Christopher Hitchens once wrote of George Orwell that what made the latter such a powerful and effective anti-imperialist was that as someone who had served British imperialism in Burma he had carried out its repressions, and its spirit had come to pervade some of his most inner and unconscious sensibilities. Any critique Orwell developed of imperialism, therefore, had to be particularly thorough-going for it needed to operate not only on an intellectual level but in terms of a more inward protean reformation: *he had to kill the imperialist inside him* – "he had to suppress his distrust and dislike for the poor, his revulsion from the 'coloured' masses who teemed throughout the empire."[91]

I suspect something similar was true of Rembrandt. He had been a purveyor of masculine power and masculine oppression, but at the same time that immanent, inward experience of how such power was made manifest, how such exploitative instincts were carried – provided a deeper and more authentic dimension to the type of female suffering he was seeking to depict. He understood the dilemma and the pathos which was inherent in the victim's situation, not only for his deep sense of aesthetic identification with the victim herself, but also because he felt something – immanently, organically – of the nature of the power which called such oppression into being and perhaps even craved it. It was a power by which he had profited in his life. So, in his picture *Woman Bathing in a Stream*, there is a dualism – a dualism which once more fluctuates between freedom and oppression and which pervades the spirit of the picture itself. This scene was painted in 1654 and shows a woman, modelled on Hendrickje Stoffels, wading through a still pool of sleek, dark varnished water while raising her simple white chemise so that the fabric of the dress does not get wet. There is an element of eroticism to the painting; as she raises her dress, the dark draws into the exposed space between her legs, softening it in shadow, but this is offset by the expression on her face which is oblivious and dreamy, and her lips are pursed in the vaguest ghost of smile. She is not there to entice. Rather it is a remarkable study in intimacy; a person who, in their solitude, is allowing the unassuming flow of innermost feeling to pass across them gently, is taking an unconscious pleasure in the feel and the texture of the water, is perhaps thinking fondly of a memory or the evening to come.

And yet at the same time, this sense of unassuming lightness and freedom is countermanded by the fact that the young woman is not alone, for we, the viewers, are watching her – are privy not just to the near nudity of her body, but also the nakedness of her inner disposition and the innocence of her obliviousness. We are pressed into the role of the invisible, voyeuristic presence which is lurking just beyond her, in the undergrowth, in the darkness. There is a certain sinisterism at work, a sense of exploitation which works in tandem with the fact that in this moment the young woman is at her most relaxed, most free. The regal green, the plush ruby red, of the cloak which she has left on the side of the bank, suggests that this is not a modern figure but rather a biblical creation. Several critics have argued – persuasively in my view – that it is very likely a depiction of the biblical scene Susanna and the Elders – a scene Rembrandt had visited before. But what is different in this scene, in the 1654 version, is that Rembrandt does not depict the elders lurking in the bushes – he does not depict them in the painting at all; more radically, and more disturbingly – the viewer themselves becomes the elders, the interlopers, the oppressive presence which is cosseted in the shadows. In that same year Rembrandt also painted *Bathsheba* – another work which is attuned to the nature of female suffering and male oppression. It depicts Bathsheba receiving the note which summons her to King David's chambers – the king had sent her husband to war in order that he might claim her for himself. She is naked, and beautiful yes, but again not a Renaissance nude sculptured into an idealised object of sexual perfection. Instead her belly is slightly saggy, the shape of her arm slightly uneven. Rembrandt depicts these ordinary imperfections with a tenderness which is matched only by the pathos in Bathsheba's face – an expression of almost ethereal melancholy and resignation. As John Berger comments: "Her husband is away at the wars. (How many millions of times has it happened?) Her servant, kneeling, is drying her feet. She has no choice but to go to the king…A fatality has already begun, and at the center of this fatality is Bathsheba's desirability as a wife."[92]

The final Rembrandt I want to turn to is a painting which was done in 1666, 3 years before the artist's death. It is of a young noble woman. Her story is again a sad one. She was born in a small town by a river in the sixth century BC, and the people there lived in the shadow of a powerful empire. She was raped by the son of the king and – unable to live with the trauma and the stigma of the attack – she took her own life. The incident became one of those moments in history where a single act of injustice becomes the focal point of a broader set of grievances, providing a spark for a profound and sweeping historical change. The town was, of course, Rome, who rebelled against their Etruscan overlords and took the first step on their own imperial journey by establishing the republic in 509 BC. The noblewoman was Lucretia. Rembrandt's painting of her is perhaps one of the most powerful paintings which has ever been created. More than that, it is the work in which all the concerns which have fissured through Rembrandt's corpus throughout – the interiority of the individual, the nature of oppression, the hidden but inevitable presence of history, the subjugation of women – in this piece all these themes achieve an aesthetic flashpoint which fuses them in a moment of rapturous, otherworldly synthesis and deathly calm. Again the contrast with Renaissance depictions of the same subject should be noted. These tended to feature a bare breasted, voluptuous woman, sometimes having her clothes torn away during the rape, sometimes slipping a blade into her chest in the aftermath. Her face is often frightened or sad but strangely abstract, the eyes muted and numb, turned toward the heavens in a static and idealised gesture of suffering.

The Rembrandt painting is an altogether different animal. There is something dusky, shadowy, crepuscular and almost moth-like about it. Lucretia is in a very dark room, her bed chamber, and she is dressed in a tawny brown and pale green gown under which is a nightie, whose fine, diaphanous white silk flows down over her androgynous, childlike body. Whereas previous depictions often depicted the violent motion of the thrusted knife, Rembrandt has lingered on a stiller, more serene moment. The knife is held down by her side almost loosely. But a single trickle of blood which is coming though that fine white silk from her chest, indicates that the fatal action has already been performed. You almost don't realise it at first. With her other hand Lucretia is pulling on the chord which will summon the members of her family to her chamber before she slips away. This terrible intimacy, these private final moments by which her life is seen to ebb away, is compounded by Lucretia's expression which is filled with the most haunting pathos. It was not unusual for artists to depict the act of crying, tears streaming down cheeks and so on, but what Rembrandt does is show those full, dark pools of her eyes watering with unshed tears. Her face is pallid, sculptured by the most serene sadness, as she gazes into the dark; her lips are slightly pursed, and her eyes are kind and wise and soft and measured but infinitely sad. It is the picture of someone saying goodbye to the world without uttering a word.

When one looks at this painting, one is aware of the historical context. In the cosseted, intimate darkness of Lucretia's bed chamber, you can see the forms and outline of the republic beginning to take shape, you can register its youthful expansion across Italy as it clashed with the Etruscans and the Gauls, and later the great wars with Carthage. In the far distance you can make out the ascendency of Caesar and Octavian and the culmination of the greatest empire the world had ever known; one which stretched from the wintery wilderness of England's northern most borders to the hot baking deserts of North Africa, from the silver mines of Spain to the bustling market squares of Constantinople at the gateway to the East. All of this is pre-empted by what is taking place in that room in those final moments, a fatality which sets into motion the trajectory of a whole epoch, but in the very moment when you can glimpse the palaces, basilicas, amphitheatres and viaducts which are to be raised up across a continent and whose glories would be the mark of the *imperium* – in the very moment you can see these things in the future's distant outline, all at once they begin to fade and dim, disappearing in the darkness once more, and you are left with a young woman alone, gazing out with the sweetest sadness, dying in the gloom. The painting provides what is the most supreme and exquisite motif of the artist's corpus more generally; that is, the tragic dissonance between the inner life of the individual and the interminable, fateful shape of the broader historical process. Lucretia by her act has unleashed a startlingly new historical progression but it is one which is premised on the snuffing out of an individual life, and all of its passions, all of its glories, are ones she will never know. That fateful separation which opens up between the individual and the epoch is one which had been grafted onto Rembrandt's spiritual psyche by virtue of the tragic course of his own life; in its early stages, he was raised up by the historical moment as one of its most precocious sons, and yet as history swept forward the artist found himself floundering in its wake as he lost fame, fortune and family, until as an old man, he too was left in a room alone, alone in the darkness, his mind lit by the soft glow of his memories.

Chapter Five

Arthur Schopenhauer: The Philosophy of Nothingness

Schopenhauer enjoyed a salubrious existence but it was far from a happy one. Georg Lukacs describes him as the first philosopher of a "grand bourgeois"[93] status, which is accurate. He was born in 1788. His father was a wealthy merchant living in the semi-feudal backwater of Danzig which was to be, in his lifetime, annexed by Prussia. Heinrich Floris Schopenhauer, however, clearly had his gaze turned outward, toward the currents of Enlightenment thought which were wafting across Europe more broadly, the radical sense of republicanism, the breaking down of feudal barriers and trade tariffs and the set of economic freedoms which sanctified the individual and heralded the new epoch. For that reason, he named his new-born son "Arthur" for Arthur was a name which was shared by several European languages and perhaps hinted at the father's aspirations for his progeny, the life of a true cosmopolite, unfettered by national boundaries, devoted to the pursuit of international commerce and culture and the rich material rewards which would come with it. Indeed the son's life was from the outset characterised by this sense of cosmopolitanism as the family roamed across Europe and the young Arthur Schopenhauer was tutored in France, England, Holland, Switzerland and other places.

And yet the child's life was also demarked by negation and anomie. His father had great expectations for Schopenhauer, but was in many ways rendered remote from his son by the long sojourns his business ventures required, and although his mother was a more palpable presence in the young child's life, it was clear from an early age that their dispositions were almost organically incompatible. Johanna Schopenhauer was 20 years her husband's junior, and lacked the austere seriousness of a seasoned and professional money maker; she was more of a free spirit – a poet, novelist and *bon vivant* whose playful, aesthetic disposition made of her a natural and colourful *salonniere*, someone who was at ease in the company of people from all classes, and who communed with many of the leading lights of the epoch, cultivating close friendships with Goethe and the Schlegel brothers among others. Her son's stints in various boarding schools, being shunted from one to the next, meant that the young Arthur was never able to allow his formative relationships to settle and deepen; was accustomed to spending long periods of time in his own company and adept at inuring himself against the austere, unyielding discipline of the more indifferent school masters.

The young boy was very swiftly transformed into an old soul, a brooding, introverted child, with a stormy nature; an unusually perceptive person but one who was also prickly, obdurate and quick to take offence, displaying a fiercely independent train of thought. From an early age he must have looked at his mother, and seen in her openness and vivacity, a frivolity and flightiness which was utterly alien to his own disposition.

For certain, the young Schopenhauer would have seen his father as the bedrock of an otherwise free-flowing existence, a stabilising template of masculine certainty. His father's suicide in 1805, therefore, must have come not only as a horrific shock but also an existential disruption of much which he had held certain, and in the 2 years following, the young man worked as a merchant perhaps as a way of honouring and memorialising his dead father. However, the boredom and repetition of commercial practice proved too much for what was already a lithe and lively brain, and the young Schopenhauer returned to his studies where eventually he would study psychology and metaphysics at the University of Gottingen. His sense of brooding introversion was accentuated by the melancholy of his loss, the feeling of being so suddenly unmoored from the world, and in the figure of his one remaining parent the youth could find no solace. Rather the gulf which had always existed between Schopenhauer and his mother seemed to stretch to become insurmountable. Joanna Schopenhauer, with her buoyant, irrepressible personality, threw herself into life anew, establishing a literary salon, a bustling social life and a successful literary career. The young Schopenhauer's rigid, preternaturally serious demeanour was bound to sense in this a confirmation of the shallowness and lack of seriousness he already detected in his mother.

Such brooding disapproval was accentuated by what was very likely a sense of sexual disgust at the relationships Joanna entered into with the men around her – particularly, in the years to come, with a younger lodger. The instinctive feeling on the young man's part that she was so easily and obscenely betraying his father's memory. The death of his father, then, had caused the already introverted youth to dwell ever more on the transitory and ephemeral nature of the individual existence – "to be or not to be" was the question which pervaded his solitude – but to this was added his Danish precursor's sense of angst and betrayal; the father who was taken too soon only to be raised up and idealised, alongside the mother whose sexual life in the aftermath became a cypher for weakness and betrayal: "The funeral baked meats, did coldly furnish forth the marriage tables,"[94] so might the young Schopenhauer have been heard to mutter. For her part, this woman who had worked hard at giving her son a life, and who supported him financially as he had pursued his higher education, and would later use her contacts to help him achieve publication and recognition – for Joanna Schopenhauer her son remained an alien prospect, a gloomy, crepuscular presence which emitted little of the precious, carefree light of youth.

This, then, formed the backdrop of his early adulthood, the conditions under which his encounter with philosophy would take place. Schopenhauer was influenced by two thinkers in particular, and these were Plato and, most of all, Immanuel Kant. Kant, of course, was the giant which virtually every German philosophy student had to come to terms with; the contradictions in the Kantian system had thrown down the gauntlet and provided the impetus to the development of German idealism in the early nineteenth century. In particular it was the dualism which fissured across Kantianism – the divide between the infinite and the finite, the undisclosed noumenal object and the limited rational activity of the individual mind, the thing-in-itself and the forms and categories of the individual ego which might never bring the thing within the compass of their reason and remit – it was this contradiction with which the philosophers grappled in the aftermath of Kant's demise.

Schopenhauer's solution to it, like that of Fichte, who was writing at around the same time, was to seek some all-encompassing first principle which would synthesise both noumenal and phenomenal in a mighty but harmonious unity. A precocious philosopher, Schopenhauer was to set out the outlines of this principle and its implications in the first volume of his masterwork – *The World as Will and Idea* – which was published first in 1818 when the author was just 30, and it is probably accurate to say that the rest of his intellectual life was spent working on the consolidation and enrichment of the ideas which are laid out in this work.

That first, absolute principle which Schopenhauer alighted on was his famous concept of the will. In some ways he preserves, at least nominally, a Kantian-like division: the will corresponds to the thing-in-itself, the world as it objectively is, beyond the realm of appearances – while it is the latter, the phenomenal reality, which we encounter in and through "representation", to which human knowledge (reason) is limited. But although this certainly carries across some key features of Kantian dualism, Schopenhauer's infinite principle, the will, is able to intercede in the world, to manifest itself, in a way in which noumenal entities never could. What is the will? The first thing to understand is that it is not this or that particular will – the desire or inclination in any given person at any time to achieve a particular end, like post a job application for instance. But it is not unrelated to specific, individual wills either. It is rather an all-encompassing force, an absolute vitalism which pervades every object of the universe in its totality; it is a metaphysical, elemental power which structures being in as much as it provides the inclination to be. It is the invisible, infinite first condition of being, the impulse on which entities erupt into existence and seek to maintain their integrity for as long as they can against the other objects of the material world, and the forces of entropy and decay. This, of course, could involve a self-conscious will to life, and the existential preoccupation which comes from the awareness and fear of death; but in the broadest sense, the will principle underpins a stone or a river just as much as it underpins an Aristotle or an Alexander. It is the innermost essence, the principle of striving, the elemental tension which inheres in all being – in the rock which sits in the shade for millions of years, stubborn and intractable, before the sweeping storms and the relentless rays of the throbbing sun; in the river whose gushing water tumbles forward, perpetually achieving new form, new life, new expression – whose being, fluid and irrepressible, is carried forth on the jubilant crest of a wave. Schopenhauer writes of the will:

> The key to understanding the inner nature of things... the tremendous irresistible force with which rivers hurry down to the sea, the persistence with which the magnet turns again and again to the North Pole, the eagerness with which in electricity opposite poles strive to be re-united, and which, just like human desire is the more intense for being thwarted...What in us pursues its purposes by the light of knowledge here, in the weakest of its manifestations, strives

only blindly, dumbly, partially and immutably, yet because wherever it is, it is one and the same, both of these must bear the name will...For the name will denotes the being-in-itself of everything in the world, and the sole kernel of every phenomenon.[95]

The individual existence, then, is merely the conduit of will, that all-encompassing master principle. The distinction between noumena and phenomena is retained, but whereas in Kant, at the most fundamental ontological level, the thing-in-itself was irreconcilably alienated from the phenomenal appearance – an appearance which presupposed its distortion and irredeemable loss – in the case of Schopenhauer the will and the phenomenal world are able to enter into some form of coherent correspondence. The will is infinite. It is not of the world. And yet it manifests in every material object. Material objects come into being. They exist in space and time. The will is the necessary precondition for this existence. The will manifests as the striving every material world object contains within itself, the way in which it is driven to prolong its being. And yet when the object succumbs in space and time, when it slips into non-existence once more, the will continues to manifest in every other object, in every new creation. It is neither diminished nor added to. It does not change. The infinite shines through the veil of the finite; individual existences perish, decay and crumble; but the impetus to existence, the thing which provides the clarion call to all existence, remains immutable and eternal, and as ethereal as light. Its being lies "outside" time and space though the gravity of its presence is always in effect in the here and now. Schopenhauer's vision is a poetic one to be sure, though not wholly original. The will as infinite principle harkens back in its intellectual lineage to the "nous" of Anaxagoras, and in the modern age certainly has a strong correspondence with the vitalism of Herder and his principle of *kraft*. In endeavouring to overcome Kantian dualism, however, Schopenhauer generates a new set of contradictions. Firstly, the will stands "outside" space and time and though it manifests itself in the material world, it is nevertheless not subject to phenomenal laws. So, for example, the will is not subject to the principle of sufficient reason, for as something which does not subsist in space and time, it cannot have a cause: "The will as a thing-in-itself lies outside the province of the principle of sufficient reason in all its forms, and hence is completely groundless...that which lies outside time and space."[96] Again the Kantian legacy weighs heavy. As a result, Schopenhauer is compelled to yield to a further consequence of Kantianism: given that the will is not subject to the forms and categories of reason which structure reality at the phenomenal level, he must of necessity conclude that the will is outside the remit of reason itself. Herein, however, lies the contradiction: one cannot subject the will to rational cognition, one cannot provide a rational definition of its nature and standing in relation to phenomena, and yet, Schopenhauer has endeavoured to do precisely that by describing the specifics of the way in which the will relates to finite objects in their totality.

How can he hope to justify this paradox? The descent into irrationalism at this point is both necessary and inevitable, though Schopenhauer's justification for it is certainly theoretically adroit. It is true, he says, that rationally we are unable to comprehend the objective – that is, the infinite power which infuses the finite, individual objects of the world, because though we are driven through reason to establish the connection between this and that individual and finite object – by bringing to bear the principle of sufficient reason – we cannot penetrate beneath the complex of causation in order to rationally apprehend the will principle, for abstract rational thought demands we seek a cause for the will where in fact none can exist. For this reason, argues Schopenhauer, we are condemned to linger on the surface of the objects which we encounter; what we experience rationally is like the sleek, glossy water of a dark lake – we can make out the ripple and the direction of the waves, but we are unable to see the vast shape and shadow of that which lies beneath and sets them into motion. And yet, there is one object in the world which is unique in this regard. The human being, the human individual, is like any other object in the world, existing in time and space, and yet we, human individuals, inhabit this object imminently so to speak; we experience it as an object like any other, subject to phenomenal law and given to intellectual representation, and yet at the same time I embody will in a more intimate and conjoined way. I experience it not just as a passive and rational observer might behold an external object, but as an object which is at the same time myself, the willing subject. Schopenhauer writes:

> The body is given in two entirely different ways to the subject...It is given as an idea in intelligent perception, as an object among objects and beholden to the laws of objects. And it is also given in quite a different way, as that which is immediately known to everyone, and is signified by the word will...The act of will and the movement of the body are not two different things objectively known, which the bond of causality unites; they do not stand in the relation of cause and effect; they are one and the same, although given in two entirely different ways – immediately, and again in the perception for the understanding. The action of the body is nothing but the act of the will objectified.[97]

There are several things of note here. Firstly, Schopenhauer is setting up a mind-body interrelation which is in some way reminiscent of Spinozism (attributes). This allows for the possibility of an ontological development – one which sets into motion both individual will and bodily movement as reciprocal but individually self-determinate processes. This, in turn, helps to transcend the threshold of the finite (the two terms – act of will, bodily movement – do not relate to one another by way of cause and effect). Because they do not relate in this way, "they are one in the same" – they have the same root source; the principle of the will as the absolute. They are its unified embodiment. And yet, they can be "given in two entirely different ways". They are given in the phenomenal sense; that the body is comprehended as a physical existence suspended in space and time, and thus is subject to "perception for the understanding" – or to say the same, subject to the mental routines and categories of reason. But they are also given in as much as the body as subject is a manifestation of will in the world, and this fact is expressed through the intimate and inward self-consciousness of the individual existence. So the same event, my growing sense of hunger for instance, can be experienced at the two different levels of appearance and essence. On the one hand you, dear reader, might hear my stomach rumble, or you might be uncomfortably aware of the salivating drool which is dripping from the corners of my mouth as I behold that nourishing steak and chips right over there on the table. But while the external phenomenal reality might disclose such empirical details it cannot yield the feeling I have, my yearning, the physical need I experience to consume the food. And yet, in my inward state, I, the hungering individual, am aware of such need – almost painfully so. I am aware of the will acting through me, my empirical existence. The fact that I have teeth of a certain number and a certain shape with a particular capacity, the fact that I have a belly broiling with acids which digest fodder and a bloodstream which can absorb nutrients – these characteristics of my physical existence, given in time and space, have assumed their particular form only in as much as they have been shaped into the object (myself) which best acts as a conduit for the underlying impulse to be – the will which, in this case, is manifested through my hunger. In other words, the will comes to structure myself and all the other objects of the universe in its own most expedient image.

We are now in a position to see how Schopenhauer's ontology necessarily assumes a deeply irrationalist character. One cannot comprehend the will rationally because rationality can only operate at the level of the phenomenal, empirical existence – while the will represents the innermost kernel lodged at the heart of being. We encounter the will in as much as we ourselves are the bearers of such being; we encounter the will by way of our own interiority; in the immediacies of our most fundamental and protean yearnings. In fact, argues Schopenhauer, it is not only the case that rational thought *cannot comprehend* the inner essence, the thing-in-itself, but perhaps even more significantly – rational thought provides the means by which the underlying reality of the will principle is occluded and obscured. If it is the case that we encounter the will at an emotive level, at the level of our most immediate and intimate impulses, it must also be true that rational thought opens up an increasingly mediated gap between the raw sensations and actuality of the will and the complexity of rational thought's own network of abstraction, law, hypothesis and theorem. Schopenhauer, therefore, reaches the type of conclusion which was often in vogue in the century before, and represented a palpable and profound challenge to the cult of reason which had emerged in and through the Enlightenment, a critique which was founded by figures like Hamann. Hamann, a dyed-in-the-wool reactionary, was nevertheless a rich, rebellious, poetic and creative thinker who spearheaded the romantic vitalism which would go on to provide a cornerstone critique of the rational system building evinced by figures like Mendelssohn and Lessing. Hamann saw in the notion of a set of individuals acting in tandem to facilitate a coordinated, collective social contract, grounded in the prerogatives of a universal natural law – a stultifying perversion of the litheness and spontaneity of the human experience. States did not arise at the behest of pre-arranged social contracts but as a result of a mysterious conglomeration of inner needs which drove vibrantly, inexorably and almost unconsciously, the great streams of practical human development and wrote out across the face of history the enigmatic idiom of the divine creator. The rise of reason was antithetical to this process; the rise of reason in the world represented a soul-destroying, totalitarian machine which petrified everything glorious and living, and transformed the human soul from an exquisite, depthless mystery into an ossified cog in a broader set of mechanics.

So in Hamann too an almost gnostic antagonism emerges between immediacy – and specifically the life-affirming "immediacy" which is alleged to be found in spontaneous, practical experience – over and against the cold, clinical abstractions of reason which drain flesh-and-blood events of their unfettered joy and creative possibility. But it is the point of difference between the irrationalism of Hamann and the irrationalism of Schopenhauer which is of critical interest. In Hamann the irrationalism has a pronounced theological character, the immediacy of the experience brings the individual closer into contact with the divine power, and it is the divine power who is the source of all reality. Hamann's vitalism as a philosophical world view represents the hope to overcome man's alienation from his natural sensuousness and raw creativity which has been provoked by the despotic, impersonal caveats of a transcendental reason, a reason which exists in marked opposition to the life and vitality of the empirical world. Behind this, of course, lies the reactionary nostalgia for a feudal past premised on kinship, personal rule and organic tradition in opposition to the development of a more impersonal market economy which was facilitated by revolutionary upheaval and was more and more the provenance of the present. But despite its wholly conservative and retrograde character, Hamann's vision was nevertheless a "positive" and "optimistic" one, for it sought to initiate a "radical" change by bringing people back into alignment with the divine purpose.

In Schopenhauer's philosophy, which is equally reactionary, the tone and direction is fundamentally different. Most significantly, Schopenhauer's vitalism is not inspired by an omnipotent and personal deity but rather a blind, absolute force, and this confers upon it a deeply nihilistic character. In Hamann's case the absolute as the divine is encountered through the immediacy of experience, and thus a "radical" encounter is presupposed which imbues the individual with a sense of holy purpose even if they are not able to rationally articulate that purpose. In Schopenhauer one encounters the will most directly through the immediacies of experience too, but the encounter generates the very opposite impression; that is, it creates a sense of profound purposelessness, the ultimate awareness that all life is geared toward its own endless, blind perpetuation, and that there is, and there can be, no higher end, beyond this striving. The element of nihilism, the emptiness, the pervading sense of a life which fluctuates between boredom and despair is something which Schopenhauer lyrically absolutises by way of the will principle; in thrall to it - the animus of our innermost being - we struggle to perpetuate our existence instinctively and futilely; a blind mole toiling in the darkness is the allegory the philosopher so mordantly proffers. In the final analysis, the difference between the positive irrationalism of Hamann and the profoundly pessimistic irrationalism found in Schopenhauer can only be conceived of in terms of the conflict of antagonistic historical epochs. Hamann is hostile to capitalistic development at its outset for he is still channelling the spirit of the declining feudal world - its centuries old traditions, the organic solidarity which was fused in religious experience, the unmediated bonds between the peasant and the land, and the artisan and the guild - in the revival of these forms was held the romantic possibility of thwarting the emerging economic order based on generalised commodity production and a developing "cash nexus", an order which leaves "no other bond between man and man than naked self-interest, than callous 'cash payment'". Schopenhauer, however, was writing from the other side of the French Revolution, and was unable to entertain any hope of a feudal restoration. Rather than subvert the capitalist model – capitalism was, for Schopenhauer, already an unalterable fact – the power of his philosophy lies in the way he was able to transform the existential compulsion exerted by the working out of blind market forces which is the expression of a specific social-historical epoch – into an ontological absolute which becomes the timeless and unchanging precondition of the entire universe – i.e. the will. Schopenhauer, then, was writing in the manner of bourgeois theoreticians more generally, who tended to form what Istvan Meszaros quite correctly categorises as an "eternal present" – i.e. the historical specificity of the capitalist epoch is transfigured into a permanent and eternal fixture of human existence, from Adam Smith, who regarded all of history as merely the prelude to the realisation of the capitalist social system, to Francis Fukuyama, who notoriously described that same system as "the end of history". But – in contradistinction to Smith and certainly to the later, vulgar apologists of capitalism who were not even cognisant of Smith's qualms regarding the system – what Schopenhauer does is to inject a deep sense of pessimism into his vision; he sees (albeit unconsciously) the central tenets of capitalism – the blind competition, the remorseless individualism – as immutable factors of a transcendental human nature driven by the will, but he does not laud or celebrate these elements as a guarantor of social progress (as the ideologues of capitalism almost always tend to do). Rather he experiences in them the unrelenting hopelessness which is visited on the individual by a mighty, meaningless universe. Because the will principle is eternal, immutable, it can never be "satisfied" by its mediations with the finite; as soon as one vessel dissipates under its interminable gravity, another takes its place. For the individual human being, this is to be in thrall to a tendency which can never be sated; as soon as we realise this particular desire, as soon as we satisfy that particular need, we are at once under the compulsion of a new one. We are driven on, randomly, inevitably – plagued by a never-ending and arbitrary set of desires which arise from the miasma of the world, and which compel, move and torment us, until finally the shell-like shape of our body, exhausted and spent, shrivels away into nothingness while all the while the will continues to burn, only in new forms and on new horizons. The human existence implies being locked into such a remorseless, meaningless cycle – like Sisyphus we are all of us striving to push that boulder to the top of the hill, and as with Sisyphus it must inevitably roll back down, and we must inevitably begin to push again.

Despite the bleakness of its outlook, this vision has a profoundly reactionary and conservative core when we consider its implications. Firstly, it is reason, rational thought, which occludes and blinds us to the true nature of the will as the secret nestled at the heart of being. Secondly, everything we try to do, every high-falutin ethical end we strive to attain only helps to disguise the true impulse latent in all human activity – i.e. the blind unfolding of the will. Considered in tandem, these two conditions have damning implications most of all for political and historical projects of radical or revolutionary emancipation. If one takes Hegelianism, and the Marxism which grew out of it, one is confronted by the notion that history develops in terms of an ontology of labour whereby the evolution of more complex forms of social organisation yields the possibility, at least, of more radical forms of human freedom. In addition, both Hegelianism and Marxism argue that such a development can and must be comprehended self-consciously – i.e. subject to rational thought – so that it could be culminated in radical (Hegel) or revolutionary (Marx) practice. If Hamann's philosophy was tailored from the feudal purview as a means to combat the forms of generic rationality which were part and parcel of the ideology of bourgeois individualism and early Enlightenment thought – then the key components of Schopenhauer's ideology have been framed from a later stage in capitalist development when the ideological need has arisen to combat any social agency which has the historical capacity to revolutionise capitalism from within – and any political philosophy which might dare to articulate such a possibility in rational and historical terms. Historical development is merely an illusion by which the elemental and eternal primacy of the will is veiled. In other words, Schopenhauer's philosophy, at its most fundamental level, is a weapon trained upon Hegelianism and Marxism, perfectly calibrated to obliterate the historical dimensions in both – and, of course, is particularly precocious for the fact that Schopenhauer was writing before Marx and before the industrial proletariat emerged as a class with its own independent political programme in the middle of the nineteenth century.

If any type of historical solution to the problems of modernity is necessarily placed outside the scope of Schopenhauer's philosophy by virtue of its fundamental ontology, then one can't help but wonder if there is any element of hope or redemption which might raise the individual existence above the nihilism and empty infinity of the will principle. In fact, the means of alleviating the fug of hopelessness which is cast across his thought is provided foremostly by Schopenhauer's encounter with Eastern religion, particularly his reading of the Hindu texts the *Upanishads*, his appreciation of Buddhism – and beyond these, his encounter with Plato. Schopenhauer's reading of Plato runs along the following lines: he is prepared to accept Plato's conception of the infinite as a multiplicity of "forms" or "ideas" whose infinite unchanging ideality informs the objects of the empirical world. In Schopenhauer the Platonic forms act as a kind of mediation between the will principle and phenomena – any given "idea" is the metaphysical outline of any material world object. The form represents a type of transition stage – the eternal template which has the pure form of the specific object in the state "before" the object manifests its physical and temporal actuality. It has the guise of the finite but subsists as an infinite content – for it is eternal and unchanging in its aspect.

Such a setup provides the ontological architecture which would undergird Schopenhauer's "Buddhist" perspective. Abstract reason, which is structured on the cause and effect principle, means a person can see things "only in their interrelatedness, the final goal of which is always a relation to his own will".[98] But, argues Schopenhauer, if we are prepared to try and relinquish "abstract thought" and the principle of sufficient reason, if we wander out into the world, and stop trying to rationally derive the connections between objects, but instead just linger on this particular object; if we give ourselves over to the contemplation of this mountain, or this statue – without trying to locate it in a broader rational order – then "what is known is no longer the individual thing as such, but the Idea, the eternal form, the immediate objectivity of the will at this grade."[99] In fact, argues Schopenhauer, when one contemplates an object in this way, when one has a contemplative encounter with the infinite, abstract essence of the object which in some sense persists outside space, and time, and causality – then the subject itself experiences a radical transformation. Schopenhauer writes:

He loses himself in this object (to use a pregnant German idiom), i.e. he forgets his very individuality, his will, and continues to exist only as the pure subject, the clear mirror of the object, so that it is as if the object alone were there without anyone to perceive it, and he can no longer separate the perceiver from the perception, but the two have become one, because the whole consciousness is filled and taken up with one single sensuous picture.[100]

In experiencing the "idea" – i.e. the pure form of the object which remains untouched and uncontaminated by relation or mediation – the subject too sheds its awareness of its relation to the other, to the will. In the abstract object the individual himself is evaporated: "The person rapt in this perception is thereby no longer individual (for in such perception the individual has lost himself), but he is a pure, will-less, painless, timeless *subject of knowledge*."[101] The Buddhist component of Schopenhauer's philosophy is now fully apparent; when one, as a subject, makes the conscious decision to lose oneself in the contemplation of the object in its ideality, one is also taking part in a process which allows the individual to escape the relentless, inexorable consumptive power of the will principle as it is channelled through the material order and indeed through the individual self. In the contemplation of the object in its pristine, infinite isolation the subject is able to enter into what Schopenhauer calls "the state of pure will-less knowing",[102] and so escape the never-ending wheel of need and desire on which the individual existence is perched. To put it in the Buddhist refrain, we are able to attain *nirvana* – or to put it in another way still, the need to convert oneself into the "pure subject" is at the same time the demand for one's own dissolution, the yearning for nothingness. Hence we can see how the abstract negativity of the Buddhist philosophy is channelled through Schopenhauer's philosophy by way of the Platonic forms as the wistful, wishful hope for non-being in the face of the blinding, never-ending monstrousness of the will principle as Absolute.

Such a formulation – such a synthesis of Platonic idealism, Buddhism, Hinduism, eighteenth-century *Sturm und Drang* irrationalism and Kantian dualism – provides a heady tonic; a melancholy and vividly poetic vision which is both tragic – and in its ultimate embrace of nothingness – in some way serene. The vision Schopenhauer is endeavouring to propound is almost prophetically bound up to capitalist modernity – in its more decadent, twilight phase. The principle of the will, the striving for being, could have been given a more positive spin – an irrationalist take on the Spinozist *natura naturans* in which "nature" as self-caused activity realises a broader teleological purpose. If Schopenhauer were writing in an earlier time his will principle might have attained this type of character. But in Schopenhauer it was not the "one absolute substance" – which is really key to the character of the will principle. The will is articulated as a single unmediated absolute substance, this is true – but its behaviour and expression are not a consequence of this, but rather a consequence of the fact that it operates in a purely individualised way. The striving for being which the will manifests – is not the striving of the totality of being in its interrelated and mediate connectivity – it is only ever the striving of being of this individual object or that individual object. The will principle as absolute is as well the principle of absolute individuality. The imposition of the Platonic forms is illegitimate in the sense that they are simply grafted onto the Kantian thing-in-itself (will) almost as an afterthought thus generating a romantic and aesthetic mysticism. And yet, such a manoeuvre is wholly necessary. Schopenhauer required some way of allowing the infinite principle to graduate from a single one – the absolute substance as will and totality – to the many – i.e. to level of the individual unit by which the will is made manifest. Each individual object has a Platonic form that imparts to that object an infinity relating to it in its particularity – each object is an individual in as much as it is both a generic conduit for the will and is as well possessed of a form which is unique to it. The form persists as an infinite and eternal condition which does not enter into a relation of mediation or dependency with any other form. It remains a purely isolated individual abstraction which is raised to the lofty heights of a metaphysical eternity.

Why is this significant? It becomes clear when we reconsider

Schopenhauer's notion of "the pure subject of will-less knowing". We must remember that such a condition is achieved in and through the aesthetic contemplation of the objective form (Idea) of this or that given object. In achieving this, in its encounter with the Idea the subject loses the semblance of itself and merges with the object – Schopenhauer describes the process thus: "The Idea includes object and subject in like manner in itself, for they are its sole form; but in it they are perfectly balanced; for as the object here, too, is simply the idea of the subject, the subject, which is absorbed entirely into the perceived object has thus become this object itself."[103] Herein lies the crux, the methodological operation which provides the impetus and impulse of Schopenhauer's philosophy at its metabolic level – "the subject, which is absorbed entirely into the perceived object has thus become this object." To this, one must at once counterpose the great gain of the Hegelian philosophy which involved the cultivation of the subject-object dialectic that had opened up between Fichte's absolute ego and Schelling's natural philosophy; it was Hegel's great discovery to seize upon human labour (work) as the means by which the subject mediates itself with the object – and in so doing, generates its own subjectivity, producing itself, in and through the forms of social organisation which underpin its creative activity. In other words, Hegel's philosophy emerges as the apex of classical German idealism precisely because, in it, the subject-object dialectic which fissures across the panorama of the period is finally cultivated by way of an ontology of labour which, for the first time in the history of thought, depicts the human nature in its historical essence, as a socio-historical unfolding at the level of production – and by so doing, exhibits the logic inherent to such a process and thereby the possibility of self-consciously accruing to ourselves the powers of freedom and self-determination that such a process throws up.

Now we have already drawn attention to the fact that

Schopenhauer's philosophy was targeted against any historical account of human progress, and particularly that of Hegel, whom Schopenhauer seems to have regarded as some kind of *bete noire*. History is merely the rational illusion which serves to occlude us from the fact that our activities and thoughts ultimately only ever express the organic force and compulsion of the will principle, both eternal and meaningless. But we are now in a position to see that Schopenhauer's philosophy does not rest with the reduction of any and all historical progress to the level of chimera. Schopenhauer goes further. The only conceivable salvation to the quandary of being, the only means by which one can extricate oneself from the churning, perpetual nihilism of the will principle, is by the way in which the subject is dissolved in and through its encounter with the object – "the subject, which is absorbed entirely into the perceived object." Or to say the same thing, at the deepest most fundamental level, Schopenhauer's philosophy fuses the subject and object in an abstract identity which succeeds in nullifying the very dialectic which underpins the possibility of historical development and which forms the ontological foundation of both Hegelianism and Marxism. The possibility of redemption, of some respite and "freedom" on the part of the individual in Schopenhauer, is premised on the fact of an encounter with the Idea which dissolves the subject-object interrelation of the historical process. In other words, *salvation for Schopenhauer quite expressly lies in the way the individual is able to renounce his own individuality as a historical being.*

Such an analysis is rounded off by Schopenhauer's conception of time. In the Hegelian and the Marxist conception time enters into a dialectical and historical bind with objective matter. Leon Trotsky treats the question with his customary elegance when he writes – "everything exists in time; and existence itself is an uninterrupted process of transformation; time is consequently a fundamental element of existence...a thing...if it does not change... does not exist."[104] Time, therefore, is not something abstractly distinct from matter, but is merely its form, the metaphysical carapace of its objective becoming. However, Schopenhauer, in the words of Lukacs, preserves the Kantian-subjectivist "strictly metaphysical division of space and time" and "the restricting of their validity to the phenomenal world [and] the sovereignty of causality as the linking category of objects".[105] But, as Lukacs also points out, Schopenhauer deepens this viewpoint; by making causality the true and only means by which phenomenal objects are to be related, he raises a vision of phenomenal flux, a foment of ceaseless becoming and expiration, a domino rally in which one event physically precipitates the next *ad infinitum* – a never-ending reconfiguration of the same basic elements of matter. Such a "becoming" offers an endless repetition divorced from the possibility of any type of fundamental and qualitative change, for it merely serves to disguise the true timelessness of the will principle it overlays; thus time is, of necessity, converted to a purely formal and subjectivist property which stands in a fixed, ossified and irreconcilable opposition to matter. Time is no longer "a fundamental element of existence" for existence itself is not subject to genuine change or development and therefore time cannot grow out of it dialectically as its organic expression. Thus time is the illusion perpetrated by the proclivities of the individual mind as it founders and then runs aground on the crags of the will principle. In this way, Schopenhauer has isolated and subjectivised time, unmooring it from its objectivity, and he is then able to extrude such an ontological proposition into the realm of political philosophy with the contention that historical development is merely the ephemeral, illusory husk which underpins the true and eternal human nature as evinced by the will manifested individual. Schopenhauer writes:

> Therefore, the history of the human race, the throng of events, successive epochs, the many different forms of human life in different lands and centuries, all this is only fortuitously

the form in which the Idea is manifest, belongs not to the Idea itself, in which alone lies the adequate objectivity of the will, but belongs only to the phenomenon which falls within the range of an individual's knowing, and is just as foreign, inessential, and indifferent to the Idea itself as the shapes which they assume are to the clouds, the form of its eddies and foam-flakes to the brook, or its trees and flowers to the ice.[106]

This, then, concludes our examination of Schopenhauer's fundamental ontology. It should be apparent by this point that the *raison d'etre* of Schopenhauer's philosophy lies in the endeavour to neutralise the historical method and its social-evolutionary and revolutionary implications. The means by which this is to be accomplished require and demand a sustained attack on the Hegelian dialectic on two fronts. Firstly, the subject-object dialectic is annulled and converted into an abstract identity which is carried by the mystical-aesthetic encounter with the Idea or Platonic Form of an object, thereby neutering the possibility for historical activity and historical change by removing its basis in human labour as the mediating term in the subject-object interrelation. Secondly, the dialectic which opens up between time and matter is dissolved and these things are held apart in an insuperable opposition which renders matter timeless and impervious to genuine change – while in the same moment, divorced from matter, time is realised as a subjectivist facet of the individual ego, decoupled from historical movement, thereby removing the possibility of genuine, qualitative historical change (historical time).

Across these foundations is cast the long shadow of the will principle, a Kantian thing-in-itself which Schopenhauer provides with a vitalist slant, and which smuggles into the world perhaps the most pronounced form of nihilism ever known to philosophy. The isolated, abstract individual locked into the unremitting, meaningless but all-pervasive struggle to prolong a lonely existence set against a backdrop of an infinite, indifferent universe; such a struggle is conducted, not just at the conscious level, but is one which infuses the very fabric of being and resonates its every particle. There is, ultimately, only one respite, only one form of cosmic relief which the individual might enjoy, and that comes from the contemplative encounter with the pure form which dissolves within itself the semblance of individuality, and thus annuls the very thing which carries the will. Here we see how Schopenhauer's philosophy is guided with a certain tragic honesty; in turning away from the notion of the individual as a socio-historical being, in removing him from the chain of historical development, Schopenhauer conscientiously reaches the conclusion that without history, man is nothing. For it is nothingness which Schopenhauer's philosophy inevitably and ultimately propels him toward, and in the concluding sentence of his *magnum opus* this is made abundantly clear with desolate, echoing finality: "[T]o those in whom the will has turned about and has denied itself, this world of ours, as real as it is, with all its suns and galaxies, is – nothing."[107]

In the final analysis then, Schopenhauer's philosophy is a form of Kantianism, but one which is far less sophisticated and methodologically consistent than its progenitor, and thus the insoluble contradictions of Kantianism are reproduced in Schopenhauer only in a more exacerbated and exaggerated fashion. The problem of the thing-in-itself is handled by Schopenhauer in a rather naive way; he simply asserts his brand of vitalism and, later, superimposes the Platonic forms, in order to mediate the (noumenal) will with the world. The vitalism is ascertained by recourse to an emotive encounter with one's own interiority and from this Schopenhauer purports to deduce the will principle. The contradiction lies in the fact that the mystical derivation of will as the Absolute, on one level at least, is achieved in rational terms. Schopenhauer outlines rationally the relationship the will has to objects in the world.[108] Like Kant, Schopenhauer is compelled to articulate the will principle to the world in terms of a form-content relation. The will is the content. The form is the world of finite phenomena. In describing noumena as the content, and phenomena as the form, Kant himself was subsuming the noumenal under a rational relation[109] – i.e. a relation which was a product of the finite understanding – thus contravening one of the central tenets of his own philosophy – that is, the limits of pure reason. In placing the will and the world in a relation of form to content – Schopenhauer also contravenes his own description of the will as a thing-in-itself.

But Schopenhauer goes much further than Kant in this respect. Not only does he apply the form-content relation to the will, but he also applies the category of quantity, totality, plurality etc. Schopenhauer argues that the forms (Ideas) of objects are identical with the will on an ontological level for they are infinite and timeless but they are also multiple, persist as a totality, act as a template for finite objects – all of which is to say Schopenhauer subsumes them under rational categories, subjects them to rational description and interrelation. But perhaps the most pronounced contradiction of all comes from the fact that, in order to escape the grip of the will principle – i.e. the principle of infinity – the individual must aspire to lose himself in the infinite principle of the Idea. The Idea and the will are identical as the infinite substance. Timeless, unchanging, they provide the infinite kernel which is lodged at the heart of being. And yet, Schopenhauer has succeeded in locking them into an irreconcilable dualism – a dualism which throws into relief their contradictory qualities and aspirations. The will is one and yet the Ideas are many, the will is the infinite principle which drives being, the Ideas provide the infinite principle by which one might escape the drive of being and seek refuge in nothingness.[110] A dualism opens up in the infinite substance itself – between the will and the Idea/s. Schopenhauer – to put it as Hegel might – makes each moment dependent on the other; that is to say they are manifested as two terms in a pairing – in which each delimits the other. The will, therefore, is no longer infinite because it is limited by the infinite character of the Idea which opposes it. The Idea is no longer infinite for it is drawn into contradiction with the will which it has the potential to negate.

These deep, abiding contradictions which fissure across the very fundaments of his philosophical edifice quite naturally generate all sorts of smaller inconsistencies at the higher levels: Schopenhauer's account of nature is a case in point. Schopenhauer's naturalism is particularly problematic: every organic and individual life takes on the form most appropriate to prolong its own being in accordance to the demands of the will – bodies are merely will objectified "individuals". Every individual emerges as a fully furnished product of the will – and the species is the collective expression of the fully formed, will manifested individual. As Schopenhauer writes, "the shape and organisation of each animal species has been determined by its own will according to the circumstances in which it wished to live; not however as a thing physical in Time, but on the contrary as a thing metaphysical outside Time."[111] New species can arise to threaten older ones, of course. But these too arrive on the scene fully furnished with the capabilities granted to them by the will in order to prolong their being. This, of course (and in line with the logic of Schopenhauer's ontology more generally), works to destroy any notion of dialectical reciprocity between species – the anteater does not develop a long nose in response to changes in the environment and other species, changes which create possibilities of physical development more conducive to hunting. Nor do the ants change their physical modalities in a response to the development and refinement of their predator's abilities to hunt. In other words, Schopenhauer's ontology leads to a rather crude naturalism which quite inevitably aims at the refutation of the theory of evolution. Schopenhauer was probably not aware of Darwin's work – he died the year after *On the Origin of Species* was published. Yet he did reveal his thoughts on the matter in his criticism of the theory of Darwin's forerunner Lamarck. Schopenhauer writes of Lamarck:

> he quite seriously maintains and tries to prove at length, that the shape of each animal species, the weapons peculiar to it, and its organs of every sort destined for outward use, were by no means present at the origin of that species, but have on the contrary come into being gradually in the course of time... he overlooks the obvious objection which may be made, that long before the organs necessary for its preservation could have been produced by means of such endeavours as these through countless generations, the whole species must have died out from the want of them.[112]

And yet, these rather glaring flaws should not be made into the arbiters of Schopenhauer's philosophy in its entirety. Despite the fact that Schopenhauer's ontology is regressive, represents a retrograde Kantianism with a pronounced aristocratic inflection, and reaches conclusions which easily collapse in the face of dialectical reasoning and modern science – nevertheless, there remains something within it which retains the aura of truth and a deeply poetic power. Its writing affects a melancholy beauty which perhaps reflects something of the gloomy and uncompromising life of the writer. Schopenhauer was hugely privileged – and unlike thinkers like Hegel who were paid a professor's wage – after his short stint as a lecturer, Schopenhauer would never return to a waged existence. As Lukacs points out, such "material freedom from all daily cares provided the basis of Schopenhauer's independence not only from semi-feudal, state-determined conditions of existence...but also from the intellectual movements connected with them".[113] That Schopenhauer's philosophy worked so hard to decouple the individual from its basis in categories of socio-historical existence surely can be seen as in some part to do with the fact that Schopenhauer himself had been elevated above the immediacies of the struggle for economic sustenance vis-a-vis a waged working life – and had, therefore, been abstracted from the kind of tensions and aspirations which brought one into line with others in the same situation (and which held the possibilities, at least, of being part of more unified social and ideological struggles). But to be raised up in such a way, to be inured against the social potencies which were slumbering in the offices and the universities, the factories and the farms, was only ever freedom in the abstract, an empty freedom. If anything it rendered the individual more susceptible to the great historical upheavals of the period, the French Revolution, the Napoleonic wars which decimated Europe, the rallying cries of restoration which echoed through the halls of the Vienna Congress in the aftermath, the endless ebb and flow of revolution and reaction; for someone whose life was moneyed but transient, privileged yet at the same time rootless – for someone whose existence was unfortified by any contact with a broader social movement – the vast transformations which were sweeping across an ever darkening skyline could only have been experienced in their full, blinding force, in terms of an elemental and all-pervasive nihilism. The spectre of the will, a dark, swirling funnel passing across the panorama, and the lonely individual existence, abstracted and set adrift, blowing in the wind.

To this one must add the melancholic details of Schopenhauer's own life, the suicide of his father, the breach with his mother, the intense aversion Schopenhauer had for the niceties and social graces one had to master in order to function easily in the company of strangers. The stubborn, gloomy slant of his disposition alongside the lonely nature of his own social being;

all of this set the stage for an encounter with modernity which was both profoundly reactionary and poetically fecund. He was able to produce the eternalisation of capitalist fragmentation in and through the will principle, and thus he was able to varnish the prospect of capitalist existence with an infinite cosmological sheen. At the same time, such existence was something which impressed upon him its tragic futility and imbued him with both melancholy and dread. In exaggerating the blind forces of capitalist modernity, in emphasising the moment of abstract negativity, in absolving it of its historical context, in raising individual anomie to the echelons of eternity, Schopenhauer created the type of philosophy which was truly symptomatic of historical decay, and would most tragically resonate in times of global reaction and unfettered imperialism; a lugubrious, spectral poetry which was most alive when the forms of the future were veiled by the dark night of the capitalist epoch and it felt as though the new day might never come. In the words of Lukacs, "Schopenhauer's system, well laid out and architecturally ingenious in form, rises up like a modern hotel on the brink of the abyss, nothingness and futility."[114]

Chapter Six

Donald Trump: The Pantomime President

Donald J Trump's tale is a tale of epochs and generations, about dilapidated tenement housing and star-spangled casino palaces, about race hate and glossy Forbes spreads, about bankruptcy on route to the presidential suite. Above all, it is about the dirty trails which money leaves in its wake, the grime which lives behind wealth's golden, glittering facade. It is a story which begins at the end of the nineteenth century. Trump's grandfather, Fredrick Trump, was made of hard, flinty Protestant stuff, a taciturn, grey austere man who had made it over on a steamship bound for the US in order to invest his life savings, making a fortune as a restaurateur and businessman at the height of the gold rush. His son, Fred Christ Trump, was fated to live in less salubrious times. Trump Senior came to his own business ventures on the cusp of the Wall Street Crash, but while the times were changing, Trump Senior inherited his father's ruthless determination and his ability to turn a buck. Fred Trump was able to channel the windfall from his father's network of restaurants, brothels and bars into the grey, piling storeys – the squat rooms, the leaky ceilings – of the crumbling dilapidated tenement housing whose gloominess seemed to speak of the depression era *par excellence*. Fred Trump, like many an astute businessman before him, was an effective barometer for human desperation, and in the thirties – the very epoch of the dust bowl and the hobo, and desperation and drought – it was here when Fred Trump made his bones. A savvy skin-flint, he was notorious for pinching the pennies; rather than shell out for an exterminator to take care of the lice-filled rooms he rented, he would endeavour to do the job himself. He was known for keeping his books and cash on his person, and even as a millionaire many times over, he would keep just the one small office with a single secretary.[115] He had the immigrant outsider's sense of self-sufficiency, the businessman's need to keep things on the down and low, and the landlord's sense of self-superiority and borderline revulsion toward those he rents to, those to be squeezed and extorted.

Almost inevitably, such aversion chimed with a racist set of politics. Trump Senior flagrantly discriminated against blacks, trying to up the white count among his tenants, trying to cultivate the image of a more "respectable", "well-to-do" element, no doubts so his properties could attach to themselves higher prices. He was exposed for his racist practices, not only by the Civil Rights Division of the US Department of Justice which would eventually file a suit against him, but also by that astute and poetic chronicler of the times Woodie Guthrie, who had the misfortune of having Trump Senior as a landlord. Guthrie would croon about his odious landlord with both ire and melancholy when he sang "I suppose Old Man Trump knows/Just how much/ Racial hate/ he stirred up/in the bloodpot of human hearts."[116] It seems, however, as if Trump Senior's racism was about more than just economics; he experienced his race hate in the purest form and from the heart – so to speak. In 1927, for example, he was arrested during a Klu-Klux-Klan rally in Queens. It would be difficult to add to this melting pot of toe-curling characteristics – a veritable embarrassment of riches for any one individual – and yet, one has to include a cynical aptitude to play the broader political climate. While Trump Senior was clearly an inveterate racist, a dyed-in-the-wool right winger and a hoarder of cash on a Scrooge-like scale, he was as well a schemer of Machiavellian means, someone adept at greasing the political wheel in order to glean any type of economic advantage. Despite his hard-right affiliations, he was able to court the Democratic Party of the time, watering its bureaucratic machine with his own ill-gotten gains, and this was no doubt helpful in providing him with a steady stream of favourable loans from the Federal Housing

Administration (FHA), delivering a windfall of millions. Trump Senior would give an overinflated estimation for construction costs for properties, absorb the loan which was to cover them, and then squirrel away the surplus amount on which he would pay no taxes, using it as capital to stimulate other investments, other ventures. In the words of the investigation which exposed such shoddy practice, the tenants who would then move into such abodes, were saddled "with the burden of meeting not only legitimate costs"[117] but also the costs of the money the developer had removed from the circuit of investment for these particular properties.

While it is clear that "Old Man Trump" was blessed with something akin to intelligence, it was the type of intelligence which had been narrowed down into the most base deviousness, and which saw those outside his immediate circle merely as cogs in a broader machine to be manipulated, finessed or pressured into better yielding the cash product. There was no higher end in human endeavour than the extraction of profit – a petty, perpetual, monotonous and grinding process to which "Old Man Trump" was devoted with every fibre of his being. Gnarly, wizened, devious and cynical, he would walk the shadowlands between legality and illegality, the slow trudge-trudge of the slum landlord up a darkened staircase, approaching the door of the destitute and the desperate, indifferent to the fumes of misery he leaves trailing in his wake. Perhaps, therefore, it was almost inevitable that Old Man Trump's money making activity would neatly elide into the echelons of the criminal underworld, and when his racket involving FHA loans was brought into the light of day, Fred Trump began to rely on his Brooklyn connections more heavily including Joe DePaolo – President of Dic Underhill Co, a company with alleged mob connections[118] – and business partner and financier William "Willie" Tomasello[119] who was, according to the Federal Organised Crime Task Force, associated with the Gambino family.

If Old Man Trump was grey, flinty and largely devoid of ostentation, his wife, Mary Anne MacLeod, was an altogether different prospect. Donald J Trump's mother was from lower middle-class stock, she was born in a small township on a Scottish island. Her father ran a post office and small shop in his later years; however, with the event of the First World War the economy of their extended village had suffered, and Mary chose to emigrate to the United States in order to cleave out new opportunities. The decision, born of aspiration and bravery, implied both loneliness and a meagre economic existence, for at first she made her way working as a domestic servant in the houses of the well-to-do, but soon she would encounter her salvation, meeting the already prosperous Fred Trump and her marriage to him elevated her forever above the poverty bracket she had so long dreamed of escaping. Such escapism was an integral facet of her personality, the young maid and nanny, enamoured by the glint and glitz of the diamond chandeliers which illuminated the plush, salubrious houses she worked her fingers to the bone cleaning – and even as a lady of considerable means she never relinquished that early, illicit fascination with the workings of an upper-class elite which perhaps she never fully felt a part of. In the words of her son, she was hypnotised by the antics of the royal family back in the United Kingdom, she would watch their various weddings and processions with wide-eyed wonder, for she was "enthralled by the pomp and circumstance, the whole idea of royalty and glamour".[120] With her husband's financial resources she was able to decisively refashion herself in the style of the wealthy American matriarch, dramatised by the Jacquie Kennedy bouffant, the flashing fingers bejewelled with silver and the sleek flowing mink draped from one shoulder. All this affectation, all the gaudy glamour and crass ostentation was perhaps, on Mary Anne MacLeod's part, something akin to a magical charm, intended to ward off the memory of the poverty she had once known, the humiliation she had bridled against as a Scottish Cinderella reduced to the level of cleaning other people's houses, washing other people's children. When the British television journalist Selina Scott was greeted by the presence of Mrs Trump for an interview which took place in the nineties, Scott was confronted by a perfectly manicured, perfectly attired, perfectly coiffured creation in which "all trace of the humble Scottish lass [had been] airbrushed away."[121]

The family home too represented a kind of stubborn stand by wealth against the encroaching poverty which lurked forever just beyond the borders, of geography, of memory, of existence. The family home was a mansion with 23 rooms, 9 bathrooms, supported by 6 ivory coloured columns which flowed upward into a gable that overhung a generous front porch and was stamped with a confected crest. The Trump family crest – the mark of the *parvenu* who seeks to paper over humdrum origins with the rococo symbols of a hastily contrived, aristocratic refinery. But while the Trumps were ensconced in this ghastly monument to their own awful taste, the outer world had grown ever more turbulent, just beyond their borders economic upheaval was wracking New York, shaking the city to its foundations. In the 2 decades following the Second World War, New York had lost almost half its jobs in manufacturing. The post-war migrations of blacks and Hispanics flowing into the city found themselves increasingly locked out of the dwindling construction jobs and the unions – and though they helped provide the basis for a real estate boom with their ever-spiralling rents those newly arrived immigrants reaped none of its rewards. For them the American Dream was evaporated and what remained in its wake was the suppurating divide between wealth and poverty. The borough of Queens itself was increasingly defined by tribalism and ghettoisation; whole neighbourhoods sprang up between which invisible but impermeable dividing lines were drawn. More and more whites fled to the outer suburbs, while minorities tended to stick to their own. Fred Trump's wealth was a parasitical symptom of all of this, of segregation, the real estate boom, the shoddy tenement flats – the seismic tremors which were passing across the economic and cultural landscape of the period, and yet the Trump family home in Jamaica Estates also provided a bastion against these things, a last-ditch outcrop of wealth and whiteness which, dripping with aristocratic ersatz, provided a nod to some fantasised past, a pristine totem set against the forces of change. Trump's spiel about Mexican immigrants and the need to build walls is more than just cynically contrived demagoguery; it is part and parcel of the sensibilities he imbibed in the cultural *milieu* of his very earliest beginnings, a Queens which was simmering with the fear and anxiety that came from a sense of being overwhelmed by the "outsider" and the "undesirable", a far cry from the bawdy, colourful, raffish melting pot which characterises the area today.

The economic ruthlessness of his father, the unadorned desire for accumulation, the sense of superiority sported by the *nouveau riche* and overlaid with racist contempt – jostled for position in the young Donald Trump alongside the tasteless ostentation which came from his mother, her fixation with the gaudy, glittering trinkets which could be conscripted in the grossest displays of wealth. To this heady brew was added a strong sense of religious conformity – and every Sunday the Trump family would drive into Manhattan to worship at the Marble Collegiate church. The institution was overseen by the type of pastor which America seems to do so well. A religious entrepreneur, a holy roller who was at the same time a silver-tongued salesman, a breathless extoller of the heavenly prophets as a way to secure the more earthly variant to be measured in dollars and cents. Pastor Norman Vincent Peale – dubbed "God's salesman" – was the author of the bestselling text *The Power of Positive Thinking* which offered up the type of quackery to combine false evidence, rampant individualism and vulgar pseudo-science, all delivered in a lofty religious tone which fell somewhere between that of preacher of the prairies and wandering snake oil salesman.

Gems from this utterly, utterly awful exercise in platitude include: "Anybody can do just about anything with himself that he really wants to and makes up his mind to do. We are capable of greater things than we realize."[122] The influence of the pastor on the young Trump was profound, he was, in Trump's own words, "the greatest guy".[123] He taught Donald to confuse indelibly and forever truth with platitude, leadership with manipulation, charisma with the glib soundbite; above all, the presentation, the slick delivery, the superficial and flashy appearance was allowed to depose any deeper reality; the appearance itself was rendered sacrosanct.

Throughout his business, celebrity and political career Trump would promote the appearance above all else. An image of himself which was at the same time a fantastically contrived piece of PR placement and served to gloss over the more mundane and tawdry realities of a set of business practices which were rooted in privilege, power, illicit connection and rife corruption. Like many of history's greatest fantasists, Trump seems to have the unnerving ability to believe his own fabulations, to believe in the fantastical tales he himself spun and which speak to the heroic and extraordinary feats which underlie his climb to economic and political power. His narcissistic tendency to imbibe his own hype is what perhaps gives him such unusually thin skin; when some of his taller tales are mocked, he reacts with a petulant fury which seems almost insensible. There is, to be sure, a good deal to be mocked; the appearance he has so meticulously cultivated is always in danger of being perforated by reality itself. Trump, never backward about coming forward, does not just consider himself a businessman extraordinaire who has perfected the "art of the deal", but also a top-flight intellectual of a quite remarkable calibre: "Let me tell you, I'm a really smart guy. I was a really good student at the best school in the country."[124] In 2011 he questioned the academic credentials of the then president Barack Obama, suggesting that he was a "terrible student"[125] and hinting that Obama had managed to get into Colombia University and Harvard Law School by some nefarious means which were indifferent to merit. A true pot and kettle situation then, for Trump himself, it eventually transpired in a book by Gwenda Blair on the subject, had gained admission to Wharton School on the back of "an interview with a friendly Wharton admissions officer who was one of Freddy's old high school classmates".[126] The Freddy in question was Donald's older brother. And though it seems that Donald Trump's actual school record was undistinguished, nevertheless for years papers like *The New York Times* reported that Trump had graduated "first in his class in 1968".[127] In actual fact Trump failed to graduate with honours that year, however the rumours persisted for decades following. Was Trump the one to circulate them? Most likely – in any event he certainly didn't go out of his way to correct them. In his autobiography Trump outlines in explicit terms the fantasist's mantra: "I play to people's fantasies. People may not always think big themselves, but they can still get very excited by those who do. That's why a little hyperbole never hurts. People want to believe that something is the biggest and the greatest and the most spectacular. I call it truthful hyperbole."[128]

When we come to Trump's burgeoning business career, it is then that the "truthful hyperbole" becomes particularly intense. Over the years Trump has made significant hay recycling an image of himself as one who has a strong affinity with blue-collar America, the rugged working man who clings doggedly to the dream even in the most difficult of circumstances. In 1990, in an interview for *Playboy* magazine, Trump opined that "the working man likes me because he knows I worked hard and didn't inherit what I've built. Hey, I made it myself; I have a right to do what I want with it."[129]

Elsewhere Trump makes reference to the humble, meagre origins of his business beginnings when he recalls with gritty nostalgia just how, in 1975, his father had granted him "a very small loan" and from this, plus the sweat of his brow – "I built…a company that's worth many, many billions of dollars."[130] One can't help but note how, by this point, "hyperbole" has long since said goodbye to "truth" and sent the latter for a long vacation, as the "small" loan Trump references happens to have been for the rather portly sum of 14 million dollars. Nevertheless Trump has continued to cultivate a very different kind of image. The image of himself as a goodly grafter; a cheeky underdog, operating on a wing and a prayer – able to fashion financial success from the most meagre basic investment; the miracle of economic fire managed by the striking of flint against flint, enterprise constructed painstakingly from the bottom up. But perhaps the more apt metaphor would be that of the silver spoon; advantage fed in rich, parcelised gobbets of privilege and power to the greedy and ever open mouth of the preening second son, always ready to splash the family fortune on his next glitzy endeavour. Far from expressing any sense of originality, inspiration or imagination on his part, the basis of Donald Trump's wealth was fully rooted in privilege – the banal, prosaic hand-me-down of vast amounts from father to son in the manner of a feudal lord who wishes to fortify his scion's legacy as a way of securing the family claim. Trump's unoriginality, however, was not restricted to his cash "birth right", for he also absorbed his father's business practices and ideals almost wholesale without taking the time to formulate his own. In Trump's own words his first major deal was struck over a site located in Cincinnati – a site he had hit upon as a lucrative investment opportunity when at "college, while my friends were reading the comics and the sports pages of newspapers, I was reading the listings of FHA foreclosures… And that's how I found out about Swifton Village."[131] Again the superficial spin belies the more prosaic reality – the Swifton Village property had been acquired by his father some time before, and Trump simply took over its management, but during his time there the same familial practices of discrimination were in effect. Black residents were denied access, poorer tenants were forced out in a bid to cultivate a "better element"[132] on the road to gentrification. Donald Trump inherited not only his father's fondness for ruthless discrimination but also his tendency to cultivate contacts in the underworld; shady, subterranean figures who could be used to circumvent state bureaucracy, be relied on to exert influence behind the scenes.

According to the Pulitzer Prize winning journalist David Cay Johnston, in the construction of Trump Towers during the early 1980s, Trump was paying overinflated prices for "ready mix" concrete which was not only more expensive but also a "riskier method"[133] than the "steel girder" form of construction which was typically used in skyscrapers of the period. What did Trump have to gain? Well, argues Johnston, the "ready mix" concrete providers were almost down to a man mob outfits – and by securing deals with some of their bosses like Anthony "Fat Tony" Salerno, boss of the Genovese crime family, or Paul "Big Paulie" Castellano, boss of the Gambino crime family – Trump was as well able to procure the kind of muscle which would see the job pushed through with quick, brutal efficiency and apply the type of pressure which could secure "union peace" and a pliable and cheap workforce.[134] So, for instance, when Trump hired as many as 200 non-unionised workers to work on a demolition job in 1979 (Bonwit Teller department store) in an incident which epitomises his attitude toward both immigrants and blue-collar workers, the 200 men – the majority of whom were illegal Polish immigrants – were paid $4 to $6 per hour with no benefits. Some of them were using sledge hammers rather than power tools, were working over 12 hours a day – 7 days a week, and were sometimes lacking in elementary safety equipment like hard hats.[135] When Salerno was convicted in 1988 – the indictment against him listed the $8 million contract for concrete to be used on one "Trump Plaza" on the East Side as a part of the mafioso's racketeering enterprise.[136] In the early eighties Trump was sued by a woman with mob connections who accused the mogul of taking kickbacks from contractors in court papers and pushed for the Attorney General to mount an investigation. Trump at once settled, paying the woman a cool $500 000.

In the briefest glance at Trump's incredibly sketchy resume the mob connections pile up. From Felix Sater, a convicted money launderer for the Russian Mafia, who helped invest in the Trump Soho Hotel, to Joseph "Joey No Socks" Cinque, someone who had been convicted on felony charges pertaining to stolen art, and was a former associate of the crime Kingpin John Gotti. From Salvatore "Salvie" Testa, a "crown prince" of the Philadelphia Mob, who sold Trump the land Trump Plaza was to be situated on – to the crime boss Nicodemos "Nicky" Scarfo whose construction companies would be deployed in the building of it. The force which helped mediate Trump with the mob was the dirty lawyer Roy Cohn, a soiled hand-me-down from the era of McCarthyism resonating avarice and corruption. Cohn had come to prominence rooting out suspected communists for the sinister, witch-finding senator, and in order to make the prosecutions more palpable Cohn would claim that some of the defendants were closeted homosexuals and spies. Rampant homophobia thrived in the hothouse of paranoia he so effortlessly helped erect, thereby creating the context for the then president Dwight Eisenhower to sign a federal order barring homosexuals from positions in the federal government. What Cohn had failed to mention in an unsavoury crusade saturated with homophobic hatred – was that he himself was a closeted gay man. When Donald met Roy, way back when in 1973 at an exclusive New York nightclub, the then 27-year-old Trump was much enamoured by the slick, sharp talking lawyer who was mobbed up and demonstrated the kind of vicious, acquisitive aggression which Trump *fils* had been taught to prize his whole life long: "You made it in my father's business — rent-controlled and rent-stabilized buildings — by being very tough and very relentless."[137]

Cohn at once began tutoring the younger man in the arts of power politiquing and aggressive legal manoeuvre. Trump outlined the latest legal dilemma he and his father were facing in the deferential tones of one seeking advice; "tell them to go to hell," the older man cackled back with a mobster's hacking drawl! Indeed Cohn would be conscripted in fighting that particular suit – for racial discrimination – on the Trumps' behalf, and at once filed a $100 million dollar countersuit. The countersuit had no merit, was ridiculously inflated, and was dismissed by the judge almost instantaneously, but that was beside the point; what it actually achieved was to make the papers, to give the Trumps a media platform by which they could blast out their outrage about the perfectly true allegations made against them. And in this sense, Donald and Roy attained a certain spiritual affinity. Like Trump, Cohn was obsessed with cultivating the outward appearance, the presentation. As a true homophobe he felt in his bones that to be gay was indicative of a blemishing, "effeminate" weakness and so he countered his own homosexuality by developing a weasel-like ruthlessness, by transfixing any enemy with the ominous power of his underworld contacts or the prospect of the high profile politicians into whose ears he whispered.

At the core of Trump's being too, there nestled a fundamental inadequacy – the palliative to which would always be the gaudy posturing of an oversized bully. Trump had learnt the bullying part, stock and trade, from his father – but it seemed as though he had never been able to step out of Trump Senior's shadow. The constant spiel about in some way being a self-made man, the running off at the mouth about his affinities with the blue-collar worker – all this speaks to the unease which comes from being handed everything; instead of the "effeminacy" of homosexuality, Donald Trump's was the "effeminacy" of privilege. That was something Trump's father never really had – granted Fred Trump too had inherited money, and in no small measure, but his own father had died when he was just a 13-year-old child. Coming of age in the depression era, Fred Trump had had to be self-sufficient in a way in which Donald never needed be, and for this reason – though both men were driven fundamentally by greed – they nevertheless represent two very different archetypes of wealth. Whereas Fred Trump was most comfortable doing business in the shadows, making contacts on the sly, surreptitiously greasing the wheels from behind the scenes – Trump *fils* had come to fruition in the era of Reaganomics and neoliberalism, an epoch of casino capitalism and rampant speculation, the moment in which industrial capital was eclipsed by financial capital, when form eclipsed content, and the realities of deregulation and deindustrialisation were papered over by the flashy facade; the yuppie playboy screeching around the city in his spiv's suit and top-end Lamborghini, roaring with testosterone and ambition. Whereas Trump Senior, in his own miserly, miserable way, had been concerned with providing homes in poor areas, Donald Trump looked to expand the scope of the family business, moving from tenement housing to vast investments in luxury projects like golf courses and casinos. The casino was, in many ways, a temple to the type of wealth which Junior now held sacred, a wealth which promoted both the glitzy appearance and the reckless financial gamble all wrapped up in the whirl of the roulette wheel or the flashing, bleeping windows of the slot machine. The mob officials and enforcers were the guardians of this world, its high priests, and through tainted lawyer Roy Cohn, Donald Trump was granted unadulterated access. Whereas Trump Senior had fostered his own mob connections, looking at the men from that world wryly, seeing them as a useful means to certain ends, Trump Junior was enamoured by them – their ostentation, their gaudy displays of wealth, the simmering promise of sudden violence they held.

For him these people were objects of aspiration and glamour. Trump got to know the movers and shakers of that world and it was Cohn who helped pave the way. Trump's meetings with figures like Salerno who would build Trump's first casino in Atlantic City were facilitated by Cohn and held in the lawyer's townhouse. Trump went into the casino and the hotel business with the brassy confidence of a master of the universe, a financial savant whose charisma and flamboyance were to be fated in a glittering, profligate world of wealth whose dynamism and ruthless individualism offered soaring, stratospheric rewards. Everything was his for the taking.

Trump visited the banks, overdosed on credit time and time again, splashing the money about in a golden shower of expenditure which fell on casinos, hotels and yachts, cocking his leg over New York City, marking his moment as the man of the hour, grinning out from the pages of a thousand glossy spreads which all bespoke of his sophistication, glamour and savvy. And such affectation set into such gaudy overdrive – behind it lurked something more elemental and unformed, an oedipal impulse, the need to supplant his father's success so utterly and fully that for the first time Donald could feel himself to be a man in his own right.

Unfortunately, that's not quite how it all worked out. With all his wild excess, Trump Junior had run up $3 billion dollars in debt. His Trump shuttle airline company arced in mid-air before plummeting to the ground and exploding in flames. When Trump Hotels went public he "over-leveraged [them]... with such expensive debt, that they could never make enough money to repay bondholders...It was a great way for Trump to escape debt burdens, but it created a huge burden for his shareholders."[138] Trump lost the Plaza Hotel – a hotel which itself had lost $74 million during its first year under Trump's stewardship.[139] Trump had to declare bankruptcy several times over. He was forced to sell his prized yacht – the Trump Princess.

And perhaps most significantly of all – the jewel in Trump's crown – the Taj Mahal Casino – went into economic freefall just a year after it had opened in 1990, haemorrhaging money. What is particularly interesting is that, in order to buoy it up, Trump was forced to hand half his equity to creditors, and at the same time, Fred Trump was summoned, to prop up his helplessly flapping man-child – at once swooping in to buy millions in casino chips which could act as a loan to his son in order to help avoid default.[140] The notion of Trump as a shrewd businessman with the Midas touch, then, was always part and parcel of a massive PR campaign that Trump himself helped generate, and which offset the reality of implosion, bankruptcy and bailout; which obscured the fact that Junior's reckless gambles, flagrant exploitation and illicit working practices were shored up by a safety net of wealth and the figure of his father in the background, keeping one watchful eye on his garish progeny. It was through lawyerly weasel Roy Cohn that Trump was able to better work the press and cultivate a media image which would help mask his litany of failed ventures, for Cohn, according to one of Donald Trump's long-time political advisors, "was a master at understanding the news cycle...Roy would literally call up and dictate pieces for Page Six because [New York Post owner] Rupert [Murdoch] was a client."[141] After Cohn's death in 1986, Trump would not forgo such close connection with the media. In the decades to follow not only was Trump profusely litigious – suing ex-wives who released information in the public domain through books or newspaper articles, taking action against authors like Timothy L. O'Brien or Jacob M. Appel whose depiction of him he had taken offence to – but Trump also maintained Cohn's close connections to various media outlets so that his celebrity image would be enhanced in and through the drip-drip of various hagiographic articles which gushed about his sexual prestige or his supposed charisma, while less sensational pieces worked as little more than adverts by which he could hawk the Trump name to wealth investors. As Sydney Blumenthal notes, these two streams of propaganda increasingly converged; "the headlines fed to the *New York Post* consisting of make-believe quotes from his then mistress Marla Maples ("Best Sex I've Ever Had") became a PR platform for the licensing of his celebrated name to murky investors from Russia, China and Saudi Arabia who were looking for an American frontman."[142]

And yet, not all the media followed suit. The image of Trump as a financial *Ubermensch* who had triumphed as a result of his own ingenuity and magnetism simply stuck in the craw of some of the more satirical and critical outfits. *Spy* magazine, for example, recognised – in a spirit of lacerating irony – that Trump's glaring, overblown loudness was the inevitable product of someone whose every need had been coddled by untapped wealth and whose entitlement was apt to crack into the petulant fury of a spoilt toddler the moment his toys were taken away. "Wa-a-a-a-h! – Little Donald, Unhappy At Last – Trump's Final Days,"[143] shrieked one satirical leader, depicting "the short-fingered vulgarian" in the manner of an errant child, fists clenched, eyes streaming with hot petulant tears, having just lost control of his latest casino venture. That such spreads were few and far between probably speaks to the manner in which the lawsuit happy Donald had managed to do a number on the press, and yet *Spy's* lead headline, dripping with contempt, was redolent of a larger sensibility. The town which was closest to Trump's heart, the place where he'd built his beloved Trump Towers – the phallic manifestation of all his aspiration and vulgarity – was the place where Trump was most keen to be seen in the glamorous, splendid glow of success. And yet, the citizens of Manhattan had always been in possession of a certain kind of humour; urban, stoical, dry – with an acute detection system for the presence of bullshit. In Trump's fanciful presentation, pompousness and self-aggrandising – in the slick spiel of the used car salesman, alongside the thin skin and vengeful nature of a spiteful society belle – in all of these things New Yorkers sensed the overwhelming wreak of ordure. While Trump attempted to project a sense of self which was cool, masterful and charismatic – the denizens of New York deflated his fantasy with remorseless barbs of mockery and derision; from the debut issue of *Spy* in 1986 which featured Trump as one of the "Ten Most Embarrassing New Yorkers" to the late-night comedy sketch show *Saturday Night Life* which caricatures Trump as a presidential windbag with a repertoire of pouty patriotism and nonsensical sloganeering. Both unhinged and ridiculous, the Trump of New York folklore appears as an anomaly of vitriol and privilege, utterly abstracted from the lives of regular people. Perhaps that is what wounds and infuriates Trump most of all, in the city where he should be king, he is at best its most infamous court jester; and despite all the cash he has poured into PR and media spin, despite all his connections, nevertheless it seems that money really can't buy love (a terrifying thought indeed for a man like Trump who for years owned the "Miss Universe Organization" and has had a long track record of propositioning its contestants).[144] New Yorkers, however, have remained steadfastly contemptuous of his creepy advances and in 2016 during his presidential campaign he lost 87 per cent of the vote in Manhattan, in Queens he only garnered 22 per cent of the vote, in Brooklyn he won less than 20 per cent, while in the Bronx it was only around 10 per cent.[145]The more that Trump, in his belligerent, rancorous and semi-conscious way, sensed the hostility and ridicule of the city which never sleeps, the more he sought to lose himself in the dreams and fantasies of his own grandeur. The apotheosis of this process arrived when he made the move from colourful man-about-town to full on television celebrity in his own right, with the launching of *The Apprentice* franchise. *The Apprentice* was the latest in a strain of reality TV shows which, in their very essence, harnessed the worst of twenty-first-century capitalism. Instead of hiring costly actors, such programmes had hit upon the formula of exploiting real people as a means to extract drama. More often than not, they presented themselves as being socially progressive; so, for example, the ostensible premise was about the search for talent, but what increasingly became clear in shows like *The X Factor* or *Pop Idol* was that people who were often inadequate, desperate and delusional were being allowed through the early rounds so they could make a televised appearance and be humiliated by the judges for the voyeuristic delight of the audience. There was a performative aspect to such programmes; a thin, spurious moral veneer overlaying a process by which the bewildered and powerless were set against each other in what was often quite brutal and soul-destroying competition, only to have their fates decided by their natural "superiors" – several preening, besuited wealthy judges. It was the kind of pornographic fantasy which emanated from the millionaire mindset; a vindication of crass competition as the natural condition of relationships and progress, the sense that market values, sales, were the ultimate measure of the human good; an absolute prostration on the part of the powerless before the alter of the dollar. It was the ideology of neoliberalism condensed into a theatre of the absurd. Trump harnessed his own version of this paradigm in *The Apprentice* – here the contestants would compete in groups to do various business tasks – the most successful winning a place in the Trump organisation, the others, brutally derided, before being subject to Trump's notorious catchphrase "You're fired!"

The people who were appearing on this programme were aspirant, glib, and nearly always unlikeable, prone to the unqualified belief of the fantasist in the trajectory of his own rising star. But the ultimate fantasist on the programme was surely Trump himself. His turn to *The Apprentice* in 2004 marked the tail end of another string of failures, the series of schemes which he had engaged in and which had fallen flat like duds – Trump Airlines. Trump Steaks. Trump: The Game. Trump Vodka.

Trump Magazine. But the show portrayed the very opposite of this. Trump was able to present himself according to his own fantasy remit; a gimlet-eyed entrepreneur always able to glimpse the innovative and new, a businessman cum intellectual who had transfigured the "deal" into an art form, a serious, frowning figure whose authority was absolute. Donald Trump was always concerned about the appearance above all else. When he had lost control of his property ventures – had declared bankruptcy four times over – his media profile provided him with a much-needed solace. When he endeavoured to expand into other fields with a series of crackpot innovations which tanked one after the next, he was able to console himself with the thought of his name, his brand – himself as a personality, a celebrity – which extended beyond any particular product and its failures. *The Apprentice* marks the apogee of this process – for now the presentation had been wholly abstracted from the substance; there was no longer any material product – no property, no board game – which Trump was seeking to hawk; rather he was purveying only the celebrity image of himself. The appearance had overwhelmed everything else – the form had almost completely divested itself of any content. And in this, Trump's professional trajectory provides a microcosm of the movement of late capitalism more broadly: what was the financial crisis other than the triumph of the appearance over the reality, the form over content – the movement away from any investment in the building of houses to the investment in the financial packages which accrue to houses – the securities which attach themselves to mortgages – until eventually such mortgage debts were being packaged together and sold off in their own right to investors – with the ever illusory promise of staggering returns.

In the 1984 movie *Ghostbusters* the dramatic denouement takes place on the top of an old New York building. The four ghostbusters are faced with a malevolent Sumerian demi-god named Goza the Gozerian. The imp-like deity, eyes crackling with fire, offers our heroes a choice: "Choose and perish! Choose the form of the Destructor!"[146] The ghostbusters keep their minds blank, all accept Ray Stantz because the thought "just popped in there".[147] From the depths of Stantz's psyche, the 100-foot tall Stay Puff Marshmallow Man is conjured into being, striding down the New York streets with a goofy grin, crushing the cars and the terrified citizenry underfoot. And in one way, this is not a bad analogy for Trump's presidency. An electorate faced with an existential choice: Trump conjured up from the darkest recesses of the American conscience collective; a figure in which the racism and protectionism of the 1930s is materialised, alongside the casino capitalism of the 1980s and the unbridled speculation which was fully unleashed in the early twenty-first century – and finally the culture of reality TV and the garish boardroom boss in which the exercise of power wed to humiliation is glibly repackaged as the intelligence and ingenuity of progress. A 100-foot Trump, grinning, gurning – fully unbound – crashing across the streets of the city, and the country, which has for so long rebuffed him. The fact that Trump has been raised in this way, summoned like a spectre to the highest office in the land, speaks above all to the erosion of parliamentary democracy in the epoch of finance capital. The democratic candidate, the so-called "liberal" candidate in the mould of Barack Obama or Hillary Clinton, has had their platform so thoroughly penetrated by Wall Street and big business more broadly, that the spiel they perpetrate about "change" and "hope" increasingly feels like lifeless words cast into the void. And, as everyone knows, from the void there comes monsters.

Chapter Seven

Andrea Dworkin: Radicalism Raised to Art

Alongside Leon Trotsky perhaps, Andrea Dworkin was the most reviled left-wing thinker of the twentieth century. Trotsky, one remembers, was loathed from all angles; by the liberals who saw in his philosophy a subversive salvo directed against the status quo, by the anarchists who regarded it as a thinly disguised apologia for the power of the state – and, of course, by the Stalinists who would culminate their critique of Trotskyism by driving an ice pick into the head of its founder. Dworkin also died a political death; that is, she too died for her ideals. Her demise, however, did not arrive with a single murderous flash of steel; instead it took the form of a slow-burn. Like Trotsky, she was universally pilloried – from the right-wing pundits who forced her thought into the narrow stereotype of the man-hating feminist motived only by enmity and spite, to the liberals who were unnerved by the sheer viscerality of the uncompromising "J'accuse" she flung at the mechanics of patriarchy. Patriarchy was something Dworkin knew better than most: raped as a child, then abused as a teen at the hands of cops charged with her care – she later fell foul of a violent spouse, before finding herself barrelled, with grim momentum, toward the prospect of selling her body on the streets.

Such events provided the raw material, the fabric of her experiences, and as horrific as they were, she was able to weave them into something which was so much more than a howling shriek of pain. Dworkin created a body of writing which not only examined the devastation which patriarchal power could inflict on the person who was the victim of it, but also showed how it demeaned the perpetrator, relieving him of an essential humanity. She used her deep empathy to unearth not only the tragedy of suffering, but also the possibility of human dignity and self-determination. She combined a vivid account of the experience of victims, shot through with pathos – with a systematic excavation of the forms of social existence which facilitate oppression. Dworkin's politics drew down on her an undiluted stream of bile and threat. In 1999, she was viciously attacked in a hotel, and this experience, along with the physical and mental damage which lingered in its aftermath, helped lead to a prolonged, agonised death which took place over the next 5 years. She passed away aged 58. Her death, however, was not just a product of vulnerability and victimhood but also one of strength. In the words of James Baldwin, "the victim who is able to articulate the situation of the victim has ceased to be a victim. He or she has become a threat."[148] There were few who could "articulate the situation" more vividly and with more poignancy than Andrea Dworkin.

Intercourse is, in my view, her finest and most wide-ranging work. Perhaps most importantly it is the book which presents most clearly Dworkin's philosophical and methodological approach. And it is the work which does more than any other to dispel so many of the clumsy charges which have been levelled against her. It is often argued that her scope was narrow, laborious and repetitive; and yet this book begins not with the recitation of political dogma, but with a blistering analysis of one of Tolstoy's lesser known novellas, *The Kreutzer Sonata*. The novella tells the story of a man on the train who has a conversation with a stranger. In the course of the exchange, the man explains how he was once married, how the relationship with his wife soured, and how eventually he killed her in a jealous rage after surprising her with her lover. Although he was acquitted of the crime, the killer/husband now haunts the trains, looking for others to talk to, in a search for meaning and redemption. Dworkin's view of the novel is a complex and contradictory one: "The story is dense, passionate, artful, crazed with misogyny and insight."[149]

It is insightful because it demonstrates, with sublime artistry, the antinomies of patriarchy in and through the sexual act. It shows how the perpetrator is simultaneously raptured and repulsed by the object of his desire; how the need to fuck can become enwrapped with the need to kill. Specifically, Dworkin notes, the story was able to locate the element of repulsion which the killer had toward his victim "not in the woman's body, nor in her inherent nature, but in sexual intercourse, the nature of the act: what it means; the inequality of the sexes intrinsic to it; its morbid consequences to the dignity and self-esteem of men".[150]

Dworkin uses such insight to furnish a broader ontological narrative, laying bare the grinding, driving mechanics of intercourse against a background of patriarchy. Under such conditions the man is often impelled to reduce the woman he desires to the level of an object, the material means by which his desire can be sated: "The woman must be reduced to being this sexual object to be pleasing to men who will then, and only then, want to fuck her; once she is made inferior in this way, she is sensual to men and attracts them to her, and a man's desire for her – to use her – is experienced as power over her."[151] And yet, the man who thus desires – experiences a loss of being in his own right; for what he desires, he has as well objectified, has rendered less than human. Consequently, he finds himself in thrall to an alien, inhuman power – one which has ceased to share his essential humanity. It is this which drives the visceral feelings of repulsion, fear and disgust which underwrite the patriarchal project at its most elemental level: "She is this danger, has this power, dominates him, directly as a consequence of her inequality, the meaning of which is in her reduction to a sexual object."[152]

Now before anyone seeks to traduce such an argument, one should confront the organic perspective of the rapist or the abuser themselves: the often held and deeply enshrined conviction that the victim reposes in herself a subversive, insidious power which she wields against him. How he is the one to have been infiltrated *by her malevolence* – he the person to have been relieved *of his independence and self-determination*. How often does the criminal assert that the victim has "provoked" him – by wearing a short skirt, by exposing an area of flesh, by playing on his hapless sexuality – thus forcing him into a set of conditioned responses he is unable to suppress? And how frequently is such an attitude generalised in legal terms – how regularly do we hear from judges who have set attackers free – because (so the men in robes infer) the victims have set the behaviour of those who have hurt them into motion by their "sultry" and "slutty" natures?

Dworkin's ontology of intercourse provides the basis for one of the most inventive and intriguing accounts of the status of virginity. Why is it that patriarchy prizes such a condition in women? If, argues Dworkin, patriarchal conditions set the basis by which "intercourse" manifests woman's status as an object – as a repository for male desire; and if this necessitates the loss of equality and humanity of the female in male eyes – then it inevitably follows that only in her virginal state can the woman appear to the man as a living personality of an equal status. Dworkin writes:

> Equality means physical wholeness, virginity – for the woman, equality requires not ever having been reduced to that object of sensuality in order to be used as a tool of men's desire and satiation in sex. What is lost for the woman when she becomes a sexual object, and when she is confirmed in that status by being fucked, is not recoverable.[153]

Such arguments are regularly dismissed with a curt wave of the hand as ludicrously extreme – and yet one can never escape the sensation that one has with so much of Dworkin's work – *that there really is so much in it*. How her analysis helps to explain behaviours which at first glance appear bizarre. In today's world, for example, you can purchase online an "artificial hymen" if you are so inclined, and women can sign up for operations which offer "virginity repairs". The cult of the virgin is quite clearly in effect. Moving from the surreal to the mundane, Dworkin's analysis has cultural undertones of the more everyday type.

Consider that particularly unkind sensibility which young men are so regularly tutored in: the girl sleeps around, and so she is someone you can enjoy and make the most of (as an object of pleasure), but she really isn't the type of woman you should introduce to your mother. Doesn't such an ugly sentiment chime with exactly the kind of dehumanisation which Dworkin's account of the relationship between virginity and sex exposes?

In the sixth chapter Dworkin brings the analysis to bear on the historical figure of Joan of Arc, or as she was alternatively known, "Joan the maid". In this context "maid" is derived from "maidenhood" or virginity, and her virginity was an integral part of her political and religious identity, something to which Joan clung fiercely. It was not the case, Dworkin argues, that she (Joan) sought to pacify and appeal to the men around her by offering them a chaste and "pure" version of womanhood; instead her virginity entailed an act of rebellion, for her refusal to submit to sex – was also a refusal to submit to the intimate and elemental process by which the superiority of men over women, in her own epoch, was enshrined. In order to coexist with her fellow soldiers – all of whom were men – in order to effectively lead them, she could not appear to them as a "fallen woman" whose life was "bounded on every side by the constraining domination of sexed men".[154] Her virginity allowed Joan to appear to those men as an equal; she wore the same uniform as they, she slept in the same quarters. Such "intractable male identification", argues Dworkin, "expressed not in the usual female submission to the male but in an attempted coequal bonding with him, was central to her quest for freedom".[155]

Her struggle to establish herself as a free being was couched in profoundly religious terms too. Joan communed with the sacred dead; with the ghosts of saints and martyrs who provided her with inspiration and a sense of righteousness as she led the French troops into the heat of battle in order to pulverise the English armies over and again. It was the voices of the dead which provided her with succour and solace as she crouched huddled in a dank cell, having finally been captured and brought to her knees. Her virginity took on a holy aspect therein; it placed her at the end of a line of religious martyred women she herself venerated, and at the same time, the assertion of this right to a fundamental physical privacy in a brutal and male dominated world underpinned what can only be termed the most remarkable and heroic proto-feminism: "This right of physical privacy was never articulated as a right, and for women it barely existed as a possibility: how did Joan even imagine it, let alone bring it into physical existence for herself for so long?"[156]

Joan's very being then, freely chosen, freely actualised, was a blemish in the smooth, untrammelled flow of patriarchal power, and when she was finally defeated, the English soldiers turned her over to the Inquisition rather than deal with her themselves, for she appeared to them as somewhere between warrior and witch; though she was defeated and shackled, they still felt a sense of unease and awe before the inflamed, uncompromising power which seemed to reverberate through her. It was a power which the Inquisition and its legions of cruel, rigid, sadistic priests were determined to extinguish. As Dworkin notes, one of its key demands was that Joan should relinquish her male attire, and in so doing they endeavoured to strip her of the equality which the heroism of her existence had forged: "The Inquisitors wanted her stripped, violated, submissive; out of her male clothes, the equivalent of naked, fragile, accessible, female."[157] And so it was done. Joan was stripped, beaten and very likely raped, before being burnt alive. She was perhaps around 19 years of age at the time. The church, the same church which had excoriated her before immolating her at the stake, would, Dworkin notes with terrible irony, "rehabilitate" her some 20 years later, once the strength of her achievement – the impetus she had provided to the liberation of an occupied territory – had settled into the recesses of a developing national consciousness. Later still, in 1920, that same institution declared her a saint. "Joan's story", Dworkin observes, "is female to the end, when she died, like nine million other women, in flames, condemned by the Inquisition for witchcraft, heresy, and sorcery".[158] Later Dworkin adds, "she was a hero whose biography brazenly and without precedent violates the constraints of being female until the terrible suffering of her death."[159] Something similar, perhaps, might be said of Dworkin herself.

The writer's attunement to the nature of female suffering, its viscerality, is carried over into one of the most beautiful appreciations which has yet been written of the tragic art created by the Mexican artist Frida Kahlo. The inspiration for her art, Dworkin argues, was more often than not permeated by the relationship which opens up between the socially circumscribed "macho male" and the object of his desire – the "chingada" whose destiny it is to be screwed (the word "chingada" means, quite literally, "screwed one"). Dworkin quotes Frida's husband, Diego Rivera, considered at the time to be Mexico's greatest painter. "If I loved a woman, the more I loved her," Rivera admitted, "the more I wanted to hurt her. Frida was only the most obvious victim of this disgusting trait."[160] Throughout his life Diego neglected and demeaned Frida, he cheated on her with, among others, her own sister – often during the periods when Frida was pregnant with his children, and when her already damaged health had yielded a series of brutal, bloody miscarriages. It is this combination of pain, viscerality and the underlying hatred which so often seems to infiltrate love; all of this Frida experienced and was able to syphon into her art;

she "painted the suffering, enraged; she created an iconography of the *chingada* that was resistance, not pornography; knowing herself to be the screwed one, she made an art of passionate rebellion that shows the pain of inferiority delivered into your own body – the violence of the contempt".[161] Of the work *A Few Small Nips*, painted in 1935, Dworkin describes it in terms which are as volatile, glittering and magnetic as the art of Frida herself:

> A naked woman...is on a bed, gashed all over; she is alive, wide-eyed, her body animated in curves and subtle living contortion; a man stands upright next to the bed, he is fully dressed, even wearing a hat, and he holds a knife in his hand; he is aloof, indifferent, blank; and the blood in blotches and smears is all over her body and spreads out over the walls and over the floor in spots and smears even past the boundaries of the canvas to the frame. Kahlo shows the unspeakable pain of being alive and female, penetrated like this.[162]

It is perhaps this, more than anything, which Dworkin and Kahlo hold in common; the ability to make visible the invisible; to graphically reveal, with great sadness and the most profound pathos, the inner lives of women whose suffering is sometimes so commonplace and ubiquitous that it appears to melt into the background of the everyday. Both Dworkin and Kahlo are able to tear the veil away, to reveal the visceral truths which propound patriarchy, and the dignity and humanity of those who struggle against it. Frida extolled such truth in and through the fantasy forms of a highly individualised, magical realist aesthetic; Dworkin was able to raise them to the light by means of a broader and more conscious political exposition. For this reason she brought upon herself the chagrin, ire and almost infantile sense of rage which is exhibited by those who sense dimly, unconsciously, a challenge to the world they know – to the status quo, and the power and security they derive from their unquestioning, unknowing place within it. For people like Hugh Hefner and Larry Flynt, and their respective publications, *Playboy* and *Hustler* – for such institutions and men, who are nothing but children grown gargantuan in the garb of wealth, entitlement and power in which they have been outfitted; for such people their whole lives were nothing more than an extended adolescence by which they were taught to see women's bodies as their most prized, precious toys, to be manipulated, explored, spread-eagled, penetrated and then discarded, whenever and however they saw fit. Naturally this was overlaid by the cosmetic philosophy of liberal individualism: the women – and let's also add to this the children for many were underage – who fell within the remit of their power, due to destitution, due to the desperate need for some kind of recognition, due to the idealised and utterly misplaced expectations of the life that awaited them; such figures were imbued with a full and comprehensive freedom which spoke nothing of their economic disenfranchisement; weren't they, after all, just following the American Dream? The joyless drabness of embittered, ugly (it is always "ugly" – for the inability of the woman to conform to the man's sexual expectations is a crime in itself) feminists like Andrea Dworkin who presented a vocal challenge to this point of view – could only ever be seen as the puritanical assassins of a sacred freedom.

Dworkin helped unmask such commonplace justifications, and she helped channel and amplify the voice of generations of people who, more often than not, had been rendered mute by the media mainstream consensus. None of this means that there aren't knots of ambiguity in her own work. Dworkin never asserted that all heterosexual intercourse was rape, or was automatically oppressive, as her critics were so fond of repeating. In fact she explicitly located the act of repressive or explicitly violent intercourse in a patriarchal system which was social, as opposed to generic. She explicitly derides the biological reductionism of the view which does not locate the act of intercourse in the development of a broader set of social relationships in which "the woman is subordinate to the man",[163] and which sees the act of intercourse as intrinsically repressive – "God made it so, or nature did, according to the faith of the explainer...Both conceptual systems – the theological and the biological – are loyal to the creed of male dominance and maintain that intercourse is the elemental (not socialised) expression of male and female, which in turn are the elemental (not socialised) essences of men and women."[164] But at the same time, even though she comprehended the human essence as a network of social relationships, nevertheless her philosophical approach was what one might describe as existential in character; that is to say she posited subject and object as isolated and individual categories which then proceeded, in their interactions, to exemplify patriarchal relations at the point of intercourse; the subject objectifies the "object", and in so doing, loses the semblance of himself.

In adducing the subject and object relation as one of exploitation, however, she was unable to show how these categories (subject and object) are themselves formed through social-historical processes developed over many epochs, that the individual subject is merely a particle of a broader historical dynamic. She was unable to show how the subjugation of women by men – how the formation of patriarchy – was achieved over a prolonged period as a result of a deeper and more abiding process. It was one which saw a more advanced division of labour emerge based on a higher degree of productive technique, a social division of labour which saw not only the formation of the first class relations, but also a split between the women who were increasingly assigned to the domestic realm, while the men took control of the direct process of production and distribution on the land. The great Marxist anthropologist V. Gordon Childe suggests that early neolithic villages had a division of labour between the sexes, but it was one which did not imply any "industrial specialisation".[165] Childe argues that both genders contributed in equal measure to the direct production and reproduction of economic life: "The women would till the plots, grind and cook the grain, spin, weave and manufacture clothes, build and bake the pots, and prepare some ornaments and magical articles. Men on the other hand may have cleared the plots, built the huts, tended the live-stock, hunted, and manufactured the needful tools and weapons."[166] Because both genders were locked into the direct means by which the society produced and reproduced its own existence, the role of women in developing technology is revealed as being highly pronounced. According to Childe, productive techniques such as the "threshing and winnowing"[167] required to separate wheat and barley from the husk, alongside the development of a rudimentary form of "biochemistry – the use of the micro-organism yeast – and also a specially constructed oven…were, judged by ethnographic evidence, the work of women".[168] In addition women are to be credited with "the chemistry of pot-making, the physics of spinning, the mechanics of the loom, and the botany of flax and cotton".[169] Childe, following a host of other anthropologists, argues that the often decisive role of women in the direct productive process was exhibited in social custom by the fact that often "kinship is naturally reckoned in the female line, and the system of 'mother right' prevails."[170]

It is with the invention of a more sophisticated type of plough, Childe argued, that women's role in the direct processes of production was fatally undermined. Hitherto the directly "productive" labour was divided in the way that "whereas women normally hoe plots, it is men who plough fields."[171] With the introduction of the new plough, however, the emphasis moved solidly away from individual plot cultivation to the tillage of fields through the use of cattle tethered to ploughs. By "welding indissolubly cultivation and stock-breeding",[172] neolithic existence had undoubtedly accomplished a revolution in productive output, but the achievement came at a price, for it deprived women of an essential role they had in the productive process; it relieved them of "their monopoly over the cereal crops and the social status that conferred".[173] It would be difficult to exaggerate the gargantuan and truly tragic consequences of this shift; it marked, in the words of Friedrich Engels, "the world historical defeat of the female sex".[174] As men began to exert more sway over the means of production, as they gained more fully the control over the surplus product which the harvest yielded, they also began to achieve a political hegemony; that is, they started to make more and more of the decisions about how production should be organised, how technology should be developed, how it should be protected in the crucible of conflict, and how trade relations should be negotiated with other peoples. The women, especially those who were not members of a ruling elite, were still pressed into productive roles in the fields, but it was now their husbands who determined the future of the household, assuming the roles of heads – of patriarchs – able to command their wives and the children, more and more the bearers of a legal power which could reduce and condemn the latter to a life of domestic drudgery. In the field of culture, the same rapid and terrible extirpation was achieved; in the rich religious life a series of splendid, powerful mother creators are eventually succeeded by their male counterparts, and sometimes in the bloodiest of fashions. In the Babylonian tradition, for instance, Tiamat, the primordial goddess of the salt sea – is eventually flayed by the storm god Marduk who goes on to form the heavens and the earth from her dismembered body. In this myth, in particular, one notes that the male's creative power in production – in the creation of the world – stems directly from the most savage disempowerment of the female and the harnessing of her body as merely an objective material to be utilised in the production process itself.

In the capitalist epoch, such a separation – the separation of women from a direct intervention into the productive process on a society-wide basis which had come into effect over 5,000 years ago – is fundamentally undermined. Under industrial capitalism women are sucked back into the processes of direct production on an unheard of scale, for they come to appear alongside millions of others in the abstract guise of sellers of labour power before the market. A coherent and wide-reaching feminist movement can emerge only when labour has reached this level of abstraction – such that gender particularity at the level of socio-economic existence is increasingly dissolved in the abstract quantum of labour time – in labour in its commoditised form – which is then concentrated in the new industries which were everywhere springing up, pulling women *en masse* into the processes of production *as direct producers* once again. The first women's rights convention took place in 1848, held at Seneca Falls in New York and many describe this as the genesis of the modern feminist movement. What is interesting is how many of the women involved in the convention – which was fighting for women's suffrage among other issues – actually came out of the abolitionist movement which had been gaining momentum in the US from the 1830s onward. Women like Abbey Kelly, who would later agitate for equal rights for women, would speak eloquently and incisively on the injustices of slavery, but simply the fact of speaking as a woman on a public platform to a mixed audience was advertising powerfully the cause of women's rights and independence too. The US abolitionist and the feminist agenda, then, was in some sense symbiotic; both movements were delivered as twins. They were both concerned with a universalising agenda, but the impetus to the ideology was provided by the fact that the same universal abstraction was more and more achieved at the level of social being; i.e. through the commodification of labour on a mass scale and the creation of a working class which was universal in its aspect.

None of this is to say that capitalism is able to eliminate the pervasive effects of patriarchy. Capitalism itself is a double-edged sword in this regard. In the creation of a modern working class, it provides a great impetus toward the empowerment of women. At the same time it adapts the patriarchal standards which have accrued over millennia to its own idiom. The woman's body becomes in some sense culturally "commodified"; that is, it is increasingly presented as a commercial object ripe for appropriation and possession, something to be exploited and utilised alongside any other. Such a vision is realised, not only in more extreme forms of pornography, but also in the everyday depictions of female flesh which advertising draws upon. In addition, at the purely economic level, the pay which women receive in any modern economy for a specific job – average conditions pertaining – is still almost guaranteed to be substantially lower than that of a man. In the UK, for example, the gender pay difference stands at 15 per cent with women, on average, earning almost £5,000 less[175] than their male counterparts in full time employment. In the domestic sphere the situation is also skewed. Taking the example of the UK again, it was estimated that women carry out on average 60 per cent more unpaid work including "adult care, child care, laundry and cleaning"[176] in comparison with the males of the same family. This translates into an extra 10 hours per week of unpaid labour performed by women in the home. And, far more visibly, across the board one sees in the highest echelons of political and economic power that women figure far less than men; they are, almost uniformly, a reduced presence in the various parliaments and board rooms, political think tanks and religious organisations, military command centres and the elite levels of the civil service, not to mention women are far less likely to become heads of state.

Nevertheless the transition to industrial capitalism, by universalising the role of women in the directly productive process, does create the possibilities for female liberation which were hitherto unimaginable, and it does so by binding the liberation of women to the question of class. By assimilating the role of women into the processes of capital reproduction at the most fundamental economic level, by proletarianising them on a vast scale, capitalism not only locks them into the direct means by which society produces and reproduces the conditions for its own existence, but furnishes them with almost unlimited potential power therein; for they, along with their male counterparts, are the one group which – though subsumed under the capital-labour power relation and in thrall to its exploitative consequences – nevertheless hold the possibility, at least, of taking control of society's economic organs, the factories, the shops, the workplaces in and through a collective revolutionary mobilisation. The potential to regulate and determine their outputs on a conscious, collective scale which encompasses the needs of the vast majority of the people, i.e. the very people who keep those institutions ticking over on a day-to-day basis. To say the same, in the modern epoch, the full and thorough-going liberation of women is bound, of necessity, to the liberation of humanity as a whole in and through the working-class struggle against capitalism.

Dworkin's sublime ingenuity lay in the way she used what is essentially an existential method to illuminate the oppression of women. At the same time, *because she does not seek the historical roots which underpin the creation of patriarchy – she, Dworkin, is unable to conceive of the historical forces which inhere in the fabric of the present, and which have the potential to transcend it.* Dworkin is unable to show how the question of female emancipation becomes inexorably fused with the question of class struggle and emancipation under the capitalist social system because she is unable to unearth the roots of patriarchy as a historical phenomenon; she is therefore compelled to pose the question of women's oppression as a relationship between an isolated male subject which reduces his female counterpart to an object and in so doing comes to constitute an entire social system which is premised on the disempowerment and suffering of women. Because Dworkin's subject-object dialectic constitutes a form of existentialism, it shares certain traits with Sartre's thought and the Heideggerian philosophy which in many ways gave birth to it. It gives life to the lonely and beautiful tragedy of the individual consciousness set adrift in modernity. It is an individual consciousness which is female centric, and speaks to what it means to be rendered a mere objectivity for another subject in a manner which is profound and shot through with pathos.

But because it is profoundly ahistorical, because it cannot reveal the true social basis for the formation of the individual subject as oppressor nor object as oppressed – it inevitably unmoors both categories from historical development more broadly. For the same reason it is unable to seek within the historical present the living social agency which has the possibility of transforming those forms of social existence which continue to sustain patriarchal relations. And because Dworkin frames patriarchy as the opposition between subject and object on an external, existential basis – she is unable to register any of the real historical changes which have erupted in the process of class formation in the capitalist epoch, and the very real strides in female emancipation they have helped set the basis for. She registers the terrible shredding power of extreme pornography which, under capitalism, pumps the male orgasm out on an industrial scale, through an endless number of digital images and videos, all fuelled by the pain and subjugation of a million silent female screams – and yet she is unable to account for why the same system has led to a vast increase in the level of female rights. She cannot, in lieu of her philosophical model, seek these changes in an ontology of labour – the transition from one mode of production to the next, the historical movement by which labour attains an abstract form as a commodity and therefore sets the basis for a radical reformation in the possibilities of female emancipation. Voting, abortion rights, property rights, modern divorce rights and so on – such achievements are premised on a profound historical transition; they simply wouldn't have been conceivable in the midst of the Dark Ages with the level of productive technique and the system of social relations which pertained. But Dworkin does not conceive of such gains as bound up, even indirectly, to a shift in historical horizons – and so she articulates them in terms of vague mirages which have just been offered up by cunning patriarchs, deceptions which have no real substantiality: "Life can be better for women – economic and political conditions improved – and at the same time the status of women can remain resistant, indeed impervious, to change... the status of women relative to men does not change."[177]

At the intuitive and literary level everything in Dworkin's prospectus is attuned to the possibilities of human emancipation, and the recognition that the end of patriarchy will put an end to the suffering of women, but also the experience of men who are in thrall to the desperate, compulsive need for violence and degradation which their own self-loathing generates. And, as well, it will end the pain of the men who are themselves victims of patriarchal behaviour and norms. It seems as though no human being, no artist, no writer – has ever so vividly and consciously sketched out the consequences of patriachy, and the pathos and struggle of those who bleed because of it. For Dworkin was someone who lived and bled as a consequence of it, a living emblem of both subjugation and resistance. And yet, because her philosophy was existentialist in character, despite its theoretical depth and profundity, she could not locate at the heart of capitalist patriarchy, the historical logic which had driven it to assume this form, at this point in time; consequently, she could not locate within it the historical possibilities by which its reformation, its revolution, might be achieved. For all that was done to her, for all the hate which was slung at her, and for the heart and courage she manifested in the face of it, her methodology inevitably came up short, leading to a nebulous, wistful, conclusion – one which attains more than a whiff of despair. Toward the end of her searingly powerful book she concludes: "How to separate the act of intercourse from the social reality of male power is not clear."[178] This too adds to the tragic tinge which imbued Dworkin's work, and her life.

Chapter Eight

William Blake: Avenging Angel

He is around 6 or 7 years old, but he is small for his age, and walks with a slight stoop. He is walking through a packed London street. All around, people are busying themselves – a queue of women has formed around a street water pump, big bawdy market men shout out in cheerful voices hawking their wares, birds in cages squawk indignantly, a dog dashes along the pavement having slipped its leash, and a large carthorse clops lazily across the sun-drenched pebbles of the winding road. A colourful clatter of sounds and voices and scents permeate the hot, hazy air, and yet the boy remains aloof from the hubbub and the commotion, he walks in the shadows afforded by the overarching walls, and he walks alone. He is not by any means poor, but his clothes are dishevelled, his face is streaked with dirt; there is a slight flinch in his posture – his gaze turned downward, his eyes dreamy and timid. Other people have not been kind, the children at his school tease him and sometimes worse, because he is different – the things he says, the way he speaks – so he tries to remain quiet and invisible, but they find him anyway. They always do. As he walks, the street widens, opening into the gladed green of Peckham Rye, and beyond that the distant hills of Croydon, only the young boy notices none of it, for a shadow has fallen across his face, his small lips puckered in a slight frown. Even though he is only a child, all at once he seems more than his years, an old soul. From above there is a rustle. Automatically the boy looks up. Above him is the biggest oak tree he has ever seen. Its branches fan out in every direction. Behind it, the sun is high in the sky, a blazing ball of white, and its light threads through the leaves of the tree, splitting and fissuring into a thousand tiny pinpricks of bright.

As the boy's eyes adjust to the brightness, he is able to make out – within each fragment of light – the image of a face, the image of a serene figure gazing down at him, smiling benevolently. The tree is full of angels. And the young William Blake smiles back. It was not the first time the young boy had had a vision. His parents were dissenters, Protestants who had separated themselves off from the Church of England, and though their precise affiliation is not known it seems they may well have been influenced by some of the radical religious energies of the time like antinomianism and Muggletonianism. To the tightly regulated, conservative caveats of the established order – to the systematic and often inhibiting rules which subsumed and ordered the lives of the congregation *en masse* – these creeds invoked an individualised, rebellious and ecstatic vision, the sense that salvation was to come about – not through the imposition of law from above – but by the cultivation of a rich, private spiritual universe on the part of the individual of true faith. A direct and personal mediation with God which did not require the intervention of official church doctrine. For this reason dissenters such as Blake's parents were often regarded by polite society as somewhere between dangerous subversives and asinine cranks, and no doubt the stigma of difference rubbed off on their precocious and introverted young son and marred his early school experiences. At the same time, however, the parents offered their child a model of creativity and independence of thought at home, with religious poetry, imagery and discussion saturating their sunlit house on Broadstreet in a busy corner of Soho, flooding the air like music. If the world outside felt repressive and hostile and inhibiting, the parents offered the young child a compassion and kinship which was out of keeping with the patriarchal template of the period where children were to be seen and not heard. William's vulnerability was apparent to his parents, a contemporary comments that Blake's father withdrew him from school because of the mistreatment he encountered there, because his son would flinch terrified before physical punishment, for he "so hated a blow".[179] His mother took up William's education in earnest, home-schooling the boy, until the age of 10 when the parents, appreciating the child's gifts for the artistic, made the decision to allow William to enrol in a drawing school on the Strand and 4 years later to become an apprentice of the engraver James Basire of Great Queen Street. Though it seems they allowed their son a remarkable leeway in terms of following his own calling, nevertheless young William's brooding intensity and the depth of his burgeoning imagination would sometimes unsettle his parents, and this was particularly true when it came to his visions. At the age of 4 he glimpsed the face of God outside his window. Sometime later, he saw the prophet Ezekiel. And when he saw the angels festooning the tree forming a lattice of glittering winking silver, he at once reported the vision to his father. This was one of the only occasions where James Blake considered using corporal punishment against his son, so unnerved by William's account his father was.

For the young boy then, the reality which he encountered more and more took on a dual form. There was the richness of feeling and thought which characterised his home life, the poetry of the Bible, the family discussions which touched upon the divine, the intimate, candle-lit ceremonies in which he and his siblings were encouraged to partake, all under the watchful, loving eyes of their parents. And then there was the external reality, the cold light of day, the harshness of school life, the arbitrary discipline of the masters, and the cruelty of other children. Such polarities pertained in the world more broadly. Around the corner from where William lived was the looming shadow of a poorhouse, and near to this was a grimy abattoir filled with the hot shrieks of frightened and dying creatures. To the more salubrious south, however, was Golden Square, adorned with the fine regal buildings inhabited by the great and the good, clean, breezy and serene. And yet the historical panorama of the period was anything but tranquil; the Industrial Revolution was in free-flow, tearing up the old trades, sucking vast numbers of workers into the newly formed factories, subserviating the individual to the dictates of steel and steam; all that was old and venerable and time-honoured seemed on the verge of perishing. On the horizon the storm clouds of the mighty French Revolution had already begun to gather. For the boy growing up, William would have apprehended these changes intuitively, semi-consciously, in the muttered conversations of those around him, in the anxieties of his own parents. As a hosier, the economic position of William's father would have been particularly susceptible to the changes in manufacturing brought about by the increase in factory output. More broadly, when the young child went for one of his long, languorous walks through the sunny market squares, as the people bustled around going about their business as usual, the boy – who was possessed of such a delicate and heightened aesthetic sense – could not but have tasted the chill in the air, must have everywhere sensed the shadows creeping closer from the edges.

For young William Blake, there was always a world within a world. The violence and the fragmentation and the furore of the external world with all its contradictions and conflicts was redeemable by a deeper reality, a world of imagination, a divine world, and from a very early age, his condition and nature – his introversion, his sensitivity, his aesthetic disposition – attuned him to its presence. Through his visions he would glimpse it momentarily. The young boy was increasingly using his religious vision as a palliative to the contradictions which were erupting everywhere in the reality he encountered on a daily basis, and so, at the age of 10, when Blake was sent to drawing school, it was about more than just developing a technical talent the boy happened to possess, it was about enhancing an elemental aspect of his very nature, crystallising his encounter with the world. Because of the precarious economic conditions of the time, the fact that his parents were not moneyed – it seems they could not sustain for their son a long-term education in the arts at one of the more prestigious schools, so apprenticing William to the engraver James Basire was perhaps the only logical choice, for it meant the boy could continue to work within a creative *milieu* while also learning a trade, specifically the technique of engraving in plate. It was through the practice of this craft that William Blake absorbed the art of Renaissance masters like Raphael, Michelangelo and Durer. His early work involved taking their drawings and creating engraved copies of them, committing classical forms to the permanence of hued copper or silver.

Later Basire sent Blake to various abbeys and churches in London so that he could copy images from the stained-glass windows and the funereal effigies; alongside the burgeoning optimism and the lucent humanism of the classical Renaissance, the young man added an appreciation of the morbid and the melancholy – the dark shadows of the gothic and the medieval which imbued ancient churches creaking with ghosts. And this contrast between the light and the dark, with all its Manichean connotations, was to provide one of the centrepiece motifs of Blake's artistic repertoire and philosophical purview, as he worked the influences of the sacred and profane into his own compositions as a means to illuminate his rich inner life. The artist cultivated his art in the context of the plebeian craftsman of yore "surrounded by iron pots for the boiling of the oil, pans for warming the copper plates, tallow candles, racks of needles and gravers, fine linen cloths to strain in the plates, old rags for wiping the ink off the plates, pumice stones to polish the plates, feathers for smoothing the ground of varnish on the plates".[180] For Blake the workshop and the small printers press became both an apothecary and a temple – it provided the sacred space in which he could combine colour and form, thereby opening the doors to a world within a world, the doors of perception, of the imagination; and now he was no longer merely seeing the visions – he was creating them.

As an artist and a craftsman in his own right Blake opens up a short-lived printing business with a fellow apprentice before striking out on his own. In the same period his life as a young adult is blighted by its first major tragedy, the death of his father in 1784, and following on its heels – perhaps more shockingly – the death of his beloved younger brother Robert in 1787. It seems that William had developed an almost paternal fondness for his sibling, and had taken to instructing the young man in the arts of engraving and drawing. Perhaps Robert's nature, soft and pliant, allowed the more introverted and brooding older brother – who had acquired a prickly reputation for quarrelling with his fellow apprentices – to yield to the type of tenderness which was always such an integral part of his nature, and informed William's attitude over the years to both children and animals. In any event, their relationship was curtailed when Robert contracted what was probably tuberculosis and died shortly thereafter. His older brother tended him in his final days. And in the moment when Robert sighed and slipped from life, William experienced another vision, watching as his younger brother's spirit ascended to heaven, "clapping its hands for joy".[181] A more perfect melding of the melancholy and the rapturous one could not hope to find and in the years which followed, Blake communed with his brother's spirit and it is said that the deceased Robert provided William with the inspiration he required to create a new form of etching technique.

Blake's art from this early period is singularly distinct. He produces illustrated poetry such as *Songs of Innocence and Experience*, religious treatises such as *All Religions are One*, commercial work including illustrations for works of other authors such as Mary Wollstonecraft, and his own sketches, paintings and engravings; through these multiple mediums certain themes and motifs shine out. In one of his earliest works,

Oberon, Titania and Puck with Fairies Dancing (1786), the artist depicts those three characters from Shakespeare's *A Midsummer Night's Dream* – their bodies in full flow, whirling under the stars – and already some of the elemental qualities of Blake's aesthetic are in play. First there is the influence of the Renaissance masters, particularly Durer but most of all Michelangelo. The images of the figures dancing are bathed in the white, their bodies marbled and perfectly proportioned, their faces serene and statuesque gazing out with transcendental joy. The devotion to physical form which was the preoccupation of both classical Greek art and the individualism of the high Renaissance is exhibited with a deft, almost light touch – an effortless, playful sense of genius – but the technique is complemented by a corresponding emotional tone. The innocence of awakening, the sense that the figures who are dancing are for the first time becoming aware of their own powers, and delight in such a sense of themselves, and this again provides a nod to the Renaissance period when the philosophy of humanism was being welded to a glorious explosion in scientific technique and the vistas of a new world were sharpening on the horizon.

Blake, however, was not working from within the Renaissance period, but from the purview of its melancholy aftermath, when the new forms of capitalist development had become more pronounced, and the cultivation of scientific technique had reached such a stage as to lead to the strangulation of the individual labourer and the skilled artisan of old by the manacles forged in the furnace of the new industries. As someone whose labour activity was itself grounded in the artisanal mode Blake was, like his father before him, attuned to the threat of the factory, the remorseless mechanical march of the conveyer belt, the way in which human spirituality and creativity could be crushed by the hissing, grinding contraptions of the machine. Inevitably, therefore, to the element of Renaissance optimism, the celebration of the creative powers of the new human – there is added a darker, more melancholy vision; an atmosphere of pervading threat which seems to encircle the human actors, the haunting glimpse of a future chock full of ominous portents. To return to Oberon, *Titania and Puck with Fairies Dancing* – alongside the characters, bathed in the ethereal pallid light from the stars, dancing with such free-flowing innocence and optimism – at the same time the trees and grass which form the borders of the scene seem to flow toward them in melancholy waves of dark greens and blacks. There is something fragile, something transitory about their existence – the interplay of light and dark is not sharply defined as in the *chiaroscuro* of the Baroque – rather the darkness has the muted, lurking menace of a gothic fairy tale. For this reason the characters seem more like pagan figures, dancing in the dark, their joys fragmented, fleeting and evanescent; they are children of the night.

The contrast between innocence and ominousness provides one of the abiding motifs of Blake's compendium. In 1789 he publishes his *Songs of Innocence* – a series of poems which would later appear conjoined with the 1794 publication of another set of poems – *Songs of Experience*. In *Innocence* we are treated to a delightful homily to existence which focuses on the life of a lamb. Blake begins by questioning the origins of that life: "Little Lamb who made thee/Dost thou know who made thee/Gave thee life & bid thee feed. By the stream & o'er the mead; Gave thee clothing of delight, Softest clothing woolly bright; Gave thee such a tender voice, Making all the vales rejoice!"[182] The cadences are soft and lilting, the questions come gently, floating across you with the tenderness of a warm breeze, and the overall effect is one of harmony – the lamb resonates in unity with its environment when "all the vales rejoice". The poem conjures up a sense of innocence, a state of grace untrammelled by mediation or malevolence and the second stanza of the poem reveals the source of such unadulterated goodness: "Little Lamb I'll tell thee, Little Lamb I'll tell thee! He is called by thy name, For he calls himself a Lamb: He is meek & he is mild, He became a little child. I a child & thou a lamb, We are called by his name. Little Lamb God bless thee. Little Lamb God bless thee."[183] *The Lamb* is a beautiful, tender ditty which is compassionate and gentle, but avoids sentiment because of its language, the lulling, nursery rhyme perfection of the simple phrases. And yet, despite the simplicity, the poem also gives us a profound glimpse into Blake's religious vision. The lamb is associated with innocence and spiritual harmony in a natural environment which has not been structured according to the tenets of civilisation and the state, and for this reason, the natural goodness which abides in us all has not been tainted or corrupted. This has a certain Rousseauian inflection, which is enhanced when the goodness which is godly is also identified with a "little child". Here, however, Blake's vision becomes more uniquely his own, for the child in question is not merely an archetype of innocence as in Rousseau, but also *the child* – the divine power which is manifested as a specific child – Jesus Christ. The emphasis on Christ the child is important – Blake goes on to say: "He calls himself a Lamb...He became a child. I a child & thou a lamb." In other words, Blake's vision is radical for it cyphers the experience of God through childhood and nature, and ultimately ourselves. Drawing on a more radical Protestant tradition, the encounter with the divine world is not mediated by obeisance before a set of rules provided by a creator whose existence is as a remorselessly alien power *out there* set against ourselves, but by the awareness of Christ the child, the innocence which is an integral part of divinity, and which we can access by slipping into the deeper spiritual recesses of our own being. Through prayer, through art, through song. It is a quietist form of religion in which the world resonates with divinity if only we are able to peel away the outer layers of rule and commandment which conceal it from us.

But Blake is the poet *par excellence* of antipodes, of oppositions, and as soon as we turn to *Experience* we find what is perhaps his most famous poem of all – *The Tyger*. In this poem, all tenderness has been evaporated in favour of an almost spectral malevolence; the hidden hand of a dark creator at work behind the curtain of the universe. In the timeless words of the first stanza, Blake asks the same question of the tiger which he has of the lamb – who created you?: "Tyger Tyger, burning bright, In the forests of the night; What immortal hand or eye, Could frame thy fearful symmetry?"[184] In alluding to the answer, Blake turns to the imagery of the Industrial Revolution, images of fire and metal at work in some terrible celestial forge: "In what distant deeps or skies. Burnt the fire of thine eyes? On what wings dare he aspire? What the hand, dare seize the fire?...What the hammer? what the chain, In what furnace was thy brain? What the anvil? what dread grasp, Dare its deadly terrors clasp!"[185] The rhythmic, rhyming relentlessness of the lines moves with a dread perfection, the interminable blows of a hammer striking against iron, working closer and closer to the moment of inception, the flashpoint of being, whereby the deathly, beautiful tiger is called into creation and all of the universe resonates and weeps in the instant of its awakening: "When the stars threw down their spears. And water'd heaven with their tears: Did he smile his work to see? Did he who made the Lamb make thee?"[186] They are, quite simply, some of the most powerful, evocative and sinister lines ever to have been penned, and they contrast so vividly with the burbling gentleness of *The Lamb* that the reader can all too easily find themselves muttering the same question under their breath – "Did he who made the lamb make thee?" The contrast between the two poems involves most profoundly the contrast between two differing religious outlooks. On the one hand, the deep humanism of the dissenter tradition in which God is immanent in the spiritual substance of humanity itself and requires only a personal awakening on the part of the true believer through his or her own spiritual and aesthetic journey. On the other, a God who poses in terms of a dark infinity, an implacable and alien force before which we stand as finite, frail scurrying creatures, trembling beneath its resonating power – and yet inexorably alienated from its mysterious veiled nature; able to know it only by its effects in the word, effects embodied, first and foremostly, in its most terrible and beautiful creation, that burning tiger which stalks through the night. The first vision of God offers up an imminent, almost Spinozan form of theology, the second operates according to the terrain of the Kantian sublime. The first vision encourages self-discovery and self-determination. The second is more conducive to abasement and prostration before power. In *The Lamb* and *The Tiger*, the duality which Blake, from a child onward, had detected in the world around him, the duality between the outer world of unfreedom and the inner world of the imagination, between the newly industrialising society and the artisanal world of yore, between London's striking poverty and glittering wealth, between the powerful elite and the huddled masses – this duality was now grafted onto the religious realm such that the figure of God himself was rent asunder. At this stage, it is perhaps not quite true to say that Blake is talking about two different gods but that gnostic element, that duality, is already latent in the ambiguity of that one whispered question: "Did he who made the lamb make thee?"

Another key dissonance between *Songs of Innocence* and *Songs of Experience* lies in the historical timeframe. *Innocence* was published the very year the French Revolution broke out, and Blake, like so many radicals of the day, was intoxicated with hope. *Experience* was published several years later and in the interim much had happened. France had been invaded and had declared war on Austria. The king, who had been at the centre of the counter revolution which was brewing on an international scale – and had encouraged his counterparts in Austria, Prussia and Bohemia to retake France in the name of Royalist Absolutism – had been dethroned and decapitated.

Whether Blake supported the regicide is not known. In a poem penned a few years before – *The French Revolution* – Blake uses an elegant, archaic language which strikes at the heart of Absolutism, diagnosing its irradiating, sclerotic effects on both the individual personality and the epoch. The poem opens with the lines "THE DEAD brood over Europe: the cloud and vision descends over cheerful France; O cloud well appointed! Sick, sick, the Prince on his couch! Wreath'd in dim."[187] The "dead brood" which hangs over Europe is a reference to the mighty and yet unworldly and inhuman spectre of the European monarchies which exude the type of dark power and stultifying ignorance that nestles not only in the cold bones of the ossified figure of the regent himself but seems to seep into the landscape of the country more broadly by way of an "appalling mist", palling the terrain in a deathly, grey hue:

> And appalling mist; his strong hand outstretch'd, from his shoulder
> down the bone, Runs aching cold into the sceptre, too heavy for
> mortal grasp—no more. To be swayed by visible hand, nor in
> cruelty bruise the mild flourishing mountains. Sick the mountains!
> and all their vineyards weep, in the eyes of the kingly mourner; Pale
> is the morning cloud in his visage.[188]

Despite its grotesque description of the figure of the monarch, the poem itself operates along biblical lines which work toward the reclamation of paradise in and through a spiritual uplifting, a rapture of the soul. The conclusion of the piece has a distinctively pacifist flavour in which even the absolutist tyrant of old is rehabilitated and repositioned in peace "beneath morning's beam".[189] Events in the real world, however, were rushing onward and showed little sign of achieving such harmony or reconciliation. The revolutionary moment had tilted to the left, as the pendulum of political influence swung from the Girondins to the Jacobins, and the Paris masses were mobilised in the defence of the revolution. Eventually, though, a more centralised state began to emerge which increasingly sought to secure political balance by striking out not only at the forces of the old reactionary regime but also the radical forces that were hostile to the development of a political dictatorship. To paraphrase a writer of the times, the revolution had set about devouring its own children. In March 1784 the left-wing Hebertists had both their wings and their heads clipped by the neat, precise and lethal swish of Madame Guillotine. The following month it was the turn of the right-wing tendency, the Indulgents. In this way the centrist Committee for Public Safety sought to seal its stranglehold on power and raise itself above factions and the mass movement. Whereas in his 1790-91 poem *The French Revolution* Blake could still use the name Voltaire to represent revolutionary freedom, only a few years later he was associated with what the poet had come to regard as an unholy trinity – a triumvirate which consisted of Newton, Bacon and Locke.

For the rationalists and materialists of the sixteenth, seventeenth and eighteenth centuries had become, for Blake, the ideological arbiters of a new state power which had facilitated a vast upheaval, transforming the old guilds in a process of social reconstruction which resulted in the supremacy of industry and a reserve army of paupers and labourers who had been displaced from their traditions, communities and organic ties to the land. A new inhuman world was being raised, a systematic, mechanised, inanimate leviathan which would pervert and contort individual vitality and creativity in the heat and vapour of its own interminable operations. For Blake, those who constructed great, rational, mechanistic systems in thought were the inevitable corollaries of this, they were achieving in the mental arena what was already at work in the material world, the subordination of men to the lifeless caveats of an alien, inhuman power. For sure, figures like Voltaire were justified in their aghast protest against the arbitrary cruelty and corruption of the *unenlightened* absolutisms of old. But when they went further, when they tried to build new remedies, new ways of transforming society's structures according to the clinical paradigms of reason, when they attempted to impose the indifferent abstractions of rational thought upon whole communities of palpitating, flesh-and-blood people – then the inevitable result was, and would always be, the blade of the guillotine, raised high, glinting in the sunlight, ready to fall and sever individual conscience and autonomy once and for all. The French Revolution in its tragic trajectory had in some way fulfilled the old gnostic prognosis, only it was reason which was placed in the role of the "demiurge", a false god which offered up its sinister chimeras, and served to separate and obfuscate humanity from its true spiritual content by subjecting existence to a series of punitive, rigid and external laws. In a sense Blake's romanticism was both prophetic and retrograde; it was prophetic in as much as it detected with great aesthetic insight and pathos, the tragic consequences of a society which was increasingly being structured according to the impersonal imperatives of a generalised market economy, a capitalist economy; but at the same time it contained more than a whiff of the reactionary, for Blake had come to the conclusion that any attempt to rationally transform society on the basis of collective, revolutionary action would automatically end up in some form of totalitarian dead end. For this reason, to Blake's introverted personality, was inevitably added an introverted set of politics – he had sympathy for and occasionally fraternised with figures in more radical circles, like Mary Wollstonecraft, William Godwin and Thomas Paine, but he could never be a "politico" in the way they were, could never feel himself at home in the salon or the coffee house or the clandestine basement meeting, seeking to incite collective action, plotting for a better world. Instead his attitude was invariably more contemplative and melancholy, his thoughts fell inwards, his protests were more and more addressed to heavenly beings rather than earthly ones.

But what could prove to be something of a restriction in terms of active, positive politics – provided something of a boon for Blake's aesthetic development. In disdaining coherent and collective political action in favour of the timeless inner spiritual revelation, Blake was in effect renouncing the future in favour of the present; instead of concentrating on political schemas by which social groups might actively refashion the social hierarchy, Blake's aesthetic focus fell almost wholly on the individual in the here and now; the pain and the pathos of the chimney sweep, galley slave, prostitute or vagabond. Isaiah Berlin – apropos of the new brand of militant Russian revolutionary who had arisen in the mid-nineteenth century – suggested that such figures were often prepared to "sacrifice the present to the future, to make men suffer today in order that their remote descendants might be happy; and condone the brutal crimes and the degradation of human beings, because these are the indispensable means toward some guaranteed future felicity".[190] This type of charge – one of frigid utilitarianism – could never have been levelled against Blake. The suffering of this or that individual encountered during his wanderings through the smog smeared streets of London in the late eighteenth century was such that it overwhelmed him absolutely and all at once, rendering him insensible with rage or sadness, overloading his senses, providing the raw material which he would syphon back into the vivid, volatile and humane elegance of his poetry. The journalist Paul Foot writes of just this type of incident:

In London in the 1790s, like in London today, it was commonplace to see a woman being beaten up in the street, and equally commonplace for embarrassed or irritated bystanders to pass by on the other side...Walking in the St Giles area, and seeing a woman attacked, he [Blake] launched

himself on the scene with such ferocity that the assailant...
thought he had been attacked by the 'devil himself'.[191]

Blake's poems exhibit both the pathos and rage which comes
from fleeting individual encounters of this type, raised by the
poet to the level of eternity. Sometimes it is done with a deathly
softness, and an adroit, almost gentle turn of phrase, which
nevertheless strikes at the heart of exploitation. Consider the
way Blake effortlessly conjures up the condition of the most
vulnerable of all, the poverty-stricken children of London's
underclass, the sweeps whose small, emaciated bodies are
perfectly suited to filtering the dust-clogged funnels of
chimneys. He envisages "thousands of sweepers, Dick, Joe, Ned,
and Jack" and all of them "lock'd up in coffins of black".[192] Their
poverty, the working existence they are consigned to, becomes
a kind of living death; for what was a chimney – to that set of
children whose life expectancy was so meagre – other than a
coffin in black? In the next moment, those same children are
released by an angel, and the poet pictures them moving "down
a green plain leaping, laughing, they run, And wash in a river
and shine in the Sun."[193] This tender, heavenly glimpse of what
childhood should entail is not allowed to congeal into sentiment,
however, for the poet at once employs a bitterly ironic twist:
"And the Angel told Tom, if he'd be a good boy, He'd have God
for a father, and never want joy."[194] What constitutes being "a
good boy"? Blake answers – it means fulfilling one's duties on
earth: "And so Tom awoke; and we rose in the dark, and got with
our bags and brushes to work."[195] The pathos of the children
is compounded by the deep bitterness of the poet toward the
religious establishment; those who preach heavenly rewards
as a means to absolve the suffering of children in the here and
now, the adults who fashion those chimney shaped coffins and
have the children marched toward them with a feeling of duty
in their young hearts. Again the poem is simple, tender, pithy

and yet shot through with pathos, and remarkably revealing; like that woman on the street, the condition of these children is commonplace such that it has been rendered invisible in its ordinariness, and it takes a poet of Blake's genius and dualistic dimensions to strip away the facade of the everyday, and reveal both the horror and the humanity underneath.

In the poem *London*, Blake famously lays bare the suffering of the city, in a series of stanzas which have a grim, almost Dickensian flavour – the streets wreaking poverty and desperation: "I wander thro' each charter'd street, Near where the charter'd Thames does flow, And mark in every face I meet, Marks of weakness, marks of woe."[196] The poem has a strong historical aroma; this is clearly the London of the late eighteenth century with its rapidly expanding slums, the towering tenement housing blocks leaning in from every side, the narrow streets, the rivulets of dirt and sewage which flow across them streaming toward the broiling, sullied waters of the Thames. But along with the stultifying toxic physical atmosphere, there is a fug of ignorance and helplessness which has settled on the consciousness of the citizens themselves. Just as in *The Chimney Sweeper* Blake is concerned with how people accept the world which has been presented to them by the church authorities or the state power – the outer world with its rules and regulations and inherent injustices – and are unable to see past this to the deeper spiritual realities: "In every cry of every Man, In ever Infant's cry of fear, In every voice, in every ban, The Mind-forg'ed manacles I hear."[197] The famous reference to "mind-forg'ed manacles" perhaps adumbrates what some Marxist thinkers have come to describe as "false consciousness", but it is also specifically Blakean, for again he is focused on the inner consciousness of the downtrodden individual, thereby hoping to incite a spiritual awakening, seeking to thwart oppression in and through the moment of sacred revelation. But the most characteristic element of this poem, the one which is more

Blakean than anything else, is the sheer sense of pity the lines exude. The "infant's cry of fear", the "hapless Soldier's sigh", the "new-born Infant's tear", the "chimney-sweeper's cry"[198] – if one had to choose what is perhaps the most remarkable quality in Blake's aesthetic corpus, one could do worse than reference his attunement to the suffering of others; his ability to outline it in clear and yet desperately tragic terms, thereby transmitting it to you also. Pity was a value he appreciated in others, it seemed to him not something which diminishes and degrades like some type of ad-hoc emotional charity, but something profoundly and spontaneously human. One can't help but recall the rather lovely and melancholy anecdote related in any number of Blake biographies, whereby Blake was recovering from rejection and heartache, and took solace with a friend. "Do you pity me?" – he asked that same friend, and when she – Catherine Boucher – responded affirmatively, Blake said simply "Then I love you."[199] There is something naive but so completely heartfelt in the poet's response, and a year later the two were indeed married.

Pity he has above all things. I think this also speaks to the tragic nature of his own disposition. When he writes about human suffering he seems to be living it once again on behalf of the blighted lives he raises in poetry and prose. But such deep running aesthetic and emotional sensibilities had taken root in a man whose religious disposition had made him singularly unqualified to contribute to the conscious and political struggle against injustice in terms of a practical reformation of society. As the years went on, the revolution degenerated into the complete tyranny of the single individual Napoleon Bonaparte, and any sympathy Blake had for the type of clandestine revolutionary struggle conducted on the part of radical groups who were attempting to follow the path of the Jacobins must have reached its nadir. The landscape of Europe had been wracked by war. For the 12 years following 1793 the British Isles were on lockdown and England found itself in a pitch black, life and death struggle with the emperor, as Napoleon's armies swept across country after country in Europe. Although England was not itself overrun, nevertheless the atmosphere at home grew fearful, stifling and oppressive. The vast sums of money required to finance the war machine, alongside the food shortages which had been provoked by French blockades meant that food prices soared yet purchasing power declined, and the rumblings of hunger and disaffection became ever more ominous. At the same time, a sense of vicious patriotism was promulgated; the enmity and spite toward the French abroad was translated into a mood of suspicion and derision to those at home who refused to march to the tempo of the war effort. From 1794 it became legal to arrest radical political leaders without trial. In 1795 parliament passed measures which made it virtually impossible to hold public meetings advocating reform. As the thunderclouds of war flashed intermittently above, a feeling of paranoia and fearfulness settled on those on the ground; strangers were greeted with tight-lipped suspicion, conversations were guarded and curtailed for state spies were everywhere; Pitt's government saw the hidden hand of foreign conspiracies around every corner, and at work in every shadow. Blake himself became a victim of the crepuscular political climate. In the early nineteenth century and its perilous economic conditions, he found himself unable to sustain an independent workshop and was forced to seek patronage by moving to the small countryside village of Felpham. The fiercely independent artist bristled under the more conservative leanings of his patron William Hayley, but the most notable incident was when Blake came across a soldier in their back garden. Accounts differ, some say the military man was loitering, some say he was urinating in the bushes – but whatever he was doing was sufficient to drive Blake into such a rage that the diminutive but volatile poet grabbed the surprised soldier before frogmarching him to the local pub where the army was being quartered. The soldier was, from all accounts, a large man who was rather taken aback by the much smaller individual who had set upon him with such fury; he was "the King's soldier", the soldier protested in a shocked stutter – to which the insensible Blake muttered darkly – "Damn the king, and you too."[200]

Of course, reading about it now the whole incident retains a certain comic inflection, but Blake's reference to the king, uttered in such company and such conditions, could have had, quite literally, mortal implications. He was tried for high treason and sedition. The soldier brought with him another solider to act as a witness for the prosecution and both men embellished details and offered up falsehoods which were, according to William Hayley, "happily exposed"[201] by Blake's legal defence. Blake's time in the countryside seems to have been alienating and miserable, and the debacle with the solider and subsequent trial capped it off. Blake averred that the government itself had "sent the soldier to entrap him",[202] and while this seems unlikely it does speak to Blake's general mood, and the political context in the country more broadly. At the conclusion of the trial, Blake at once left for London. Travelling those country roads at night, passing the small villages whose flickering shadows were outlined before the ghostly fire of gas lamps, Blake would have been aware that a legion of soldiers would have been garrisoned at every one – watchful, ready, perpetually on standby. The landscape which was so beloved by him, now blanketed in darkness, must have felt foreign, alien and full of foreboding. It was around this time that he wrote *Jerusalem*, and we have in that poem the famous contrast between England's "green and pleasant Land" and those "dark Satanic Mills". The sense of the apocalyptic is carried over into his art too; of course it was always a feature, but in this period – the period of the European wide wars – the feeling that one is living in an end of days becomes all the more pronounced. From 1803 to 1810 he paints the series of paintings known as the Red Dragon Paintings, the most famous of which is *The Great Red Dragon and the Woman Clothed with the Sun* (c 1803).

In this watercolour image a scene from *Revelations* is depicted where:

> there appeared a great wonder in heaven; a woman clothed with the sun, and the moon under her feet, and upon her head a crown of twelve stars: And she being with child...And there appeared another wonder in heaven; and behold a great red dragon, having seven heads and ten horns, and seven crowns upon his heads...and the dragon stood before the woman which was ready to be delivered, for to devour her child as soon as it was born.[203]

Blake's image does justice to this sinister evocation. In the foreground, the dragon is painted with its back to us – in the very moment it has fanned out its wings, covering the sky, looming over the figure of a supine woman who is bathed in yellow; it is the Manichean image of a vast figure of darkness about to blot out the sun. The interplay is one between elemental cosmic forces, couched in the language of the apocalypse, but it also draws on Blake's own epoch; it harnesses the way in which the sacred, ethereal light which is emitted by the individual personality is on the verge of being devoured by the dark spectral forces which are everywhere erupting on the horizon; the forces of industry, the forces of war, the forces of reason. Blake, in this moment in time, must have felt himself a locus point in that very struggle, must have felt his own prophetic and spiritual vision on the verge of being torn apart by the social and political darkness which was amassing against it. Blake's painting, that dragon whose face is not visible but whose head is topped with a blood-dimmed rim of red, is all the more terrible because we see only the back of the creature; the woman below however – she can see its face, and her own is transfigured in a look of ecstasy and horror, for she is being made witness to that which the human gaze simply cannot behold. Once again, we are back with the Kantian noumenal/sublime in that celestial forge where the hammer blows of some dark, invisible, indecipherable creator strike against a darker material still, a material from which is called forth both the tiger and the dragon.

It is the tragedy of Blake's existence that while he felt the suffering of the oppressed in the very depths of his being, while he was able to articulate it with the poignancy and soulfulness of poetic genius – nevertheless he was unable to enjoy the solidarity of a broader political movement, and his struggles and his rebellion remained – in the course of his own lifetime – a very private affair. As his biographer Peter Ackroyd points out, though he had some financial success with his commercial engravings, he "remained quite unknown in his lifetime",[204] and a work like the *Songs* which inspired and captivated generations of schoolchildren throughout the twentieth century (including the current writer), was printed by Blake himself, out of his own pocket, in terms of a meagre number of issues which sold very few. Alongside his introverted, private disposition, it was his political romanticism which cost him an abiding contact with any contemporary social movement. He believed that the great system builders, the rationalists and the materialists of the sixteenth, seventeenth and eighteenth centuries, had helped clear the way for the oppressions of the modern state, and while there is certainly some truth in this – such *philosophes* were often engaged in the unconscious attempt to rationalise the emergence of a modern market economy and its social implications – Blake nevertheless declared *all* systematic, generalised, totalising overviews of the social world to be fallacious: "To generalise is to be an idiot. To particularise is the alone distinction of merit. General Knowledges are those knowledges that idiots possess."[205] Such irrationalism, however, is inherently problematic. If one wishes to resist or prevent endemic injustice – that is, injustice which is entrenched and society wide – one does so best when one is first able to raise a coherent image of that society in the mind;

to lay bare in thought its structures and relationships, to depict the social agencies and interests which facilitate exploitation and to reveal those elements which are subject to that exploitation and have the inclination or ability to better resist or subvert it. One must know what the object, the social world, is in order to fundamentally transform it for the better. In the modern age, therefore, system building in theory, in philosophy, holds a necessary relationship to social revolution in practice – if such revolutionary energy is not to falter, dissipate and collapse in on itself.

Of course it was the loneliness and alienation, his sense of a private universe, the feeling of isolation from any broader, more coherent political movement – which helped sharpen the sense of aesthetic pathos of many of Blake's greatest works. But perhaps some part of him, unconscious, unacknowledged, longed for a more systematic approach to the central problems humanity faced; issues of injustice, redemption, revolutionary sacrifice. He never departed from his radical romanticism – his acerbic contempt for reason, and his elevation of the aesthetic imagination into the infinite substance *par excellence* – but in his later years there is a shift in the character and form of his work. In short it becomes more systematic. Blake tries to distil the essence of the human condition by creating a mythological cosmology in which its key elements, symbolised by various supernatural actors, are set into collision. Perhaps the most famous example of these "prophetic books" is the *Vala, or The Four Zoas* which Blake worked on from the years *circa* 1797-1807; in fact two editions of the poem were penned but neither was ever completed. The Gnosticism which was always a strong component of Blake's religious thought is now more fully realised. The epic poem begins with the figure of Albion – a symbol of universal humanity, humanity in an unadulterated state – which has somehow fallen and "must sleep in the dark sleep of death".[206] The fall creates a type of cosmic rupture, and from the initial state are emanated "the four zoas".

These entities are Tharmas, who symbolises natural instinct and vitality, Luvah who represents love, passion and emotion, Urizen who is the demiurge of reason, and Urthona who symbolises imagination and inspiration. Each of these eternal entities/qualities has its own earthly avatar but perhaps more importantly the "Four Mighty Ones are in every Man" and they have, therefore, a certain historical resonance. Urizen, of course, has come to supremacy in the modern age – the fallen age – in which the spirit of reason, science and experiment predominates and thereby precipitates the alienation of humanity from itself. And yet the soul of the individual is so ordered that the other emanations/elements are eternally part of it, forever in effect. One can restore the cosmic balance, one can unite the four zoas and return the soul to a higher unity but it is only the power of Urthona – the power of the imagination, of inspiration – which has the potential to do this. In another epic poem, *The Book of Urizen*, Blake describes how Urizen (Satan, the fallen god) finally recognises his error – the inadequacy and oppressiveness of reason – and such awareness arrives when Urizen himself is overwhelmed by the kind of emotion that Blake holds so dear. Urizen is overcome in a supreme moment of pity.

...for he saw
That no flesh nor spirit could keep
His iron laws one moment,
For he saw that life liv'd upon death
The Ox in the slaughter house moans
The Dog at the wintry door
And he wept and called in Pity
And his tears flowed down on the winds.[207]

The cosmological reconciliation of Urizen with the other elements/emanations – is really about Blake's motif *par excellence*; that is the need to accomplish a revolution on earth in and through the subordination of reason to the imagination on the part of the individual. Ackroyd would describe *The Four Zoas* as "one of the most extraordinary documents of the decades spanning the eighteenth and nineteenth centuries"[208] while the literary critic Northrop Frye said of it: "There is nothing like the colossal explosion of creative power in the Ninth Night of The Four Zoas anywhere else in English poetry."[209] And yet, despite its archaic, apocalyptic beauty, and the celebration of love and imagination which powers its core, nevertheless the poem is, at times, rambling – lacking in both direction and cohesion – and eventually it peters away into nothingness. Blake was never able to complete it. And this was more than a coincidence. There is a forlornness to the lines which in some way reflects the existential gulf which had opened up in Blake's political thought: between his ardent desire for a revolutionary awakening on the part of mankind as a whole – and the fact that the basis for such an awakening was confined to the lonely universe of the individual consciousness in and through his aesthetic activity. In this lies the tragic dichotomy of Blake's romanticism. In contradistinction to contemporaries like Wordsworth, Blake was irreconcilable; he did not grow more reactionary as he got older, rather his radical spirit burnt with a fervour which was sustained by that indelible sense of pity for the oppressed and an incandescent feeling of rage against the injustices of the oppressor. But the tragic divide between his aesthetic and religious consciousness and the possibility of political action grounded in collective social-historical agency could not be traversed. Consequently – as he entered the twilight of his life – his hope attained a melancholy hue, and the revolution he so ardently wished for was increasingly displaced such that it was almost fully focused on a group of heavenly actors and the titanic struggles they enacted against a backdrop of celestial darkness; beautiful, infinite and yet entirely remote. The revolution he hoped to call into being on this basis was always going to be an exercise in futility, but his poet's pathos and tragic beauty has helped record the lives and dreams of the oppressed, and transfigured the spirit of an age into the guise of eternity.

Chapter Nine

The Political Psyche of Hillary Rodham Clinton

There is a particularly telling scene in a recent episode of the American political and legal drama *The Good Wife*. The protagonist, Alicia Florrick, is accompanying her husband on a tour bus as he campaigns for the US presidency. In an unguarded moment, after hours on the road, she happens to reveal her frustration: "You know what the nightmare is? ...Being on a bus in the middle of Iowa."[210] Alicia is, at this point in the series, in the midst of an existential crisis, ruing her life choices and lamenting possibilities lost. Unbeknownst to her, however, her comments are caught on camera, leaked on the net, and at once her husband's approval ratings in Iowa start to plummet. The campaign swiftly moves into gear; an advisor directs her to make a public apology as a means of damage limitation – she was tired and just wanted to get home, she should say – one of her children is ill, she should say – thus appealing to the homespun, maternal demographic and getting back in the voters' good books. When Alicia finally comes to make her apology, she says precisely what is required; she explains she is sorry for any offence but she was under pressure, desperate to return home, worried about a sick child – something to which "every mom can relate".[211] And yet, as Alicia delivers these lines there is a disconnect between the words themselves and the tone of her voice; the words are familiar and invite sympathy and complicity, but the voice is strangely empty – smooth, toneless, dead. The scene is telling. Alicia is lying, of course – but her lies have been compelled by the logic of the political system more broadly; a system whereby every misstep or gaff is analysed by a group of PR experts who then rationally calculate on the basis of statistics and demographical analysis – what the most favourable and voter friendly response would be. To paraphrase the sociologist Max Weber, Alicia has been divested of her own voice, made to speak in the artificial language of a group of professionals, an idiom which is indifferent to her inner life, alien to her true feelings and sensibilities. This is the reason why her voice sounds so bereft, so inhuman. In speaking those words, Alicia places herself at odds with her true self. The scene has a certain dramatic leverage for it expresses, with genuine artistic conviction, the contradiction between the manufactured PR persona and the authentic, inner self – a contradiction which so often comes to underwrite the modern political personality.

What makes Hillary Clinton such a remarkable and chilling prospect, I think, is that in her – such a contradiction has ceased to abide. There is no longer any authentic, inner personality which is suppressed by the exigencies of the outward political performance. Rather, she has become her spin. She has become the sum total of lies, half-truths, glib aphorisms and demagogic platitudes which her PR process calls into being. There is no longer any deeper, buried content beneath the shell – there is only the shell – or at least if there is something underneath, search there and all you will find is the unending blackness redolent of the deepest nihilism; for nothing she says matters in itself, in terms of its own content and truth – but only if it can be hitched to the wagon of her unlimited ambition and the trajectory of her own political star.

Take, for example, her attitude to the black population in the US. As a child of the sixties, the young Hillary was not unexposed to the dignity and the grandeur of the civil rights movements; she attended protests, and wrote her undergraduate thesis on the community organiser Saul Alinsky. In her own words, "probably my great privilege as a young woman was going to hear Dr Martin Luther King speak,"[212] and she even got the chance to shake the hand of the great man himself. When the tide had turned, however; when the rippling currents of change – of free love, black power and anti-war – had flagged before the decades of stultifying economic malaise and neoliberalism; when the vibrant and optimistic horizons of the sixties had melted away before the harsher, more austere panorama of years which saw a marked rise in black poverty and black incarceration – Hillary Clinton simply recalibrated her political brand. In the 90s, it was not community activism which was her focus and the realities of economic inequality, but rather the spectre of gangs, and her rhetoric attained a particularly vehement, fearmongering and distinctively Republican flavour. This was in the period when husband Bill Clinton was looking to cement his own presidential legacy through a series of "tough" criminal justice reforms, expanding the prison system and shredding the net of social welfare; in the context of such initiatives which decimated black communities in particular – Hillary proved adept at using the racially coded and enflamed rhetoric which might "justify" them, describing members of gangs[213] as "super-predators", almost sub-human creatures with "no conscience, no empathy".[214] The cut and thrust of such campaigning has – given her need to mobilise the African American vote in 2016 – been conveniently relegated to the distant past; once again, and without batting an eye, Hillary was able to hitch her bandwagon to the growing momentum of powerful movements from below like the "Black Lives Matter" campaign.

To be clear, none of this means Hillary Clinton is a racist. Racism – though irrational, atavistic and repellent – demands some particle of genuine belief on the part of the person who espouses it; they must, one feels, believe in what they say. The political psyche of Hillary Rodham Clinton, however, is unable to raise itself to the level of such belief – even in terms of the toxic. Ideas, for her, are merely the array of tools by which her path to the top is to be fashioned, they can have no real merit or power outside that objective. Consider her "feminism". It allows her to pitch more convincingly to younger voters, endowing her with a veneer of progressivism, suggesting that she is something more than the conventional political package, fortified by Wall Street wealth and connections, and made sleek and glossy by the slick lubrications of the most up-market PR firms. Hillary's "feminism" allows the lie to linger that she is actually prepared to go to bat for sections of the disempowered, that she is willing to speak out, stridently and morally, for those who might otherwise remain neglected and invisible: "Every survivor of sexual assault deserves to be heard, believed and supported."[215]

Strangely enough, this was a line of thought to which she failed to cleave when Juanita Broaddrick, a nurse, accused Hillary's husband of raping her in 1978. "Bill Clinton, Ark. Attorney General raped me and Hillary tried to silence me. I am now 73...it never goes away,"[216] tweeted Broaddrick in 2016. In his book on the Clintons, in a chapter entitled "Is There a Rapist in the Oval Office?" – the late Christopher Hitchens makes the case for what a highly credible witness Broaddrick is (among other things, her accusation pertaining to Clinton's biting her on the lip during the assault closely resembled an account of another woman's sexual encounter with Clinton, and Broaddrick's bruised face was observed by several independent witnesses at the time of the alleged rape). Despite the powerful and persuasive nature of such allegations, however, Hillary maintains the stony, dignified silence of a public figure who is clearly high above the fray and won't deign to comment. The same type of silence, incidentally, which she maintains toward Paula Jones and Katherine Willey, who accused her husband of sexual harassment and sexual assault respectively. Hillary has been somewhat more vocal, however, on the subject of her spouse's litany of extra-marital affairs, choosing to describe one of his paramours – according to the Pulitzer Prize winning investigative journalist Carl Bernstein – as "trailer trash".[217]

One of the many perversities in this whole sordid tangle of

exploitation and power is the fact that Hillary Clinton – on a much more minor level it is true – is herself a victim; a victim of her husband's infidelities, the breach of trust and the public scrutiny and sense of humiliation which have come with it. But the one thing which is clear, which insider accounts verify over and over, and which the victims of her husband's sexual rapaciousness and weasel-like mendacity also confirm – is that Hillary Clinton has been an active participant in the silencing of the women who have come forward in whatever capacity. Detailed accounts have emerged – including one from the legal watchdog organisation *Judicial Watch* – which testify to the way in which Hillary Clinton created a "war room"[218] staffed by figures in the administration like James Carville and George Stephanopoulos for the express purpose of smearing and discrediting any individuals whose testimonies might mar the public image of the Clinton crusade – particularly the legion of women who could speak to her husband's infidelity or sexual misconduct (or worse). Why was Hillary Clinton prepared to go to the wall for someone who had betrayed her with such flagrancy and such frequency? Again, the answer revolves around questions of entitlement and prestige; even Hillary's most personal, intimate relationships were of necessity subordinated to the trajectory of her commercial and political success; even the most human of concerns was, with her, made to genuflect before a glittering, unyielding fetish for power.

In an illuminating piece for *Harper's Magazine*, Doug Henwood describes the relationship between Hillary and Bill as something which resembled not so much a love affair but rather a well-crafted commercial and political strategy, a joint business venture – "the Clinton enterprise"[219] – by which the two major shareholders pooled their political, cultural and financial capital in order to triple the value of their individual stocks. While other lovers might have murmured sweet-nothings to one another across a candle-lit table, the Clintons' truest aphrodisiac always lay in the eroticism of their entitlement. In private moments they would make reference to the prestige and cachet their future held; the seat of supreme power – the highest office in the land – which, to them, was theirs by virtue of destiny. "Eight years of Bill, eight years of Hill"[220] – Hillary would simper and coo. One receives an impression of the Clinton union, not simply as a marriage of two people, but also the marriage between a patrician sense of old money and entitlement with the more modern and clinically ruthless values of a capitalist super corporation: the Clintons fused in a single political machine, sleek, purring and primed for power. For this reason, the profligate financial capital exercised by the denizens of Wall Street was always going to be a significant motor in the Clinton drive to success. When Bill Clinton ran for office in the early nineties, in the words of *The New York Times* journalist Stephen Labton, he was able to "tap into a well of Republican financial and political support" by embracing Wall Street – "collecting millions of dollars from a growing cadre of Wall Street bankers and corporate executives"[221] thereby. And in the early years of the Clinton administration bankers and financiers were rewarded thoroughly for such contributions, with CEOs like Goldman Sachs' Robert Rubin being appointed to senior White House positions. In a 2016 article, financial insider Chris Arnade wrote of his time working on Wall Street and the influence the Clintons managed to cast onto the trading floor:

> I owe almost my entire Wall Street career to the Clintons. I am not alone; most bankers owe their careers, and their wealth, to them. Over the last 25 years they – with the Clintons it is never just Bill or Hillary – implemented policies that placed Wall Street at the centre of the Democratic economic agenda, turning it from a party against Wall Street to a party of Wall Street.[222]

It should come as no surprise then, how, according to *The*

Washington Post, the Hillary "campaign and allied super PACs [Political Action Committees] have continued to rake in millions from the financial sector, a sign of her deep and lasting relationships with banking and investment titans".[223] Indeed, according to the same article, "donors from Wall Street and other financial services firms have given $44.1 million to support Hillary Clinton's campaigns and allied super PACs, compared with $39.7 million in backing that former president Bill Clinton received." In other words, Hillary has managed to reach something of a milestone, even out-vying her husband in his gambit for the favour and finance that the super corporations of Wall Street and their ilk can bestow. Yet despite the clear and available evidence of this, Hillary has once more adjusted her rhetoric to a more radical mood, to suit the feelings and sensibilities of the millions of ordinary people who feel ripped off by the financial flagrancy of the banks and the huge state bailout allotted to Wall Street of which they themselves bore the brunt. "No bank is too big to fail," declares Hillary, her features set in a gaze of gimlet-eyed determination, "and no executive too powerful to jail,"[224] – she adds with the same steely ominousness. Of course, no executive *has been* jailed – at least not on her watch.

The sheer gaping gulf between her actual political record and the rhetoric of spin which her campaign weaves is nothing short of flabbergasting. In a sense, when someone is so profoundly abstracted from living reality by the unslakeable demand of their ambition and the unstoppable momentum of a vast political machine – then the lines between fantasy and reality inevitably start to blur and fray in their own heads; they begin to believe the absurdity and bluster of their own campaign hype. One is reminded of Hillary's infamous pitch to the explorer Sir Edmund Hillary, informing him that her own mother had named her Hillary in his honour – having been inspired by his achievement. Somewhat later, a sharp-eyed member of the press happened to notice that Mrs Clinton was already 6 years old at the time her "namesake" achieved the climb which would make him famous throughout the world (and thus a person of interest to a mother searching out baby names). Or, on a somewhat more perturbing note, there is the claim Hillary made in 2008 – relaying an account of herself alighting at an airfield in Bosnia in 1996 and having to brave gun fire. "There was supposed to be some kind of a greeting ceremony at the airport...but instead we just ran with our heads down to get to our vehicles,"[225] she explained with a wry, world weary chuckle, displaying the type of grim fortitude and gallows humour of those who have been compelled to put their convictions on the line even at risk of their lives. Unfortunately, however, real time footage later emerged of the event, which showed not only the notable absence of bullets but also Mrs Clinton taking a leisurely stroll before being met by a little girl who handed her a greeting card by way of welcome.

To an absolute sense of ruthless, hard-headed pragmatism – to the ability to speak, calmly and soberly, any untruth in service of the political campaign – the corollary seems to be a certain saccharine sentimentality and a vulgar capacity for self-aggrandising fantasy. Both these elements – the pragmatic and the sentimental – are key components of the political psyche of Hillary Rodham Clinton. Consider how, in the campaign for the presidency in 2008, Hillary hit a more personal note in her speechifying. "It's about our country" – she said in a halting whisper, her voice beginning to crack: "It's about our kids' future. It's about all of us together. Some of us put ourselves out there and do this against some difficult odds...I just believe so strongly in who we are as a nation."[226] The bathos is palpable; Hillary, eyes swollen with tears, is on the verge of breaking down – but not simply for the rather trite, chest swelling patriotism she has extolled – "I just believe so strongly in who we are as a nation" – but also because she has such epic sympathy for herself and is so profoundly moved by her own sense of nobility and self-sacrifice – "Some of us put ourselves out there and do this against some difficult odds."[227] The whole speech sort of melts into this demagogic, emotional, self-regarding sludge. Now consider how easily she moves from such gushing sentimentality to an entirely more sinister, pragmatic and ruthless agenda, when in the course of the same campaign she had these ominous words for the Iranian people – "I want the Iranians to know that if I'm the president, we will attack Iran (if it attacks Israel)…we would be able to totally obliterate them."[228] How effortlessly the transition is made from a simpering and demagogic appreciation of the people whose votes she wants to attract in one country – to the bellicose, almost genocidal longing to "obliterate" the population of another. Again, bathos and belligerence walk hand in hand, in the crucible of a tawdry and depressing set of PR theatrics devoted to the unbridled and naked pursuit of votes.

And through it all the same depressing commitment to the politics of power and wealth is evinced. If Hillary was able to bow before the citadel of high finance in an act of political obeisance which put even the Republicans in the shade, she has shown a similar commitment and devotion to global politics in pursuit of the most hawkish, militaristic imperial stratagems. Her record is blazingly clear. She voted for the Iraq war. She accused the Saddam Hussein regime of having explicit ties to Al Qaeda, the very same fiction the Republicans had promoted in the drive toward war following 11 September. She backed the military intervention in Libya. She urged Obama to bomb Syria. She was in favour of the most recent pulverisation of Gaza on the part of the Israeli war machine. As Michael Crowley observed in *Time* magazine: "On at least three crucial issues — Afghanistan, Libya and the Bin-Laden raid — Clinton took a more aggressive line than [Defence Secretary Robert] Gates, a Bush-appointed Republican."[229] Again what is astonishing is not simply the way in which such politics seems to shill for the most powerful vested interests, but the way the shamelessness of her 2016 campaign sought to occlude her political record in light of an American public which had grown increasingly weary and disillusioned by decades of international conflict. The spin machine once again went into overdrive bolstered by an increasingly supine mainstream media.

In a widely disseminated interview, Hillary implied that the reason why she voted for war in Iraq was because this was the only conceivable way she could help prevent...the war in Iraq. By voting for war, so the paper-thin rationale goes, Saddam Hussein would have been pressured to allow the weapons inspections to be fully carried out before a full scale invasion was actually mounted: "The very explicit appeal that President Bush made before announcing the invasion, that getting that vote would be a strong piece of leverage in order to finish the inspections."[230] On this basis, a more pacific and diplomatic solution might have been arrived at by the time of the final hour, unfortunately George W. Bush jumped the gun and invaded prematurely (one has to admire the casuistry here for she has also succeeded in shifting all blame onto the unpopular and now defunct Bush regime – they didn't wait to finish the inspections but pushed ahead with the invasion anyway). The same perverse, rather Orwellian inversion has been achieved in terms of her politics on Israel. The fact that Hillary has been so consistently hawkish with regard to Israeli foreign policy, her support for the 2012 bombardment of Gaza, her opposition to all boycotts or sanctions levelled against the Israeli state in response to its ever more murderous military incursions – this is then transmuted, through the darkest PR alchemy, into the claim that Hillary is the best person to broker a peaceful solution to the Israel-Palestine conflict. It is *precisely because she is so pitiless* toward the Palestinian people that she has the ear of the Israeli leadership and is better able to curb its "excesses".[231] Again, one is struck not only by the mendacity of it, but also the utter disregard for the shelled civilians who have been made the victims time and time again. Shakespeare's

213

Timon of Athens says of gold that it makes "wrong, right; base, noble; old, young; coward, valiant".[232] Quite so – especially when said "gold" has been funnelled into a multi-million dollar PR media machine which never sleeps, which cycles out spin on an industrial scale with precision, calculated ruthlessness and a supremely bureaucratic indifference to truth.

And in some sense Hillary herself is the visible embodiment of that machine, standing at the podium, garbed in a high powered business suit, her words as elegant, slick and crafted as her perfectly coiffured hair – speaking in slow, measured tones which inevitably build up to the type of saccharine promise which might have been snatched from an up-market, self-help guru: "In America when we stand together...*there is* no barrier too big to break."[233]

Hillary is, to be sure, an effective speaker; controlled, with a perfect sense of poise, and a soft spoken but compelling delivery which resonates with audiences, and causes them to squirm in anticipation, even if she hasn't offered up anything beyond vague generalities – beyond those barriers which are so very big and that America is so very great. Like any practised PR impresario she understands that tone is everything, and hers has been modulated through years of public engagements. Like many of the most skilled speakers, she is able to sense the mood of the audience, its ebb and flow, and adjust her pitch accordingly. At the same time, while it would be churlish to deny she is a strong speaker, there is an element of the inhuman in her speechifying which she is unable to rid herself of. The sheen of her flawless appearance, the small, perfectly controlled head movements and arm gestures which suggest something robotic, the words which arrive wrapped in feeling but with a dearth at their core; all of it speaks to something vaguely inanimate, the sophisticated emanations – channelled through a human actor – of a billion and one PR calculations, performed behind the scenes, by a vast media apparatus which has tested every demographic, registered every voting trend and tailored the words, the tone – even the personality of the speaker – in turn. When one looks at Hillary Clinton one is not just seeing a person but also a product; the highest product of the PR process, a product which has been equipped in every possible way with the means by which political ambition and political power are to be achieved. Every possible way, that is, but one – the presence of any genuine belief.

Was it always to be thus? When one scans Hillary's political resume it is difficult to conclude otherwise, and yet, there is one anomalous event in the history of her campaigning and the axis of her ambition. In 1993 Hillary fought to introduce a new healthcare bill. It was, by far and away, the most radical proposal of her political career. Employers were to be offered certain incentives to provide workers with healthcare. Workers were to be organised into different sections with the possibility to hammer out at the negotiating table the kind of health packages they might enjoy. Those on the lowest incomes were to be given some level of free healthcare. Providers would then compete on this basis; so, the hope went, costs would be kept down. This was a form of managerial capitalism with a heavy state inflection; a Keynesianism in the medical sector, so to speak, and it was surprising – not simply for the radical nature of the reforms relative to Hillary's political colours up to that point – but also for the way in which the bill was put forward. In his *Harper's Magazine* article Doug Henwood refers to it as "an impossibly complex arrangement"[234] while the political scientist Martha Derthick described the bill's complete and utter sense of "political naivete".[235] It was drawn up in a somewhat secretive, haphazard fashion, a bill which went against the grain of the normal political consensus. Perhaps that was the reason why it suffered from disarray and hadn't been subject to the same level of meticulous organisation as some of Hillary's other campaigns. Perhaps it was the bill which had managed to mobilise what little youthful idealism Hillary had left, the bill which she would fight for on the basis of the integrity of the idea, the fact that it might make some positive difference to the lives of a lot of people – rather than the immediate calculus of her own career prospects.

In the event, it was met by a vitriolic reaction on the part of Conservatives, libertarians and especially the high fliers in the health industry whose profits were endangered. By the fall the following year, moneyed interests and lobby groups had ensured that the bill was shot down in flames. Perhaps too that was the moment in which any last vestige of idealism was extinguished in Hillary, leaving in its wake the certainty that political ideals which are not hitched to the processes of corporate power and elite self-interest are doomed to be exercises in futility. If you really want to get something done you have first to be in a viable position to do it, only somewhere along the line it is not so much the "something" to be done which seems so important, but rather the "position" itself which begins to take centre stage. An article from *The New York Times* shows how, by 2006, Hillary's relationship to the health industry had undergone the most radical of surgical procedures: 13 years on from her attempted healthcare reform she was "receiving hundreds of thousands of dollars in campaign contributions from doctors, hospitals, drug manufacturers and insurers" while at the same time many of "the same interests that tried to derail Mrs Clinton's health care overhaul [were] providing support for her Senate re-election bid".[236] Hillary had, of course, reached accommodation with the big companies by promoting legislation which would extend private health insurance packages and shield doctors from more pricey litigation, among other things. By this point, however, the political psyche of Hillary Rodham Clinton had long since calcified; her ambition and the belief she carried in the inevitability of her own ascendency – elements of her political make-up throughout – were now rendered as absolutes. Nothing else mattered. And, over time the allegations against her husband, her own role in the bloody mire of Iraq, the lies, the half-truths, the slanders and the sleaze – all of it could be forgotten or glossed over; after all, people have short memories, and when all's said and done, the past is the past – "thoughts which should indeed have died. With them they think on? Things without all remedy. Should be without regard: what's done, is done."[237]

In the run up to the election for the leader of the Democratic Party in 2016, only one senator came out to endorse Bernie Sanders – the more radical candidate who wished to take Wall Street to task – whereas scores came out in favour of Hillary along with more than 160 House Representatives.[238] In a presidential election which had one of the lowest turnouts in US history, the Republican candidate Donald Trump eventually won the ticket to the White House. And yet, Hillary's premonition – those "8 years of Hill" – has hardly been quashed, with the rumours abounding that she is already preparing herself for the next presidential challenge in 2020. Despite her most recent misstep, still Hillary stands – immaculately attired, forensically ambitious. And above all – at one with the political machine.

Chapter Ten

Chronicle of a Coup Foretold: The Backlash against Jeremy Corbyn

The political landscape of Britain in the early twenty-first century was shaping out to become a grim, grey terrain. It was a place where politics was increasingly monopolised by parties of the centre-right and their figureheads – a never-ending series of bright-eyed automatons, computer coded simulacrums programmed in the latest PR prosody, caught in a perpetual loop, compelled to blink out at the camera while generating the same robotic references to "hard working people" and "the great British public" and "a better Britain". No soundbite was too anodyne to be synthesised, no mantra too glib to be rehearsed *ad infinitum*. Speechifying became not so much a question of human emotion but PR production, as the political machine became ever more refined in the art of creating the innocuous and the bland. Behind the facade, political practice grew ever more corrupt, and perhaps this is what happens when belief itself is not to be won through the sublimity of the idea, but through a faithless investment in the professional dissemination of the populist phrase. Increasingly one can believe in nothing, for your own political voice is rendered toneless and hollow; separated from yourself, refracted through an alien prism, gilded with artificial life. A voice echoing back from the podium a series of digitised words which unspool across a ghostly flickering screen. What remains after the death of the genuine political voice besides the dull, unwavering certainty that a seat of power is yours, by virtue of your position, your class, your elevated nature – the fact that you are at one with the party machine? What is left other than the perks and the privileges, the financial rewards and the sycophantic group of underlings who hope to rise in your wake?

While the voice of Westminster droned on in its smooth lifeless, uninterrupted monotone – "a good Britain", "a better Britain", "a great Britain" – *in actual Britain* we saw the tendrils of corruption thicken and lengthen from behind the scenes: the surreptitious connections which formed between big media outlets and the higher echelons of the police were brought to the fore in the hacking scandal, the ever increasing financial privileges politicians had wheedled from the public purse were laid bare by the expenses scandal of 2009. Such pressures were compounded by the most cataclysmic event of all, the global financial crisis of 2007-08. To which the political class responded with the same organic uniformity, the same smooth, lifeless monotone: one which spoke of "overspending", "tightening our belts", and how "we are all in it together". At which point the Labour Party and Conservatives signed up for an economic policy[239] which promoted the same set of austerity politics and the public were promptly landed with a £1.3 trillion debt which fell disproportionately on social services and the poor, while the bankers and businesspeople whose hawkish speculating had precipitated the crash continued to see their property portfolios grow and their bonuses bloat.

The unanimity of voice and policy was extended beyond the fundaments of economic planning. Both parties more and more shared the same vision of society, the same sense of the people in the classes below them – who they increasingly imagined in terms of a single homogeneous block – a traditional, indigenous rump – a "white working class"[240] – which had been for years neglected and demeaned and was now brimming with plebeian rancour. For both parties this nostalgisised and fantastical vision of a time immoral social entity was not only a repository of some elegiac notion of "pure Britishness" but also became a fetish which materialised their own class prejudice: the idea that the working classes are innately nationalistic, xenophobic and reactionary. It was assumed in advance that workers were only ever concerned with the most parochial and immediate set of self-interests, but this standpoint was then presented in terms of a progressive concern for the neglected and marginalised. At the same time, such an ideological vision gave both parties licence for developed and sustained attacks on immigration, for the "white working class" was the victim of a "liberal elite" who had allowed the immigration numbers to flow unrestrained into the country and therefore contributed to the depletion of jobs. Perhaps even more significantly, the more existential notion was purveyed that this "white working class" was dying as a result of having its healthy British cultural values diluted and swamped by the influx of foreigners.

In the broadest terms a calcification of politics was achieved: each party signed up to the same economic austerity line, though the Conservatives were, of course, more extreme in its application, and each party purveyed the view that the most grievous political problem of the age was not the system of unbridled finance which had been unleashed by the rise of neoliberalism, but the issue of immigration. It was this which truly threatened national cohesion. Despite the fact that governmental departments and think tanks had rendered the economic boons of immigration from the poorer countries which had joined the EU in the time following 2004[241] in terms of objective statistics, despite the fact that many of the refugees were not so much seeking British benefits but fleeing from British bombs and the wars which had been opened up across the Middle East, nevertheless the Labour Party, the so-called party of internationalism and working people, went out of its way to genuflect before the ignorant and the base, combining the demagogic with the downright absurd when they released a decorative mug which read: "Want tough control on immigrants! Vote Labour".[242]

It is necessary to review these elements, to show how, by 2015, mainstream politics – the politics of the two major parties –

was increasingly articulated in the language of PR, harmonising themes of anti-immigration and pro-finance, condensing the interests of an exclusive political elite into a single voice, a flow of unthinking, humdrum patriotism interrupted only by the regular and ominous vignettes issued against immigrants, benefit claimants etc., – all those who found themselves at the bottom of the pile. The same voice was carried by the media, dominated by slick, savvy professionals who had disproportionately enjoyed the advantages of a "public school" (private) education[243] and the system of networking such education facilitates. Glitzy high fliers, media savants, who tended to evince the type of organic, pristine disgust for the majority of people whose lives they were so remote from. And yet such lives were parodied and caricatured by such an elevated select, by the endless series of programmes they produced and which told of a dirty, belligerent, parasitic underclass, breeding widely, drinking heavily, brawling profusely, spilling out onto the streets in an uncontained profusion of beery, vomit stained ignorance.

It is necessary to review all these elements to show how they come together so seamlessly in an organic ideology which had grown increasingly pervasive, whereby the differences between the ruling political wings of Labour and the Conservatives had increasingly thinned to nothing. It is necessary to remark on such a consensus, in order to understand the cataclysmic impact of the man whose voice has now shattered it.

Corbyn's rise to power was, superficially, the result of a fluke; an ironical joke on the part of the younger generation of Blairite politicians who voted for Jeremy Corbyn to take part in the Labour leadership election as a way to demonstrate their own tolerant open-mindedness. Never for a second believing he could win, this small coterie of up and coming politicians treated the older back-bencher with the same type of condescending politeness they might have granted a distant, doddering elderly relation. Then something odd happened. Corbyn's gentle, persistent conviction began to garner support. More and more, younger people in particular, started to flood into the party, enthused by his message. Upended, like fishes suddenly tossed upon the sand, the younger Blairites were compelled to gulp in shocked indignation from the sidelines, as Corbyn went on to win a landslide victory and become the new Labour leader. At once, the faint tone of condescension evaporated and something sharper and altogether more visceral took its place. Again, what is so fascinating is the sheer uniformity of purpose which swept across the upper echelons of power, from the Conservative Party and much of the right-wing press, to the BBC and many of the broadsheets, and even those Labour politicians on the front benches who were actively serving in Corbyn's cabinet. What could he have said, what could he have done, to have provoked such a deluge of loathing and bile from virtually every section of the political class across the board? In the event it is simple enough. He was in the position to finally interrupt the ideological unity which the ruling elite cultivated with such glib, toneless soundbites through the years. And Jeremy Corbyn was able to do this by speaking in his own voice: one which was fundamentally ordinary – in terms of its kindness, compassion and gentle humanity.

It wasn't "immigrants that drive down wages", he argued, but "exploitative employers".[244] And it wasn't "immigrants who put a strain on our NHS" – in fact it was immigrant labour which has helped sustain it over and against "the politicians who have failed to invest in the training".[245] Likewise it wasn't immigrants who had created a crisis for housing, but rather "a Tory government that has failed to build homes".[246] With the same, persistent, humane conviction Corbyn argued against renewing the superweapons which were a legacy from a cold dead war, and suggested that such money would be better spent on the NHS and other social services. Across the broader panorama, the spectre of poverty was increasingly stalking the streets with hundreds of thousands now turning to foodbanks, while others had been swindled out of their pensions. At the same time the perpetrators – croaking, cocky capitalists like Philip Green – were snapped on their yachts leering out at journalists with bloated insouciance. The Tory palliative, the thin ideological facade of "we are all in it together" was cracking month by month, day-by-day, and beneath it could be glimpsed the grotesque, almost Dickensian contradiction between the struggling majority and an increasingly parasitic super elite. In such a context Corbyn's quietly passionate sense of justice and his attunement to the suffering of those at the bottom was a potent formula, but beyond this he put forward a coherent economic policy which before had previously been *persona non grata* in the realm of the political mainstream – that is, he put forward a policy of anti-austerity, which argued that the rich financiers and the tax-shy super conglomerates should be the ones to foot the bill for the crisis which they had set in motion.

In outline it is a relatively simple message, and for those who were struggling on the minimum wage, for the majority of people who were seeing a thankless working life stretching out into the distant echelons of old age (having the retirement limit pushed back), who saw no chance of being able to afford their own house, and were experiencing an NHS which was dying a slow death due to the efforts of creeping privatisation; for these people, or the next generation – as they might better be termed – Corbyn's words contained a significant power and the promise of dignity. To hear such a voice which resounded with authenticity, which had not been greased with the synthetic emotion of the PR production, which spoke simply and truthfully against the consensus, which shattered the semblance of unity and self-satisfaction on the part of a ruling elite which had for so long shaped the political discourse in its own image – to hear Corbyn speak could be an enlivening, and on occasion, a moving experience. The flow of support into the Labour

Party at the grassroots level swiftly became a flood, thousands became hundreds of thousands so, at the time of writing, the Labour Party is now the largest mass party in Europe. And it was a movement which was vital and young, for it galvanised the very people who had only known the Labour Party under the grinning, creepy auspices of Tony Blair and his political progeny. The consensus which Blair had helped to create, which had been ossified through decades of disillusion, war and support for business on the part of both big parties – meant that by the time of 2015, an atmosphere of apathy had settled upon the electorate, such that the winning party, the Conservatives, won only around 24 per cent of the votes of those eligible to vote overall.[247] And though the number of people voting was up by around 4 per cent from the 2010 election, it was still the fourth lowest electoral turnout in modern UK history – with the Labour Party itself receiving the third lowest percentage of votes it had ever garnered.[248]

So a sense of apathy, compounded by economic crisis, and a Labour Party which had exhausted its programme of Blairite "modernisation" and had limped to an electoral standstill: all of these factors created the basis for a rupture in the ideological consensus, an implosion of the centre ground, which would have quite seismic ramifications. It fell to an elderly politician to provide the voice which would shatter the consensus, which would provide the nodal point by which a new type of class politics could be refracted – one which rejected the hegemony of austerity, and behind it the monopoly the most privileged exerted over the mechanisms of the political system. He, Corbyn, was able to do this by simple, quiet truth telling, by explaining patiently but with profound conviction, that it was not necessary to bleed the people at the bottom dry, that immigration was no bad thing, and that those who had been amassing billions in tax avoidance and tax evasion should finally be made to pay out something of what they owed. If such a message were to be disseminated through a neutral press, how could it fail to command the attention of those at the bottom who were feeling the pinch of austerity on a day-to-day basis? For this reason, the press had to be anything but neutral, and the reaction of the ruling elite to the Corbyn phenomenon more generally can only be described as pathological. There was, of course, the standard red-baiting stuff, Corbyn was a Cold War warrior who hated Britain, wanted to destroy the country, and the press were able to bolster such claims with hard evidence; on Remembrance Day – the day to commemorate those killed in wars – Corbyn, they argued, had clearly not bowed low enough.[249]

But the farcical was combined with the altogether more sinister – accusations of anti-Semitism, racism more broadly and sexism. The suggestion was that since Corbyn had become leader, these things had somehow grown rampant within the party. Any connection between anti-Semitism and Corbyn's politics was entirely unfounded, so instead many commentators tried to allude to his support for the Palestinian cause and his criticism of Israeli military policy, as a way to make the leap. As is often the case in modern politics, anti-Zionism was deliberately and provocatively conflated with anti-Semitism. In addition, commentators drew attention to alleged anti-Semitic behaviour which some members had displayed, and sometimes such behaviour was elaborated with good reason. Clearly the Labour Party, like any other political organism, does not exist in a vacuum, and its members are not immune to the taint of prejudice. So, for example, in response to an intensification of the bombing of Gaza, one MP Naz Shah saw fit to make the comment – "the Jews are rallying"[250] – which is quite clearly anti-Semitic in tone. But the Conservative Party too was far from unaffected by this most nasty and atavistic of all forms of racism. In 2011, for instance, one of its MPs – Aidan Burley – decided to celebrate a wedding by organising a Nazi themed stag night. The difference between these cases is that in the Conservative example Burley was quietly disciplined and then stood down some 3 years later. There was a brief spattering of media coverage regarding the MP's behaviour and then the whole thing seemed to dwindle to nowt. In the case of Naz Shah, however, the coverage was plastered across the board, and with it came more prolonged insinuations – ever since Corbyn's election, the Labour Party was a fundamentally dangerous place for Jews, they suggested. It did not matter that Corbyn had a long and exemplary record of condemning racism including anti-Semitism. The "spontaneous", shrieking hysteria of the press overlaid a more methodological endeavour; the attempt to consciously and carefully depict a political party which was being rotted at the roots by anti-Semitism. Such an endeavour became ever less exacting in the level of evidence it required; consider the mournful example of the lugubrious Ken Livingstone – who seemingly feels the pathological need to insert arbitrary comparisons with Hitler into many of his TV snippets – and who made some incongruous and rather out of place (with regard to the issue they were discussing) remarks on how early Nazi Policy was aligned with Zionism, in as much as elements in both had argued Jews should be relocated to Palestine in the early 1930s. In the furore that followed, the bumbling Livingstone tried to defend his comments on the ground that the Holocaust Memorial at Yad Vashem in Israel also draws attention to the way in which Nazis and Zionists had entered into talks in the early 1930s about how best to facilitate the mass emigration of Jews to Palestine. This is factually true and historically verifiable. Livingstone's comments were insensitive and out of sync, but in no way anti-Semitic. The media din, however, was so overwhelming, so unanimous in its conviction that any position which didn't condemn the hapless politician smacked of anti-Semitism itself – that the historical content which supported what Livingstone had actually said went almost entirely overlooked.

The right wing of the Labour Party at once got in on the act.

Ostensibly to provide a show of just how seriously they regarded anti-Semitism, what was supposed to be a dispassionate and objective examination of what Livingstone had actually said very quickly degenerated into the same emotional grandstanding, with one of the key figures of the committee – shiny new Blairite Chuka Umunna – arriving at the point where he ceased to question Livingstone altogether, instead offering flammable but dogmatic rants on just how guilty of anti-Semitism the ex-Labour Mayor was:

> You did help reduce poverty and inequality, you did improve the housing situation in our capital city, but you're not a historian, you're a politician and by needlessly and repeatedly offending Jewish people in this way, you not only betray our Labour values but you betray your legacy as mayor.
>
> All you're now going to be remembered for is becoming a pin-up for the kind of prejudice that our party was built to fight against.[251]

To recapitulate, what effectively took place was the following: some cases of genuine anti-Semitism were discovered and acted upon, while others – alleged – were taken as fact, when a mood of hysteria, whipped up by the press, more and more came to stand in for an objective examination of what had actually been said. All of this was syphoned into an image of a party which was brimming with toxic anti-Semitism and presented Jewish members with a real danger to their safety. Finally, this poisonous mirage which the press, in collusion with the right wing of the Labour Party, had so meticulously cultivated – was then said to have been the direct result of Jeremy Corbyn's election as leader. What the press weren't so keen to reference was that, in the case of Naz Shah, the anti-Semitic remarks in question had been made in 2014 – a year before Corbyn was to become leader. In addition, the movement behind Jeremy Corbyn was attacked on several other levels. It was adduced that his leadership had inaugurated an era of racism in the party more generally. Corbyn chose to split the post of one of his shadow ministers, Chi Onwurah, so that her role would be shared by another. Ms Chi Onwurah – a black woman who also happens to be a supporter of the right-wing tendency within the Labour Party and thus an opponent of Corbyn's leadership – then went on to suggest, without any evidence whatsoever, that the logistical decision to reorder the structures of a particular party position was very likely related to "racial discrimination".[252] Again what matters here is not the evidence. It mattered not a jot Corbyn's fine, persistent campaigning against racism from the backbenches over several decades. It did not matter that Corbyn is perhaps one of the only parliamentary politicians who you will find in a black and white photo from the eighties, which shows him being dragged away by police while he is holding a placard protesting about the racist, apartheid regime of South Africa. All that mattered was that the smear had been achieved and the press at once helped it to set by publishing a slew of articles which gave complete prominence to Onwurah's views.

More "proof" of the insidious authoritarianism of the Corbyn regime was provided by Seema Malhotra, a person Corbyn had chosen for the role of Shadow Chief Secretary to the Treasury. She eventually resigned from this role, and assuming she had left her office thereby – the office was then entered into by Labour staff. This was made the subject of an official complaint on the part of Ms Malhotra – again leaked to the press – which suggested that such an entry helped provide evidence of an ongoing "campaign of intimidation and harassment".[253] Malhotra too had declared herself to be an avowed opponent of Corbyn. What we have here, then, is a whole raft of Labour MPs colluding with the press in a sustained campaign of calumny and slander against an elected leader, a leader who has been elected precisely because of the fact that his voice had broken the political consensus by emphasising the type of politics which explicitly expresses the interest of the majority at the lower economic end of society rather than the minority at the top. The campaign against Corbyn was eventually graduated into an out and out coup against the democratically elected leader, which took place after the referendum on the EU had happened and the decision of the country to leave had been returned.

Again, the whole thing was a contrived, cynical manoeuvre founded on barefaced lying. Many of the numerous politicians who took part in the coup appeared on the TV channels in order to spin what was quite clearly an anti-democratic violation of the will of the majority of the party members into a noble and self-sacrificing gambit, a conscience driven decision to resign in protest in the face of the dark, sinister forces which had so transfigured a once beloved party. Every aspect of the performance was contrived. The rebel MPs asserted that their action was the result of the individual conscience pushed to insupportable limits, an authentic gesture of spontaneous protest, but the whole affair had been orchestrated in combination with a large PR firm[254] many months in advance. In addition, the "spontaneous" resignations occurred once every hour with almost clockwork precision, carefully crafted so as to create the most sustained and ongoing impact in the media. This wasn't the first time the belligerent MPs had resorted to these kinds of tactics. In fact they had spent the whole year fulminating. In January 2016, for example, the BBC played an interview with the MP Stephen Doughy. During the interview the MP seemed to get more and more emotional before, with a dramatic flourish, he announced his resignation live on air. Eventually it emerged that the resignation had been arranged in advance[255] with the political editor of the BBC news team. The incident not only adumbrated the kind of artificial, PR inspired stunt that the plotters would later make prolonged and repeated use of; more than this, it also exhibited the behind the scenes links between the media and the political class and demonstrates the organic sense of loathing which the Corbyn movement inspired in them. Most profoundly of all however, it shows the sheer level of contempt which these people evince for the general public. They understood that the people out there do not possess their talent as leaders, as a select elite, to know what is best for the country and to make the big decisions which impact on the lives of everyone. For this reason the vast majority exist to be moulded by a combination of PR spin and gaudy theatrics, and it was such a sensibility which underpinned the whole set of "principled" "spontaneous" resignations which took place. Despite the on-camera tears from people such as the MP Angela Eagle, despite the hand wringing, more-in-sadness-than-anger tone which so many of them struck, none of these MPs had any real intention of sacrificing their position and privilege on the basis of some fundamental moral principle. Rather, through a combination of disruption, smear and slander, they were making a last-ditch effort to blacken Corbyn's image irreparably in the public eye, and thus jettison him from power – at which point, one can safely assume, this ruling elite would have taken back the reins of party control and it would be the smug, complacent process of business as usual, with no small emphasis placed on business.

The trouble was that Corbyn refused to stand down. Instead he appealed to the mandate the membership had given him less than a year before. In response members rallied around him, and many thousands more joined the Labour Party. They understood very well that what was taking place was a coordinated attempt on the part of a privileged elite to displace a democratically elected leader whose policies were out of sync with their own class power. Again the right Labour MPs played every dirty trick in the book, with the media again acting in the role of confederates. Now the MPs, increasingly desperate, increasingly shrill, endeavoured to slander the new membership – they were not legitimate political actors, but "Trotskyite infiltrators",[256] the spore of a series of far-left parties which wanted to first co-opt and then destroy. While the papers carried vivid accounts of such claims, they failed to reference the fact that these parties generally had a membership which could be numbered in the hundreds. Had they much larger numbers, the last thing a group like the AWL (Alliance for Workers' Liberty) would do would be to become part of the Labour Party. The MPs then moderated their denunciations – perhaps the majority of the new members were not from far-left parties – nevertheless they were being manipulated by individuals of that ilk.[257] Again, the allegation nicely draws into alignment two broader motifs on the part of the rebel MPs – the ability to resort to the crude lie without blinking, but also the underlying logic – that the people on the ground are dupes and idiots – and are always susceptible to manipulation by the force from above. But all the fulminations, all the lies failed to dislodge the leader. The rebel MPs floundered – they had not expected Corbyn to withstand such a coordinated onslaught, and now they were forced into a leadership election, against a figure whose support – despite every attempt against him – had gone from strength to strength.

It is said that any given group of people eventually end up with the political representative they deserve. One might question the universal applicability of the axiom but in the case of the rebel MPs, it proved true beyond a shadow of a doubt. They expected their coordinated, visceral attack to generate the kind of force to displace Corbyn, and return to themselves the control of the party machine. When this failed to transpire, when the movement from below rallied to support its representative, the rebel MPs were faced with a leadership election which they did not want, because only a minority of the membership would support them. The first candidate they floated – Angela Eagle – expressed perfectly their sense of disorientation; thrust into the unenviable position of challenger, her leadership bid was a disaster which lurched from the tragic to the comical. As she forlornly pleaded with the populous in a plaintive whimper to acknowledge her leadership abilities, even the anti-Corbyn press couldn't be trusted to muster up the type of stamina required to sit through a whole segment[258] of her prosthetic spiel. But if Eagle embodied the sense of disorientation on the part of a group of rebel MPs who now found themselves flaying in political limbo, the next candidate they raised up was a more deliberate, more considered choice – expressing their collective sense of mendacity and ambition in and through a single well-polished political persona. Owen Smith's early career was a testament to privilege and entitlement and the classical career trajectory of an upper-middle-class high flier. He began his career working in media – not on some parochial, small town station of course – but at once in a position for the BBC. From there he became a special political advisor for the Welsh Secretary of State – before synthesising both these experiences – the media aspect and the political – when he became a lobbyist for the global pharmaceutical giant Pfizer. This was a company which desperately required a fleet of such people in order to spin the various scandals it has found itself embroiled in – from the children it had experimented on and killed in Sub-Saharan Africa – to the rather closer to home case of a subdivision it had acquired which sold insulation containing asbestos right up to the time of the early 1970s.

Smith's whole record, then, wreaked of pragmatism over principle in order to facilitate the climb of the career minded individual up the greasy pole. Having only ever moved from one career triumph to the next, it probably seemed that the leadership of a major political party was the next inexorable stage on his career resume. But he intuited the problem which the rebel MPs understood as a whole, the membership was so overwhelmingly in favour of Corbyn because he, Corbyn, had broken with the political consensus on which they, the privileged, had been weaned. The dilemma was not insoluble. Precisely because of his privilege, precisely because of his years working in PR and media, he understood the fact that the vast majority of people had to be finessed, had to be handled, by those who had a proven track record – that elite minority who were always destined to excel. From the purview of Smith's politics, the solution was, in fact, quite simple. All he need do was replicate Corbyn's political programme – he need only announce himself as breaking with the same political consensus, as having a strong commitment to the politics of anti-austerity on his own account – and this way he could dip into Corbyn's pool of electoral support.

At the same time, he could use every opportunity to disparage Corbyn, feeding off the press allegations that the party had become a dangerous and malevolent space for dissenters and minorities, and all the while he peppered such campaigning with the dogmatic mantra that Corbyn was simply "unelectable". It was of course Corbyn's policies of anti-austerity which made such an "unelectable" politician so attractive to so many hundreds of thousands and so offensive to a coterie of career politicians but when Smith began to ape those same policies, those in the higher echelons of the Labour establishment did nothing to savage him in the way they had Corbyn. Why? Simply, they scented in Smith a species after their own breed: they understood this political player was prepared to do and say whatever it took to be rid of Corbyn: once he had co-opted Corbyn's politics in order to exercise Corbyn's presence, Smith would discreetly and gently begin to reverse his anti-austerity line and return the party to the political programme which reflected the politics of those at the top. Smith's mendaciousness on this score is not simply a product of unbridled entitlement and cataclysmic ambition. It was also the product of the sheer exhaustion of the right-wing tendency within the Labour Party after the Blairite years. The old mantras of "modernisation" and a "third way" had evaporated in the shelled, smouldering wastelands of Baghdad and Helmand, while New Labour slogans had little charge in the face of the rapacious march of big business and the increasing spread of poverty back at home. Smith was compelled to adopt a Corbyn-esque set of politics precisely because the words of New Labour now turned to ashes in his mouth. And every lie, every slander, every cynical manoeuvre, every behind the scenes machination the rebel MPs embroiled themselves in was conducted for the same reason – even they had ceased to have faith in their own political voice; for that reason, dissimulation and sabotage was all that remained.

The membership, however, were not taken in by such a transparent ploy. All the polls suggested that people were still flocking to the party in support of Corbyn. In the same period the rebel MPs were bolstered by the support of the Labour bureaucracy which actively attacked the democratic rights of the membership. Using the red-baiting line of "Trotskyite infiltrators" to provide the pretext, it pressed ahead with a motion to prevent people who had only been members for 6 months or less from voting[259] (thus annulling much of Corbyn's support). If such members still wanted to vote, they would have to re-register and pay a £25 fee. This was perhaps the most brazen effort yet – the Labour bureaucracy through the National Executive Committee was supporting the rebel MPs by first removing those who would vote against them. But more than that, by trying to disenfranchise the poorer elements, it reveals something which the plotters understood at the fundamental level of their being – all the tripe about Corbyn being "unelectable" aside, this was never about his personality, but the set of policies he advocated which had opened up a class rift. The anti-austerity programme he had floated expressed at an organic level the interests of the working classes and the poor. The majority of those politicians at the top were appalled, disgusted, repelled by such a programme – for they had attended the finest schools and elite universities before being jettisoned into apprenticeships at the most prestigious media, business or political outfits, and then finally taking their allotted place on the benches of the House of Commons. That one of their number was prepared to rally so openly and so flagrantly in favour of the empowerment of the vast masses of people whom they felt in their bones should remain subordinate to the interests of a tiny elite – could only ever have galvanised their instincts of superiority, disgust and, most fundamentally, fear. Behind the cynical smarmy smiles of these slick career politicians lurked the sense and spectre of class war – they understood with their honed class instincts the dangers of the movement which Corbyn was inciting, which provided him with his political mandate; they understood in the same way the hardcore patricians of the Roman Republic sensed the threat posed by the tribunes Gracchi, or the way in which the oligarchy of medieval Florence regarded the leader of the wool labourers Michele di Lando during the *Ciompi* unrest. The sense of a set of polarising social contradictions marked the rise of such figures, and the rise of Corbyn's star in our own age is not so different.

This is the reason for such a vicious counter-mobilisation against Corbyn; the illegal and immoral endeavour to strike at voters' democratic rights, the slanders carried through a media whose journalists are overwhelmingly from the public schools, the labour politicians themselves who would rather see the party run aground than suffer the indignity and angst visited upon them by a man whose policies are so out of kilter with their own class instincts. And yet, despite the fact that such people had recourse to vast sums of money, had a grip on the bureaucracy of the Labour Party at its highest level, had the ear of a sympathetic media whose political tone chimed exactly with their own interests – despite all this, when the dust had settled and the results of the election between Corbyn and Smith had been tallied, Jeremy Corbyn was again returned to power by another spectacular landslide, 62 per cent of the vote.[260] When one considers the objective trajectory of Corbyn's leadership and the development of the rebellion against it, not only do the contours of a deeper class antagonism become apparent, but so does the potential of the movement from below which has rescued Corbyn and so powerfully thwarted the attempts from those above to snatch back control of the party political process. That this presents in terms of a vivid class context naturally provides the motive for those who have carried out the coup to portray it as a response to some isolated, individualised aspect of Corbyn's personality, to disguise their own class-based attacks in the garb of purely practical concerns about Corbyn's "electability". But the Labour Party has now mobilised over half a million members making it the largest political party in Europe today, and this is precisely because, under Corbyn's leadership, it has succeeded in expressing the interests of those from below.

But if it is increasingly apparent that these events and behaviours are a product of class struggle to all and sundry, one sometimes wonders if Corbyn himself is fully cognisant of this or ever has been. In the early phase of his leadership he appointed figures like Angela Eagle, Owen Smith, Hillary Benn, Lord Falconer, Chris Bryant, Heidi Alexander – a selection of politicians who had evinced strong Blairite convictions more generally in much of their policy making history, advocating privatisation of the NHS (Alexander, Smith), voting for the war in Iraq (Falconer, Eagle, Bryant, Benn), voting for tuition fees at some point (Eagle, Bryant), refusing to oppose the Tory Welfare Bill (Alexander, Benn, Bryant, Eagle, Smith) and so on. Naturally the coup which took place started from a position of some strength because it involved these people – the very people who Corbyn himself had put into positions of power at the higher level of the Shadow Cabinet. They were in an ideal position not only to belittle publically, and at every turn, the type of politics he was pressing, but also to arrange the action which was intended to remove him from leadership. Which, of course, they did – and which failed so spectacularly, when Corbyn was rescued by the growing militancy and outrage of the movement from below. But, during the debates with Smith in the run up to the election, one was aware of the note of conciliation that Corbyn struck with regard to his opponent and the coup plotters more generally. Corbyn praised Smith's abilities, argued that they wanted the same things, and even offered him a place in the cabinet, should he, Corbyn, win the re-election. To Smith and the others, the same people who had smeared him with the insinuations of complicity with racism and anti-Semitism, Corbyn explained how they were "part of the same Labour family",[261] and that whatever happened, after the election their differences would have to be forgotten and they would have to all rally together in the fight against the Conservatives.

Watching this, one felt one's heart sink alongside a creeping sense of pessimism. By describing Labour as a "family" the sense of class polarisation which underpinned these events was rendered murky, but perhaps more importantly, what the plotters had done was rendered forgivable. This was not simply a difference of opinion which was fought out on the terrain of rational ideas; it involved a sustained slander which was then graduated into an open assault on the democratic rights of party members in the form of an actual, active coup. If the leader had not been offering a more radical left programme, if he had been a member of the political mainstream – and those in his party Shadow Cabinet had orchestrated this kind of action – no doubt there would have been an almost universal sense of outrage on the part of the political classes across the spectrum. Instead, the politicians and commentators talked in grave tones about how the coup plotters had had to act according to their conscience, overlooking the fact that few of them had one. How different it was from the leadership of Neil Kinnock which in the early eighties sought to purge the left-wing tendency Militant from Labour's ranks, not on the grounds that said trend had orchestrated a coup in order to displace the leader, or had levelled slanderous accusations against him in the mainstream press – but on the grounds that their ideas were "contradicting" the "party constitution". In 1983 the leadership expelled five members of Militant's editorial board. Three years later another nine people were pushed out, including a Liverpool Council Deputy Leader, and a district Chairman. The process intensified over the following years and in total 125 members were purged, many occupying significant positions. This, of course, was part of a broader process, the consolidation of a shift to the right which would reach full fruition under the leadership of the ghastly, grinning Mr Blair, our twenty-first century denizen of death and destruction in the Middle East. But what is important to note is that Militant sympathisers were attacked and expelled quite ruthlessly on the basis of their left political line as opposed to any concrete action they had taken against the leadership. If we fast forward some 30 years, we have a situation where a coup has actually been enacted, and the leader who was the victim of it nevertheless invites the plotters to remember that they are all part of the same "labour family". Jeremy Corbyn is a kind, decent, reasonable man who evinces a sense of faint distaste and aloofness to the more savage and Machiavellian manoeuvrings which are so much a part of modern politics. He began his stint as the leader of the opposition calling for a "nicer" type of politics, a well-intentioned though perhaps naive gambit which was met by sardonic derision on all sides. And it was perhaps for this reason that Corbyn has not pushed for the wide deselection measures advocated by many of his supporters toward the wayward rebel MPs. The MPs, for their part, immediately began their machinations once more – this time the deputy leader, Tom Watson, started to promote the idea that the broader section of MPs should have more power when it comes to selecting those who should serve on the front bench; this, he averred, would give the poor, beleaguered coup plotters some "dignity" as – their coup deflated – they chose to return to the fold, out of great principle, devotion and commitment to their lucrative careers. Of course, Watson was once again trying to bolster the power of the MPs over and against the grassroots membership, and endeavouring to set up a situation in which Corbyn's main team would be selected by the very group that so despise Corbyn. His political power would be crippled in advance. The press too began their machinations: in choosing a new Shadow Cabinet which was not manned by those determined to see him destroyed, Corbyn was demonstrating truly totalitarian sensibilities. Again, that utter sense of entitlement, even after everything they had done – the expectation that the plotters would return to the very highest positions. How different it all was from their behaviour toward Militant.

Perhaps too there is something else at work here. Having for years imbibed the atmosphere of far-left politics, one comes to realise that when a radical left programme actually comes close to attaining some degree of public significance – dare I say – even power, the politicians who are carrying it are sometimes subject to the type of disorientation of mountain climbers who are rendered dizzy by the thinning air up toward the peak. There is a sense that now you are standing toe-to-toe with the establishment, that you must try to convince them that you are reasonable and decent, that the changes you wish to make are sensible and in the best interests of the majority and not the subversive, nihilistic kind which belong to the hysterical media caricature of a progressive position. This is a pattern which seems to play out over and over albeit across a host of very different historical examples. In Chile in the early 1970s, for example, a left government had come to power on the back of a vast, popular mobilisation, but even as the forces on the right, including the leadership of the military, more and more began to plot against it, Salvador Allende and his ministers increasingly turned a blind eye to the dangers. When the workers occupied factories, when they armed themselves in response to fascist

mobilisations and bosses' strikes, when the workers created their own forms of organisation out of the desperate, last-ditch struggle for survival, Allende described such measures as an act of "crass irresponsibility".[262] Allende's government professed faith in the military and exhorted the people to believe in them as the best means to restore order and unity, while at the same time that same government pleaded with the workers to disarm and demob. In so doing, of course, they cleared the path for the very kind of counteraction which would destroy them, without qualm or hesitation, when the time was right.

The situation which led to the Pinochet coup of 1973 was underpinned by the most volatile social contradictions and a social system which was itself in the process of imploding, so it was admittedly at something of a remove from the contemporary British political scene, even one which has been wracked by the type of economic crisis and austerity we have experienced. But what is similar in the two cases is simply the following: the one social agent which was capable of rescuing the leader from the abyss was, of necessity, the movement from below. Ultimately, Allende chose to disdain it until it was too late – because, despite his socialist politics, as a child of the middle classes and as a practised parliamentarian, he was unable to throw off the organic sense that real political change could only ever issue forth from the group of the educated, privileged minority who shared a background similar to his own. It was they, in the last analysis, in whom he chose to repose his faith, just as it was they who facilitated his destruction. I do not know how far along this path Corbyn will tread. I only know that should he hesitate, should he consistently and benignly forgive his enemies within the party by calling for unity – as opposed to empowering the grassroots membership and using it as a fulcrum by which those people can be deselected and their influence restricted in every conceivable manner; should the Labour leader pursue the politics of moderation and conciliation, those who are arrayed against him will be neither moderate nor reasonable nor humane. And they will not, for a moment, hesitate.

Endnotes

1. Sigmund Freud, "Character and Anal Eroticism", *Complete Works, 1890 – 1939*. Available: http://staferla.free.fr/Freud/ Freud%20complete%20Works.pdf

2. Thomas Carlyle, *On Heroes, Hero–Worship and the Heroic in History*. 1841. Available: http://www.gutenberg.org/ files/1091/1091-h/1091-h.htm

3. Herbert Spencer, *The Study of Sociology*. 1873. Available: http://oll.libertyfund.org/titles/spencer-the-study-of-sociology-1873

4. Leon Trotsky, *The History of the Russian Revolution*. 1930. Available: https://www.marxists.org/archive/trotsky/1930/ hrr/ch04.htm

5. In the same place.

6. In the same place.

7. In the same place.

8. In the same place.

9. In the same place.

10. In the same place.

11. In the same place.

12. Hamdan Azhar, "2016 Vs. 2012: How Trump's Win And Clinton's Votes Stack Up To Romney And Obama". *Forbes*, 29 December 2016. Available: https://www. forbes.com/sites/realspin/2016/12/29/2016-vs-2012-how-trumps-win-and-clintons-votes-stack-up-to-obama-and-romney/#794419201661

13. Lori Robinson, "2008 Voter Turnout". *FactCheck.org*, 8 January 2009. Available: https://www.factcheck.org/20 09/01/2008-voter-turnout/

14. "Post–Election 2016 Recap & Resources". Penn State University Libraries. Available: http://guides.libraries.psu. edu/post-election-2016/voter-turnout

15. Serena Marshall, "Obama Has Deported More People Than Any Other President". *ABC News*, 29 August 2016. Available: http://abcnews.go.com/Politics/obamas-deportation-policy-numbers/story?id=41715661

16. Meghan Behrent, "The enduring relevance of Victor Hugo". *International Socialist Review*, May 2013. Available: http://isreview.org/issue/89/enduring-relevance-victor-hugo

17. Victor Hugo, "KING LOUIS XVII", *ODES*. 1818–28. Available: http://www.gutenberg.org/files/8775 /8775-h/8775 -h.htm#link2H_4_0005

18. In the same place.

19. Something which, incidentally, would have never appealed to Blake.

20. James Michael Donovan, *Juries and the Transformation of France in the Nineteenth and Twentieth Centuries* (Chapel Hill: University of North Carolina Press, 2010), p.70.

21. Victor Hugo, *Last Day of a Condemned Man*. 1829. Available: https://ebooks.adelaide.edu.au/h/hugo/victor/last_day_of_a_condemned_man/index.html

22. In the same place.

23. In the same place.

24. In the same place.

25. There is a section where the condemned man speaks of a "happy" childhood, but why it was happy we never really find out.

26. Victor Hugo cited in Graham Robb, "Victor Hugo". *The New York Times of the Web*, 1997. Available: http://www.nytimes.com/books/first/r/robb-hugo.html

27. In the same place.

28. Victor Hugo, *The Hunchback of Notre-Dame* (Hertfordshire: Wordsworth Classics, 1993), p.83.

29. In the same place, p.120.

30. In the same place, p.122.

31. In the same place, pp.276-7.

32. In the same place, p.126.
33. In the same place, p.126.
34. In the same place, p.195.
35. In the same place, p.197.
36. In the same place, p.426.
37. In the same place, p.429.
38. Victor Hugo cited in Meghan Behrent, "The enduring relevance of Victor Hugo". *International Socialist Review*, May 2013. Available: http://isreview.org/issue/89/enduring-relevance-victor-hugo
39. In 1821, for instance, Hugo had refused to accept any economic help from his father and endured a year of dire poverty as a result.
40. Victor Hugo cited in Meghan Behrent, *"The enduring relevance of Victor Hugo"*. International Socialist Review, May 2013. Available: http://isreview.org/issue/89/enduring-relevance-victor-hugo
41. David Hancock Turner, "Les Miserables and Its Critics". *Jacobin Magazine*, 18 January 2013. Available: https://www.jacobinmag.com/2013/01/les-miserables-and-its-critics/
42. Victor Hugo, *Les Miserables* (Great Britain: Penguin Books, 2016), p.1051.
43. In the same place, p.1054.
44. In the same place, p.1066.
45. In the same place, p.158.
46. In the same place, p.157.
47. In the same place, p.1063.
48. In the same place, p.1065.
49. In the same place, pp.78-9.
50. In the same place, p.81.
51. In the same place, p.81.
52. Hugo Chavez cited in Jenny Hendrix, "A tale of two Hugos: Hugo Chavez and the 'Les Miserables' effect". *Los Angeles Times*, 7 March 2013. Available: http://articles.latimes.

com/2013/mar/07/entertainment/la-et-jc-a-tale-of-two-hugos-hugo-chavez-and-the-les-miserables-effect-20130307

53. Meghan Behrent, "The enduring relevance of Victor Hugo". *International Socialist Review*, May 2013. Available: http://isreview.org/issue/89/enduring-relevance-victor-hugo

54. Romulo Betancourt, *Venezuela; Oil and Politics* (Boston: Houghton Mifflin, 1979), p.43.

55. Carlos Andres Perez cited in Lee Brown, "Hugo Chavez Helped Overturn Neoliberalism in Latin America". *Telesur*, 17 April 2015. Available: https://www.telesurtv.net/english/analysis/Hugo-Chavez-Helped-Overturn-Neoliberalism-in-Latin-America--20150417-0004.html

56. Sarah Grainger, "Victims of Venezuela's Caracazo clashes reburied". BBC News, 28 February 2011. Available: http://www.bbc.co.uk/news/world-latin-america-12593085

57. Georg W.F. Hegel, *The Phenomenology of Spirit* (New York: Dover Publications, 2003), p.110.

58. Karl Marx, *Rules and Administrative Regulations of the International Workingmen's Association*. 1867. Available: https://www.marxists.org/archive/marx/iwma/documents/1867/rules.htm

59. This was something which Chavez set out to address, to create a less oil dependent economy, but on this count he surely failed.

60. "Bolivarian Republic of Venezuela's Annual Report on Form 18–K to the United States Securities and Exchange Commission for the fiscal year ended December 31, 2016". Available: https://www.sec.gov/Archives/edgar/data/103198/000119312517376486/d505622dex99d.htm

61. Jorge Martin, "Venezuela: economic crisis worsens – which way forward?" *In Defence of Marxism*, 9 January 2018. Available: https://www.marxist.com/venezuela-economic-crisis-worsens-which-way-forward.htm

62. Luke Graham, "Venezuela's crisis causes its people to cut

meals and lose weight". CNBC, 20 February 2017. Available: https://www.cnbc.com/2017/02/20/venezuelas-crisis-cause-its-people-to-cut-meals-and-lose-weight.html

63. Christopher Hitchens, "The Swastika and the Cedar". *Vanity Fair*, May 2009. Available: http://www.vanityfair.com/politics/features/2009/05/christopher-hitchens200905

64. In the same place.

65. Christopher Hitchens, "From Abbottabad to Worse". *Vanity Fair*, July 2011. Available: http://www.vanityfair.com/politics/features/2011/07/osama-bin-laden-201107

66. In the same place.

67. In the same place.

68. In the same place.

69. Karl Marx, *Articles on India* (Bombay, People's Publishing House: 1951), p.29.

70. Christopher Hitchens, *Arguably* (Great Britain: Atlantic Books 2012), p.507.

71. Karl Marx, *Articles on India* (Bombay: People's Publishing House, 1951), p.24.

72. Aijaz Ahman, *In Theory: Nations, Classes, Literature* (London and New York: Verso, 1994), p.224.

73. In the same place, p.227.

74. Christopher Hitchens, "Afghanistan's Dangerous Bet". *Vanity Fair*, November 2014. Available: https://www.vanityfair.com/news/2004/11/hitchens200411

75. Christopher Hitchens, "The Vietnam Syndrome". *Vanity Fair*, August 2006. Available: http://www.vanityfair.com/politics/features/2006/08/hitchens200608

76. Christopher Hitchens, "Hugo Boss". *Slate*, 2 August 2010. Available: http://www.slate.com/articles/news_and_politics/fighting_words/2010/08/hugo_boss.html

77. In the same place.

78. In the same place.

79. George Galloway, "Hugo Chavez's death is a body blow

for the poor and oppressed throughout Latin America". *The Independent*, 5 March 2013. Available: http://www. independent.co.uk/voices/commentators/hugo-chavezs-death-is-a-body-blow-for-the-poor-and-oppressed-throughout-latin-america-8521834.html

80. Christopher Hitchens, *Hitch 22 A Memoir* (London: Atlantic Books 2011), p.103.

81. This phrase probably originated as part of a medieval Georgian chant.

82. Johann Wolfgang von Goethe cited in Blake Hobby, "Sin and Redemption" (New York: Infobased publishing, 2010), p.63.

83. Percy Bysshe Shelley, "Ozymandias". 1818. Available: https://www.google.co.uk/search?q=ozymandias&oq=ozy mandias&aqs=chrome..69i57j0j69i60j0l3.2975j0j7&sourceid =chrome&ie=UTF–8

84. Bosman, William, *A New and Accurate Description of the Coast of Guinea*. 1704. Ed. John Ralph Willis. New York: Barnes and Noble, 1967.

85. Rembrandt developed the technique of copperplate etching in order to secure a more productive output, and he was also a prolific hoarder of a variety of aesthetic commodities over the years with an eye to their future value.

86. Cited in Kenneth Clark, *An Introduction to Rembrandt* (London, 1978), p.43.

87. Jeffery Cotterall cited in Sam Marcy, *Anatomy of the Economic Crisis*, "'Tulip mania' and today's speculation". Workers Liberty, 1982. Available: http://www.workers.org/marcy/cd/samecris/eccrisis/eccris01.htm

88. Rembrandt paints another version of this subject in 1655.

89. A painting from 1642 which depicts a citizen militia gathered in their full regalia under the shadows of a dark gateway. It was not, as the title suggests, depicting a night-time scene.

90. See Mary Elizabeth Podles, "Rembrandt van Rijn's Self-Portrait as the Apostle Paul". *Touchstone: A Journal of Mere Christianity*, November/December 2013. Available: http://www.touchstonemag.com/archives/article.php?id=26-06-054-c

91. Christopher Hitchens, *Orwell's Victory* (London: Allen Lane, 2002), p.8.

92. John Berger, "Rembrandt". *Public Books*, 15 October 2015. Available: http://www.publicbooks.org/artmedia/rembrandt

93. Georg Lukacs, *The Destruction of Reason* (London: The Merlin Press, 1980), p.198.

94. William Shakespeare, *The Tragedy of Hamlet Prince of Denmark* (New York: New American Library, 1963), p.46.

95. Arthur Schopenhauer, *The World as Will and Idea* (London: Everyman, 1995), pp.50–1.

96. In the same place, p.45.

97. In the same place, p.33.

98. In the same place, p.102.

99. In the same place, p.102.

100. In the same place, p.102.

101. In the same place, p.102.

102. In the same place, p.131.

103. In the same place, p.103.

104. Leon Trotsky, *In Defence of Marxism* (London: New Park Publications Limited, 1975), p.64.

105. Georg Lukacs, *The Destruction of Reason* (London: The Merlin Press, 1980), p.239.

106. Arthur Schopenhauer, *The World as Will and Idea* (London: Everyman, 1995), p.106.

107. In the same place, p.262.

108. One should remember too that in their original Platonic guise the forms were to be the highest goal of rational thought – they were to be apprehended as knowledge and

not belief.

109. A form and content relation involves the categories of "unity", "limitation", etc.

110. It should be added, of course, that the notion of the Absolute as an antinomy – as both infinite and finite, one and many, being and nothingness – can only be overcome in and through the application of dialectical and historical thinking, but at the same time this was the very approach which Schopenhauer had sought to gird himself against.

111. Arthur Schopenhauer, *On the Fourfold Root of the Principle of Sufficient Reason* (Worcestershire: ReadBooksLtd, 2013). Available: https://play.google.com/store/books/details?id=n318CgAAQ BAJ&rdid=book-n318CgAAQBAJ&rdot=1&source=gbs_vpt_ read&pcampaignid=books_booksearch_viewport

112. In the same place.

113. Georg Lukacs, *The Destruction of Reason* (London: The Merlin Press, 1980), p.198.

114. In the same place, p.243.

115. Michelle Dean, "Making the man: to understand Trump, look at his relationship with his dad". *The Guardian*, 26 March 2016. Available: https://www.theguardian.com/ us-news/2016/mar/26/donald-trump-fred-trump-father-relationship-business-real-estate-art-of-deal

116. Woody Guthrie, "Old Man Trump". 1950. Available: https:// genius.com/Us-elevator-old-man-trump-lyrics

117. Wayne Barrett, *Trump: The Greatest Show on Earth: The Deals, the Downfall, the Reinvention* (New York: Regan Arts, 2016). Available: https://www.amazon.com/Trump-Greatest-Earth-Downfall-Reinvention-ebook/dp/B01ECUXPIM

118. Steve Villano, "The Trumps: An Incestuous Intertwining with Organized Crime". *The National Memo*, 20 March 2017. Available: http://www.nationalmemo.com/trumps-incestuous-intertwining-organized-crime/

119. Sidney Blumenthal, "A Short History of the Trump Family".

London Review of Books, 16 February 2017. Available: https://www.lrb.co.uk/v39/n04/sidney-blumenthal/a-short-history-of-the-trump-family

120. Donald J Trump cited in "But did Trump's mother make him a misogynist?" *The Daily Mail*, 15 October 2016. Available: http://www.dailymail.co.uk/news/article-3839209/She-penniless-Scots-girl-arrived-America-barefoot-ended-matriarch-married-millionaire-did-Trump-s-mother-make-misogynist.html#ixzz4bxhjCmM0

121. In the same place.

122. Norman Vincent Peale, "Norman Vincent Peale". The Motivational Thinkers Hall of Fame. Available: http://www.getmotivation.com/nvpeale.html

123. Donald J Trump cited in David Smith, "Donald Trump: the making of a narcissist". *The Guardian*, 16 July 2016: https://www.theguardian.com/us-news/2016/jul/16/donald-trump-narcissist-profile

124. Donald J Trump cited in Justin Elliot, "Just what kind of student was Donald Trump?" *Salon*, 3 May 2011. Available: http://www.salon.com/2011/05/03/donald_trump_wharton/

125. In the same place.

126. Gwenda Blair cited in Justin Elliot, "Just what kind of student was Donald Trump?" Salon, 3 May 2011: http://www.salon.com/2011/05/03/donald_trump_wharton/

127. Judy Klemesrud, "Donald Trump, Real Estate Promoter, Builds Image as He Buys Buildings". *The New York Times*, 1 November 1976. Available: http://www.nytimes.com/1976/11/01/archives/donald-trump-real-estate-promoter-builds-image-as-he-buys-buildings.html

128. Donald J Trump cited in Carlos Lozada, "How Donald Trump plays the press, in his own words". *The Washington Post*, 17 June 2015. Available: https://www.washingtonpost.com/news/book-party/wp/2015/06/17/how-donald-trump-plays-the-press-in-his-own-words/?utm_term=.

b4ff72b0d6f0

129. Donald J Trump cited in "Trump's 1990 Playboy Interview: 'We Are Being Laughed At Around The World...'". *Zero Hedge*, 1 April 2016. Available: https://www.zerohedge.com/news/2016-04-01/trumps-1990-playboy-interview-we-are-being-laughed-around-world

130. Donald J Trump cited in Harriet Agerholm, "Donald Trump has $800 million wiped off value in one year, according to Forbes". *The Independent*, 5 October 2016. Available: http://www.independent.co.uk/news/people/donald-trump-800000-wiped-off-value-forbes-2016-richest-americans-list-a7345496.html

131. Donald J Trump cited in Chrissie Thompson, "The lawsuit over Donald Trump's Cincy apartments you may hear more about". *Cincinnati.com USA Network Today*, 25 August 2016. Available: https://www.cincinnati.com/story/news/politics/elections/2016/08/25/discrimination-lawsuit-over-donald-trump-cincinnati-apartments/89269132/

132. Donald J Trump, "The Cincinnati Kid". *Cincinnati Magazine*, July 1988. Available: https://books.google.co.uk/books?id=kR8DAAAAMBAJ&pg=PA92&lpg=PA92&dq=Swifton+Village+better+element+trump&source=bl&ots=Wc3EdFkDSU&sig=OEeJIWUv8nUxB2aiA1Lao9boEak&hl=en&sa=X&ved=0ahUKEwi9x6Or5PbSAhUkDMAKHZT_DPoQ6AEIXzAN#v=onepage&q=Swifton%20Village%20better%20element%20trump&f=false

133. David Cay Johnston, "Just What Were Donald Trump's Ties to the Mob?" *Politico Magazine*, 22 May 2016. Available: http://www.politico.com/magazine/story/2016/05/donald-trump-2016-mob-organized-crime-213910

134. In the same place.

135. In the same place.

136. In the same place.

137. Donald J Trump, *The Art of the Deal*, (Arrow Books,

UK: 2016). Available: https://play.google.com/store/books/details?id=CTB8DQAAQBAJ&rdid=book-CTB8DQAAQBAJ&rdot=1&source=gbs_vpt_read&pcampaignid=books_booksearch_ viewport

138. Shawn Tully, "How Trump's Debt Addiction Crushed the Biggest Company He Ever Ran". *Fortune 500*, 31 March 2016. Available: http://fortune.com/2016/03/31/donald-trump-debt-trump-hotels-casinos-atlantic-city/

139. Christopher Cameron, "A look inside Trump's famed Plaza deal". *The Real Deal – New York Real Estate News*. 16 January 2016. Available: https://therealdeal.com/2016/01/16/a-look-inside-trumps-famed-plaza-deal/

140. Sidney Blumenthal, "A Short History of the Trump Family". *London Review of Books*, 16 February 2017. Available: https://www.lrb.co.uk/v39/n04/sidney-blumenthal/a-short-history-of-the-trump-family

141. Roger Stone cited in Jamie Weinstein, "What Roy Cohn Taught Donald Trump". *The Daily Caller*, 10 March 2016. Available: http://dailycaller.com/2016/10/03/what-roy-cohn-taught-donald-trump/

142. Sidney Blumenthal, "A Short History of the Trump Family". *London Review of Books*, 16 February 2017. Available: https://www.lrb.co.uk/v39/n04/sidney-blumenthal/a-short-history-of-the-trump-family

143. Mar Ames, "The short-fingered vulgarian cometh: When Spy met Trump". *Pando*, 23 July 2015. Available: https://pando.com/2015/07/23/short-fingered-vulgarian-cometh/

144. Tessa Stuart, "A Timeline of Donald Trump's Creepiness While He Owned Miss Universe". *Rolling Stone*, 12 October 2016. Available: https://www.rollingstone.com/politics/features/timeline-of-trumps-creepiness-while-he-owned-miss-universe-w444634

145. Sidney Blumenthal, "A Short History of the Trump Family". *London Review of Books*, 16 February 2017. Available: https://

www.lrb.co.uk/v39/n04/sidney-blumenthal/a-short-history-of-the-trump-family

146. "Ghostbusters Final Film Transcript". Spook Central. 1984. Available: https://www.theraffon.net/~spookcentral/gb1_script_transcript.htm

147. In the same place.

148. James Baldwin cited in Mychal Denzel Smith, "From 'Victim' to 'Threat': James Baldwin and the Demands of Self–Respect". *The Nation*, 10 February 2015. Available: https://www.thenation.com/article/victim-threat-james-baldwin-and-demands-self-respect/

149. Andrea Dworkin, *Intercourse* (New York: The Free Press, 1987), p.4.

150. In the same place, p.8.

151. In the same place, p.16.

152. In the same place, p.16.

153. In the same place, p.16.

154. In the same place, p.99.

155. In the same place, p.99.

156. In the same place, p.102.

157. In the same place, p.103.

158. In the same place, p.84.

159. In the same place, p.84.

160. Diego Rivera cited in the same place, p.181.

161. In the same place, p.181.

162. In the same place, p.190.

163. In the same place, p.63.

164. In the same place, pp.63–4.

165. Vere Gordon Childe, *What Happened in History* (USA: Pelican, 1954), p.67.

166. In the same place, p.67.

167. In the same place, p.65.

168. In the same place, pp.65-6.

169. In the same place, p.66.

170. In the same place, p73.

171. In the same place, p.89.

172. In the same place, p.89.

173. In the same place, p.89.

174. Frederick Engels, *Origins of the Family, Private Property, and the State.* 1884. Available: https://www.marxists.org/archive/marx/works/1884/origin-family/ch02c.htm

175. Staff and agencies, "Gender pay gap stands at 15%". *The Guardian,* 7 November 2013. Available: https://www.theguardian.com/money/2013/nov/07/gender-pay-gap-official-figures-disparity

176. Office for National Statistics, "Women shoulder the responsibility of 'unpaid work'". 10 November 2016. Available: http://visual.ons.gov.uk/the-value-of-your-unpaid-work/

177. Andrea Dworkin, *Intercourse* (New York: The Free Press, 1987), p.127.

178. In the same place, p.127.

179. James Blake cited in Penelope Fitzgerald, "Innocence and Experience". *The New York Times on the Web,* 14 April 1996. Available: http://www.nytimes.com/books/97/04/06/reviews/ackroyd-blake.html

180. Peter Ackroyd cited in John Banville, "Working Man's Art: BIOGRAPHY : BLAKE: A Biography, By Peter Ackroyd". *Los Angeles Times,* 19 May 1996. Available: http://articles.latimes.com/1996-05-19/books/bk-5746_1_peter-ackroyd

181. William Blake cited in Michael Davis, *William Blake – A New Kind of Man* (Berkeley and Los Angeles: University of California Press, 1977) p.33.

182. William Blake, *William Blake* (Middlesex England: Penguin Books, 1973), p.28.

183. In the same place.

184. In the same place, p.49.

185. In the same place, p.49.

186. In the same place.
187. William Blake, "The French Revolution", *The Poetical Works* (London: Printed for J. Johnson, No 72, St Paul's Churchyard, 1908).
188. In the same place.
189. In the same place.
190. Isaiah Berlin, *Russian Thinkers* (England: Penguin Classics, 2013), p.104.
191. Paul Foot, *Articles of Resistance* (Bookmarks: London, 2000), p.68.
192. William Blake, *William Blake* (Middlesex, England: Penguin Books, 1973), p.30.
193. In the same place.
194. In the same place.
195. In the same place, p.31.
196. In the same place.
197. In the same place, p.52.
198. In the same place.
199. William Blake cited in Peter Ackroyd, *Blake* (London: Vintage Books, 1999), p.77.
200. William Blake cited in *Trial for High Treason, 1803-4*. The Blake Society. Available: http://www.blakesociety.org/about-blake/gilchrists-life-of-blake/chapter-xix/
201. William Hayley cited in the same place.
202. William Blake cited in the same place.
203. King James Bible, "Revelation 12". Bible Hub. Available: http://biblehub.com/kjv/revelation/12.htm
204. Peter Ackroyd, *Blake* (London: Vintage Books, 1999), p.65.
205. William Blake cited in Edwin J Ellis, *The Real Blake – A Portrait Biography* (New York: Haskell House Publishers, 1970), p.375.
206. William Blake, *Blake: The Complete Blake Poems* (London and New York: Routledge, 2007), p.322.
207. William Blake, *The Book Of Urizen*. 1794. Available: https://

www.poemhunter.com/poem/the-book-of-urizen-chapter-viii/

208. Peter Ackroyd cited in Paul Foot, *Articles of Resistance* (Bookmarks: London, 2000), p.73.

209. Northrop Frye cited in Dan Miller, *Critical Paths: Blake and the Argument of Method* (USA: Duke University Press, 1987), p.257.

210. "The Good Wife Transcript" (Series 7, episode 11). *Forever Dreaming Transcripts*. Available: http://transcripts. foreverdreaming.org/viewtopic.php?f=36&t=24656

211. In the same place.

212. Hillary Clinton cited in Dan Merica, "From Park Ridge to Washington: The youth minister who mentored Hillary Clinton". CNN, 25 April 2014. Available: http://edition.cnn. com/2014/04/25/politics/clinton-methodist-minister/

213. One should not allow any suggestion that it is only black youths who are members of gangs. But Hillary Clinton made her comments in the mid–1990s, a few years after the LA riots when the mass media was focused almost pathologically on black gang warfare in urban areas (as opposed to say Ku Klux Klan mobilisations or survivalist groups in the deep south). So when Clinton used the language of "gangs" combining it with the dehumanising rhetoric of "superpredators", even though she did not make a direct reference to black people she was quite clearly drawing on a racist discourse and relaying it in a codified way.

214. Hillary Clinton cited in Robert Mackey and Zaid Jilani, "Hillary Clinton Still Haunted by Discredited Rhetoric on 'Superpredators'". *The Intercept*, 25 February 2016. Available: https://theintercept.com/2016/02/25/activists-want-hillary-clinton-apologize-hyping-myth-superpredators-1996/

215. Hillary Clinton, @Hillary Clinton Twitter, 22 November 2015. Available: https://twitter.com/hillaryclinton/status/668597149291184128

216. Juanita Broaddrick cited in Mark Hensch and Jonathan Easley, "Bill Clinton rape accuser: Hillary 'tried to silence' me". *The Hill*, 1 June 2016. Available: http://thehill.com/blogs/ballot-box/presidential-races/264988-bill-clinton-rape-accuser-hillary-tried-to-silence-me

217. Hillary Clinton cited in Melinda Henneberger and Dahlia Lithwick, "And Speaking of Perfect Unions ...". *Slate*, 21 March 2008. Available: http://www.slate.com/articles/news_and_politics/politics/2008/03/and_speaking_of_perfect_unions_.html

218. Hillary Clinton cited in Larry Elder, "The Trashing of Bill's Accusers: What did Hillary do – and why did she do it?" *FrontPage Magazine*, 26 February 2016. Available: http://www.frontpagemag.com/fpm/261957/trashing-bills-accusers-what-did-hillary-do-and-larry-elder

219. Doug Henwood, "Stop Hillary! Vote no to a Clinton Dynasty". *Harper's Magazine*, November 2014. Available: https://harpers.org/archive/2014/10/stop–hillary–2/5/

220. In the same place.

221. Stephen Labton, "The 1992 Campaign: Campaign Finances; Angry at Bush, Republican Contributors Are Helping Clinton". *The New York Times*, 22 September 1992. Available: http://www.nytimes.com/1992/09/22/us/1992-campaign-campaign-finances-angry-bush-republican-contributors-are-helping.html

222. Chris Arnade, "I worked on Wall Street. I am skeptical Hillary Clinton will rein it in". *The Guardian*, 28 January 2016. Available: https://www.theguardian.com/commentisfree/2016/jan/28/hillary-clinton-wall-street-bailout

223. Matea Gold, Tom Hamburger and Anu Narayanswamy, "Clinton blasts Wall Street, but still draws millions in contributions". *The Washington Post*, 4 February 2016. Available: https://www.washingtonpost.com/politics/clint

on-blasts-wall-street-but-still-draws-millions-in-contribu
tions/2016/02/04/05e1be00-c9c2-11e5-ae11-57b6aeab993f_
story.html?utm_term=.9bf9cc5a9281

224. Hillary Clinton cited in Christian Datoc, "Hillary: In 2016,
there's 'No Executive Too Powerful To Jail'". *The Daily
Beast*, 2 November 2016. Available: http://dailycaller.
com/2016/02/11/hillary-in-2016-theres-no-executive-too-
powerful-to-jail-video/

225. Hillary Clinton cited in Glen Kessler, "Recalling Hillary
Clinton's claim of 'landing under sniper fire' in Bosnia".
The Washington Post, 23 May 2016. Available: https://www.
washingtonpost.com/news/fact-checker/wp/2016/05/23/
recalling-hillary-clintons-claim-of-landing-under-sniper-
fire-in-bosnia/?utm_term=.cf6bc1124eef

226. Hillary Clinton, "Hillary Clinton Tears Up During Campaign
Stop". You Tube, 7 January 2008. Available: https://www.
youtube.com/watch?v=6qgWH89qWks

227. In the same place.

228. Hillary Clinton cited in David Morgan, "Clinton says
U.S. could 'totally obliterate' Iran". *Reuters*, 22 April
2008. Available: https://www.reuters.com/article/us-usa-
politics-iran/clinton-says-u-s-could-totally-obliterate-iran-
idUSN2224332720080422

229. Michael Crowley, "Hillary Clinton's Unapologetically
Hawkish Record Faces 2016 Test". *Time* magazine, 14 January
2014. Available: http://swampland.time.com/2014/01/14/
hillary-clintons-unapologetically-hawkish-record-faces-
2016-test/

230. Hillary Clinton, "Did Hillary Lie About Her Iraq War
Vote?" *The Real News Network*, 4 February 2016. Available:
http://therealnews.com/t2/index.php?option=com_content
&task=view&id=31&Itemid=74&jumival=15586

231. JTA, "Hillary Clinton Says Played Central Role in Stopping
Military Action Against Iran". *Haaretz*, 26 January 2016.

Available: http://www.haaretz.com/world-news/1.699660

232. Timon of Athens in William Shakespeare, "Timon of Athens", *The Plays and Poems of William Shakespeare* (Leipsic: Ernest Fleischer, 1833), p.616.

233. Hillary Clinton, "Hillary Clinton takes swipe at Donald Trump in South Carolina victory speech – video" *The Guardian*, 28 February 2016: https://www.theguardian.com/us-news/video/2016/feb/27/hillary-clinton-victory-speech-south-carolina-primary-video

234. Doug Henwood, "Stop Hillary! Vote no to a Clinton Dynasty". *Harper's Magazine*, November 2014. Available: https://harpers.org/archive/2014/10/stop-hillary-2/

235. Martha Derthick cited in Gareth Davies, "On Martha Derthick". *The Forum: A Journal of Applied Research in Contemporary Politics*, April 2015.

236. Raymond Hernandez and Robert Pear, "Once an Enemy, Health Industry Warms to Clinton". *The New York Times*, 12 July 2006. Available: http://www.nytimes.com/2006/07/12/nyregion/12donate.html?_r=1&

237. Lady Macbeth in William Shakespeare, *Macbeth* (London: Methuen and Co Ltd, 1977), p.81.

238. Kshama Sawant, "The (un)Democratic Primary: Why We Need a New Party of the 99%". *Counterpunch*, 21 April 2016. Available: https://www.counterpunch.org/2016/04/21/the-undemocratic-primary-why-we-need-a-new-party-of-the-99/

239. In June 2013 Labour released the news that it intended to support the government's austerity programme for the years 2015–16 – see William Keegan, "This austerity U-turn by Ed Balls is a mistake". *The Guardian*, 16 June 2013. Available: https://www.theguardian.com/business/2013/jun/16/austerity-uturn-ed-balls-mistake

240. A fictional construct which has been exploited most efficiently by the right and centre ground to attack Jeremy

Corbyn – see, for an example, Paul T Horgan, "Labour despises the white working class". *The Conservative Woman*, 25 March 2016. Available: http://www.conservativewoman. co.uk/paul-t-horgan-labour-despises-the-white-working-class/

241. Immigrants from the ten poorer countries which joined the EU after 2004 actually contributed 5 billion pounds more to the British economy than they took out in the 10 years which followed – for more, see Tony McKenna, "The Political Event of Jeremy Corbyn". *The Huffington Post*, 7 June 2017: http://www.huffingtonpost.co.uk/tony-mckenna/jeremy-corbyn_b_16967776.html

242. Cited in Stephen Bush, "Labour's anti-immigrant mug: the worst part is, it isn't a gaffe". *New Statesman*, 28 March 2016: http://www.newstatesman.com/politics/2015/03/labours-anti-immigrant-mug-worst-part-it-isnt-gaffe

243. A recent survey revealed that of the top 100 journalists only 14 per cent had been educated in comprehensive schools even though 9 out of every 10 pupils in Britain is educated at a comprehensive. For more, see Owen Gibson, "Most leading journalists went to private schools, says study". *The Guardian*, 15 June 2016. Available: https://www. theguardian.com/media/2006/jun/15/pressandpublishing. publicschools

244. Jeremy Corbyn, "Jeremy Corbyn's full speech at the 2016 Labour Party conference". New Statesman, 28 September 2016. Available: https://www.newstatesman.com/politics/staggers/2016/09/jeremy-corbyns-full-speech-2016-labour-party-conference

245. In the same place.

246. In the same place.

247. Abie Wilkinson, "Victory? Most people didn't actually support the Tories – or their harsh new policies". *The Mirror*, 9 May 2015. Available: https://www.mirror.co.uk/

usvsth3m/victory-most-people-dont-actually-5667728

248. Mick Hume, "Did the Tories really win?" *Spiked*, 8 May 2015. Available: http://www.spiked-online.com/newsite/article/did-the-tories-really-win/16954#.Wm8Qiahl-bg

249. See Christopher Hope, "Jeremy Corbyn criticised for not bowing deeply enough at Cenotaph on Remembrance Sunday". *The Telegraph*, 8 November 2015. Available: http://www.telegraph.co.uk/news/politics/Jeremy_Corbyn/11982482/Jeremy-Corbyn-criticised-for-not-bowing-deeply-enough-at-Cenotaph-on-Remembrance-Sunday.html

250. Naz Shah cited in Becky Milligan, "Naz Shah: My words were anti-Semitic". World at One, *BBC News*, 18 July 2016. Available: http://www.bbc.co.uk/news/uk-england-leeds-36802075

251. Chuka Umunna cited in Katy Balls, "Chuka Umunna turns on Ken Livingstone at anti-Semitism hearing: 'you'll be remembered as a pin-up for prejudice'". *The Spectator*, 14 June 2016. Available: https://blogs.spectator.co.uk/2016/06/ken-livingstone-faces-music-home-affairs-select-committee/

252. Chi Onwurah cited in Nigel Morris, "Jeremy Corbyn in racism row over treatment of minority MPs". *News The Essential Daily Briefing*, 22 August 2016. Available: https://inews.co.uk/essentials/news/politics/jeremy-corbyn-racism-row-treatment-black-mps/

253. Seema Malhotra cited in Daniel Boffey, "Corbyn aide accused of 'illegal entry' to MP's Westminster office". *The Observer*, 23 July 2016. Available: https://www.theguardian.com/politics/2016/jul/23/jeremy-corbyn-aide-accused-illegal-entry-mps-office

254. Lesley Docksey, "The British Chicken Coup: 172 Labour MPs against a pro–Corbyn Party". *Dissident Voice*, 5 July 2016. Available: https://dissidentvoice.org/2016/07/the-british-chicken-coup-172-labour-mps-against-a-pro-corbyn-party/

255. Stephanie Linning, "BBC under fire for orchestrating resignation of shadow minister live on air after now deleted editor's blog revealed how it was stage-managed". *Mail Online*, 8 January 2016. Available: http://www.dailymail. co.uk/news/article-3389675/BBC-fire-orchestrating-resignation-shadow-minister-live-air-producer-s-blog-deleted-revealed-stage-managed.html

256. Guy Faulconbridge, Kylie MacLellan, "Trotsky's ghost haunts Britain's Labour Party in post–Brexit vote turmoil". *Reuters*, 10 August 2016. Available: https://www.reuters. com/article/us-britain-labour-trotsky/trotskys-ghost-haunts-britains-labour-party-in-post-brexit-vote-turmoil-idUSKCN10L1V4

257. Aubrey Allegretti, "Tom Watson Sparks Row With Jeremy Corbyn Over Claim 'Trotskyist Entryists' Will Destroy Labour". *The Huffington Post*, 9 August 2016. Available: http://www.huffingtonpost.co.uk/entry/tom-watson-angers-jeremy-corbyn-fans-with-attack-on-arm-twisting-trots-infiltrating-labour_uk_57a9c626e4b089961b857cde

258. Steerpike, "Angela Eagle's leadership campaign ends with yet another gaffe – 'porridge!'". *The Spectator*, 19 July 2016. Available: https://blogs.spectator.co.uk/2016/07/angela-eagles-leadership-campaign-ends-gaffe/

259. Caroline Mortimer, "Fury as new members barred from voting in fresh Labour leadership contest by NEC". *The Independent*, 12 July 2016. Available: http://www. independent.co.uk/news/uk/politics/jeremy-corbyn-labour-leadership-membership-nec-momentum-blairite-angela-eagle-a7133556.html

260. Lizzie Dearden, Joe Watts, Rob Merrick, "Labour leadership election: Jeremy Corbyn beats Owen Smith to remain leader with 62% of vote – as it happened". *The Independent*, 23 September 2016. Available: http://www.independent.co.uk/news/uk/politics/labour-leadership-election-results-live-

2016-latest-news-jeremy-corbyn-owen-smith-a7325781.
html

261. Jeremy Corbyn cited in Lizzie Dearden, "Labour leadership: Owen Smith tells Jeremy Corbyn he needs to 'win the country' after being re-elected as leader". *The Independent*, 24 September 2016. Available: http://www.independent.co.uk/news/uk/politics/labour-leadership-election-result-latest-jeremy-corbyn-wins-reelected-owen-smith-beaten-result-a7327511.html

262. Salvador Allende cited in Mike Gonzalez, *Revolutionary Rehearsals* – ed. Colin Barker, "Chile 1972-73 – The workers united" (Bookmarks, Great Britain: 1987) p.53.

CULTURE, SOCIETY & POLITICS

Contemporary culture has eliminated the concept and public figure of the intellectual. A cretinous anti-intellectualism presides, cheer-led by hacks in the pay of multinational corporations who reassure their bored readers that there is no need to rouse themselves from their stupor. Zer0 Books knows that another kind of discourse – intellectual without being academic, popular without being populist – is not only possible: it is already flourishing. Zer0 is convinced that in the unthinking, blandly consensual culture in which we live, critical and engaged theoretical reflection is more important than ever before.

If you have enjoyed this book, why not tell other readers by posting a review on your preferred book site.

Recent bestsellers from Zero Books are:

In the Dust of This Planet
Horror of Philosophy vol. 1
Eugene Thacker
In the first of a series of three books on the Horror of
Philosophy, *In the Dust of This Planet* offers the genre of horror
as a way of thinking about the unthinkable.
Paperback: 978-1-84694-676-9 ebook: 978-1-78099-010-1

Capitalist Realism
Is there no alternative?
Mark Fisher
An analysis of the ways in which capitalism has presented itself
as the only realistic political-economic system.
Paperback: 978-1-84694-317-1 ebook: 978-1-78099-734-6

Rebel Rebel
Chris O'Leary
David Bowie: every single song. Everything you want to know,
everything you didn't know.
Paperback: 978-1-78099-244-0 ebook: 978-1-78099-713-1

Cartographies of the Absolute
Alberto Toscano, Jeff Kinkle
An aesthetics of the economy for the twenty-first century.
Paperback: 978-1-78099-275-4 ebook: 978-1-78279-973-3

Malign Velocities
Accelerationism and Capitalism
Benjamin Noys
Long listed for the Bread and Roses Prize 2015, *Malign Velocities* argues against the need for speed, tracking acceleration as the symptom of the ongoing crises of capitalism.
Paperback: 978-1-78279-300-7 ebook: 978-1-78279-299-4

Meat Market
Female Flesh under Capitalism
Laurie Penny
A feminist dissection of women's bodies as the fleshy fulcrum of capitalist cannibalism, whereby women are both consumers and consumed.
Paperback: 978-1-84694-521-2 ebook: 978-1-84694-782-7

Poor but Sexy
Culture Clashes in Europe East and West
Agata Pyzik
How the East stayed East and the West stayed West.
Paperback: 978-1-78099-394-2 ebook: 978-1-78099-395-9

Romeo and Juliet in Palestine
Teaching Under Occupation
Tom Sperlinger
Life in the West Bank, the nature of pedagogy and the role of a university under occupation.
Paperback: 978-1-78279-637-4 ebook: 978-1-78279-636-7

Sweetening the Pill
or How we Got Hooked on Hormonal Birth Control
Holly Grigg-Spall
Has contraception liberated or oppressed women? *Sweetening the Pill* breaks the silence on the dark side of hormonal contraception.
Paperback: 978-1-78099-607-3 ebook: 978-1-78099-608-0

Why Are We The Good Guys?
Reclaiming your Mind from the Delusions of Propaganda
David Cromwell
A provocative challenge to the standard ideology that Western power is a benevolent force in the world.
Paperback: 978-1-78099-365-2 ebook: 978-1-78099-366-9

Readers of ebooks can buy or view any of these bestsellers by clicking on the live link in the title. Most titles are published in paperback and as an ebook. Paperbacks are available in traditional bookshops. Both print and ebook formats are available online.

Find more titles and sign up to our readers' newsletter at http://www.johnhuntpublishing.com/culture-and-politics

Follow us on Facebook
at https://www.facebook.com/ZeroBooks

and Twitter at https://twitter.com/Zer0Books